The Curriculum Management Audit

The Curriculum Management Audit

Improving School Quality

edited by
Larry E. Frase
Fenwick W. English
William K. Poston Jr.

Rowman & Littlefield Education
Lanham • New York • Toronto • Oxford

Published in the United States of America
by Rowman & Littlefield Education
A Division of Rowman & Littlefield Publishers, Inc.
A wholly owned subsidiary of The Rowman & Littlefield Publishing Group, Inc.
4501 Forbes Boulevard, Suite 200, Lanham, Maryland 20706
www.rowmaneducation.com

PO Box 317
Oxford
OX2 9RU, UK

The Technomic edition of this book was originally catalogued as follows by
the Library of Congress:
Main entry under title:
   The Curriculum Management Audit: Improving School Quality
Bibliographical references
Includes index p. 303
Library of Congress Catalog Card No. 94-60853
Reprinted by Rowman & Littlefield Education 0-8108-3931-8

♾™ The paper used in this publication meets the minimum requirements of
American National Standard for Information Sciences—Permanence of
Paper for Printed Library Materials, ANSI/NISO Z39.48-1992.
Manufactured in the United States of America.

Contents

Introduction

LARRY E. FRASE—*San Diego State University*

THE curriculum management audit focuses like a laser on that which schools should be all about—learning. The audit is designed to determine the degree to which the written, taught, and tested curricula are aligned and the extent to which all district resources are organized to support development and delivery of the curricula. Ninety school districts have received curriculum management audits since Fenwick English developed the process and conducted the first audit in Columbus, Ohio in 1979 (English, 1988).

The audit has continued to evolve, and this book represents the most advanced thinking and practice regarding the curriculum management audit. Furthermore, this book incorporates, compares, and contrasts the principles of total quality management (TQM) with the curriculum management audit. Is there a fit between the two? If so, what is the fit? What are the discrepancies? Can a school district utilize curriculum management audit principles in conjunction with TQM and vice versa?

The chapters in this book, which share the philosophy and practice of curriculum management audits, have been written by experienced curriculum management auditors and TQM scholars. After ninety audits, we know that, in general, practice does not reflect the latest thinking regarding curriculum management. Some districts have either not determined an official curriculum or have not done it well; inequities continue to be problematic for others; productivity is down in some districts while spending is up; and in many districts the education of students is determined by political forces and powerful, although small, constituencies. In some districts, the education of students is secondary to the individual political aspirations of elected officials and the self-serving interests of professional associations.

The audit is a powerful tool designed to determine the adequacy of the curriculum—its documents, its management, and its delivery. This book presents a comprehensive discussion of the curriculum management audit, including its use, its effects, and its fit with TQM.

It may seem odd that the man who developed, implemented, and gave the curriculum management audit to the American Association of School Administrators, Fenwick W. English, is not the sole author/editor of this book. This is not the case for those of you who know Fen. True to his style for at least 25 years, the length of time I have known him, he has given knowledge, opportunities, encouragement, challenges, congratulations, and "KITA" to others. This book was designed and written by his protégés, with his encouragement and consultation. A truth he would never speak is that one day as we, the lead auditors and trainers, met in San Antonio, had to convince him to write Chapter One to lend the perspective of his 16 years work with the audit. Read Chapter One closely, he says the audit has become even more beneficial under our care. That's Fen English.

We are thankful to him for our many years of association, for sharing knowledge about the audit with us, for allowing us to help refine the audit and apply it in school districts. Most of all we are thankful for the constant guiding light he gives in an often gloomy future for education.

Overview

THIS book is composed of three sections—Part I: History, Critics, and Practical Compatibility of the Curriculum Management Audit and Total Quality Management; Part II: Curriculum Management Audit Standards and Procedures; and Part III: The Curriculum Management Audit: Research Evidence and Superintendents' Testimonials.

Chapter 1 by Fenwick English illustrates the meaning of the Audit Standards One through Five and the growth and development of the audit. This chapter provides a discussion of crucial assumptions and strengths and weaknesses of the audit.

Chapter 2 by Larry Frase presents a brief review of curriculum management auditing (CMA) and total quality management (TQM) and analyzes opposing viewpoints. This information is crucial for practitioners interested in the strengths and weaknesses of each theory.

Chapter 3 by Virginia Vertiz and Carolyn Downey presents a two-pronged review of the audit for quality indicators. First, they overlay the Downey Quality Fit Framework and the standards of the audit. Second, they overlay Deming's fourteen points with the audit. This chapter is essential to anyone desiring an in-depth knowledge of how the CMA and TQM align themselves.

Chapter 4 by Betty Steffy presents the history of the audit, which is then analyzed with regard to the following criteria: as external and internal eyes on school system management; accountability; state equity trends; the Kentucky State Education Agency involvement in curriculum management auditing; national and international use of the CMA; challenges for second generation audits; selection of curriculum; and the future of CMAs.

Part II, comprised of Chapters 5–10 presents thorough discussions of each of the five standards of the audit. The standards are defined; theories underlying teaching standards are discussed; all criteria for each standard are explained; and examples of findings and recommendations from each standard are presented.

Chapter 10, by Carolyn Downey, Virginia Vertiz and Larry Frase presents a detailed account of necessary preparation and follow-up activities for the CMA. This information is key to districts considering a CMA. Technical preparation details and samples of pre-audit press releases, internal communications, scheduling guidelines, and post-audit press releases are provided.

Part III presents Chapters 11 and 12.

In Chapter 11, Virginia Vertiz presents reactions of superintendents who have undergone CMAs by the American Association of School Administrators. Testimony from a study of the twenty-six districts most currently audited is provided. This chapter offers inside views of how superintendents see the benefits of the CMA.

In Chapter 12, Jay Kemen and Karen Gallager present the first doctoral dissertation level research findings on the CMA. This is a case study of three school districts' experience with the curriculum management audit. The results are informative and illustrate the value of the curriculum management audit in helping school districts make substantive educational improvements.

PART I

HISTORY, CRITICS AND PRACTICAL COMPATIBILITY OF THE CURRICULUM MANAGEMENT AUDIT AND TOTAL QUALITY MANAGEMENT

CHAPTER 1

Standards and Assumptions of the Curriculum Management Audit

FENWICK ENGLISH – *University of Kentucky*

THE first curriculum management audit was completed in 1979 in the Columbus Public Schools, Ohio, under the auspices of Peat, Marwick, Mitchell & Co., a big-eight accounting and consulting firm. For a school system of 83,400 students, K–12, it contained twenty findings and twelve recommendations spread over five audit standards. It was eighty single-spaced pages long. Now, consider that in 1994, a curriculum management audit was completed for the Wichita, Kansas, Public Schools, by the National Curriculum Audit Center of the American Association of School Administrators for 49,000 students, K–12. While that audit contained twenty findings and fourteen recommendations listed under the same five standards, it was over 255 single-spaced pages. While the number of findings was only eight more in Wichita than Columbus, and the number of recommendations only two more, the descriptive analyses of the actual audit increased by two-thirds.

In fourteen years of national and international utilization, the curriculum management audit has continued to increase its depth of analyses and the rigor of its analytical procedures. It has been used in state and federal courts as a source document in decisions to take over chronically troubled school districts and as administrative guidelines to promote desegregation and improve financial and racial equity in the nation's public schools. For school districts engaged in strategic planning, it has become the most sophisticated type of *environmental scan* that could be undertaken to provide an accurate data base for those engaged in the process. Above all, it has established itself as a kind of policy/operational study that is capable of dealing with the political/ personality variables that are invariably interconnected to larger organizational issues, which are described as functions, operations, or tasks. These latter indices are the fodder for most traditional administrative surveys performed by university-based consultants, accreditation groups, and consulting firms in the past. In this respect, the curric-

3

ulum management audit is a definite step *forward* because it extends this typical platform and involves the human element.

CRITICAL ASSUMPTIONS OF THE AUDIT

Like nearly all analytical procedures that are embedded in a theoretical construct or model, the curriculum management audit rests on a series of keystone assumptions. It is important to understand these assumptions because they represent, in theoretical form, the limitations of the construct and, with it, the related analytical procedures. Furthermore, all assumptions are rooted in sets of values. Such values are usually *implicit* predilections or preferences. These are always disputable, though few practitioners or lay board members ever take the time to probe deeply what form they may take. The probing is usually reserved for professorial types who feel more comfortable arguing in theoretical affairs. No model is ever *objective* in the sense that it does not make a priori assumptions about reality, the phenomena to be observed, or the interactions to be described. There is no such thing as a "completely objective" analysis of anything. Anyone making such claims is either naive, outdated, or a mountebank.

Perhaps the most central assumption of all in the audit relates to the concept of *control*. The precedent or model for auditing comes from the accounting world. Accountants assume that the agency being audited will continue to exist; that forms of control over the operations of the agency being audited are necessary to ensure its success; and that specific people will be charged with seeing to it that control is established, maintained, and extended so that dollars may be assigned to functions, tracked, and recorded accurately. It should be remembered that the root word for *accountability* is *account*. The many meanings of this word can be extrapolated from a comprehensive English dictionary as:

1 – a record of debit and credit;
2 – a statement of transactions during a fiscal period
3 – a collection of items to be balanced
4 – a statement of explanation of one's conduct
5 – a periodically rendered listing charged purchases and credits
6 – value, importance, esteem, judgement
7 – profit, advantage
8 – a statement of exposition of reasons, causes, grounds, or motives
9 – a reason giving rise to an action or other result, careful thought, consideration

10 – a statement of facts or events, relation;
11 – heresay, report: [note:oral]
12 – a sum of money or its equivalent deposited in the common cash of a bank and subject to withdrawal by the depositor. [Merriam-Webster, 1972, p. 6]

Virtually every one of these meanings is part and parcel of the curriculum management audit. Each of these twelve meanings is shown against the five audit standards (which will be explained more fully) and the three common data sources of the audit in Table 1. The table demonstrates how the twelve meanings of the word *account* are deeply embedded in the curriculum management audit. In some cases, the fiscal implications are expanded to include broader organizational functions when they are treated as though they were financial transactions.

Accountants require that an organization or agency being audited function within certain parameters that enable the auditing process to be meaningful. The context of auditing is therefore centered on ideas regarding the necessary conditions of a financial control system. These may be called the *pre-conditions* of the audit. There are four such basic pre-conditions. They may also be referred to as the "essential elements of a financial control system" (see Dearden, 1976, p. 200). They are listed next.

The Establishment of Objectives

A financial control system requires objectives or targets. These form the basis for measurement against which an existing condition is compared to a desired one. A financial control system requires priorities among the objectives. The act of comparison produces *discrepancies*. These "gaps" are descriptions of a numerical (quantitative) or narrative nature (nonquantitative). There can be no measurement or accounting

Table 1. The meanings of the word account connected to the curriculum management audit.

Data Source	Standard One Control	Standard Two Direction	Standard Three Equity	Standard Four Feedback	Standard Five Productivity
Documents	1–9	1–9	1–9	1–9	1–2
Interviews	8–11	8–11	8–11	8–11	8–12
Site Visits	4, 8–11	4, 8–11	4, 8–11	4, 8–11	4, 8–12

without objectives (desired conditions) being stated. If there are no objectives, the accountant or auditor "finds" this absence as a condition that must be established for an audit to occur. In this case, a recommendation is made to establish the necessary conditions within which an audit may be employed. This state of affairs is really a *pre-condition* necessary to engage in auditing itself. The curriculum management audit follows the same logic.

The Formulation of Plans

A plan is a tangible product representing specific actions to be taken by persons in an agency or organization, which are designed to meet the objectives or targets. These plans may be subdivided into smaller tasks, functions, or jobs and assigned to specific people. The plan is a kind of *audit trail,* against which the actions of people can be compared and judged. Discrepancies or gaps between the actions taken and those described in plans or subplans provide another set of potential quantitative or narrative descriptions for the auditors (see Kaufman and Herman, 1991).

Measuring Outcomes or Results

Sooner or later auditors come to engage in judgments about "what happened" or describe the existing state of affairs in an agency or organization. There are a variety of ways existing conditions, outcomes, procedures, and work tasks can be described and analyzed. This book describes many of them that relate to curriculum management (see also English, 1987, pp. 257–277, and English, 1988.

Comparing Results/Outcomes to Objectives

Auditors are expected to comment and evaluate what was finally accomplished by an agency or organization. The *meaning* of these conditions or affairs is set within what the organization wanted to accomplish (its objectives and its actions), juxtaposed against what it should have or desired to accomplished. The objectives actions results comparison provides the *context* within which and against which any auditor does his or her work. The theoretical construct within which auditing occurs has been called "the rational organization" (Silver, 1983, p. 77), and in the area of curriculum, "one whose significant features have been supported by valid and appropriate lines of reasoning. . . . An unrationalized curriculum is one that we may feel in our bones is good, but whose virtues we cannot readily explain or account for" (Walker and Soltis, 1986, p. 16).

SCHOOL SYSTEMS AS RATIONAL ORGANIZATIONS

The curriculum management audit assumes that school systems are "rational organizations." There is plenty of evidence that they must be. Increasing state legislation requires school systems and individual school sites to engage in the establishment of objectives, the development of plans to improve school operations and instructional processes, the utilization of measurement and testing to assess results, and prescriptive or diagnostic procedures to continually upgrade and improve operations and results. Such plans faithfully embody the preconditions for auditing to occur, thereby making auditing possible.

The *unit of analysis* (the thing being analyzed or evaluated) is normally an entire school system in the curriculum management audit. However, individual schools can be audited, along with programs within schools or even specific classrooms. The rationale for using the school system as the unit of analysis is that it is the basic unit of governance and accountability in American education. Despite the movement towards site-based management where parents, teachers, and the principal engage in rational planning and actions, no school (unless it is a school district that is possible in very small school systems) is accountable for the complete education of a child, K–12. While an individual school may be accountable for a segment of a student's education, the school system is accountable for the total education of the student. Furthermore, court actions, taxpayer suits, and the taxing function, as well as relationships with employee unions, involve the school system and not an individual school site. The curriculum management audit assumes that, for some organizational functions, a centralized approach is both necessary and economical. Other functions may be completely or partially decentralized.

EXPLICATION OF THE AUDIT STANDARDS

Since 1979, the curriculum management audit has used five standards against which information gathered by reviewing documents, interviewing system employees and parents, and visiting schools may be collected, grouped, and analyzed. It will be almost immediately seen that these five standards are intimately linked to assumptions regarding the pre-conditions required to assess agency or organizational performance as embodied in elements pertaining to a financial control system.

Curriculum Audit Management Standard One

The school system is able to demonstrate its control of resource, programs, and personnel.

The first curriculum management audit standard is centered on the control issue. That the system or agency must demonstrate it is *in control* embodies the pre-condition necessary to form a judgment regarding performance. No organization or agency can improve itself if it is not in control (cannot direct, maintain, or change) of what it does. In school systems, that means that the agency must be able to take actions to alter what people do so as to bring about conformance to its overall objectives. In schools, that means relating the performance of teachers and administrators who shape and manage the instructional process to define and continuously improve pupil learning. This assumption does not automatically mean the teacher is made into a robot, nor students into passive receptacles. It does not automatically assign inertia to the teacher-student relationship. While some potential objectives in school systems may be construed so as to *require* passivity, others may empower and provide room for teachers and students to construct their own meanings. Auditing does not require what Apple (1981) has called "the de-skilling" of the teaching cadre. In this situation, teachers are robbed of the important decisions regarding teaching content and strategies by increasing forms of social control. The audit does not require such "de-skilling." It does require that the spaces in which teachers engage in such decisions be anticipated by those in charge of system governance, i.e., the board of education in board policy. Board policy can sketch out the broad guidelines that establish the authority of the teaching staff to make such determinations. Such policies do not have to cite every specific case, but give to teachers broad potentialities to construct their classroom environments to engage in reshaping society if that is what is desired (see Brady, 1993, pp. 119–125). Auditing does not assume, nor does it require, that the teacher, as a somewhat autonomous professional, must be or should be coerced or compromised by the system for the system to be in control of itself. That some school systems within some states *do coerce* teachers is a condition often existing without any thought of auditing. Control can mean dominance. However, "bottom up" control as the sum total of teacher actions within board policy can also embody the idea. This condition can also be audited (see English, 1988, pp. 329–342). The condition that most often produces conformance and regulates teachers and students more than any other is the type of evaluation system employed by the school system or the state in which it must function. Traditional standardized, norm-referenced tests and some criterion-referenced tests definitely tend to de-skill teachers and extend the domination of the state in educational matters. Curriculum management audits can and have called attention to this state of affairs.

Common Indicators for Standard One

The common indicators for curriculum management audit Standard One are

- a clear set of board policies that reflect local and state program goals and the necessity to use achievement data to improve school system operations
- a clear set of policies that establish an operational framework for management that permits accountability
- a curriculum that is centrally defined and adopted by the board of education
- a functional administrative structure that facilitates the design and delivery of the district's curriculum
- a direct, uninterrupted line of authority from the school board/superintendent and other central officers through principals and classroom teachers
- organizational development efforts that are focused to improve system effectiveness
- documentation of school board and central office planning for the attainment of goals, objectives, and mission over time
- a clear mechanism to define and direct change and innovation within the school system to permit maximization of its resources on priority goals, objectives, and mission

Not all of the indicators will be applicable to every audit situation. They serve to establish benchmarks of what is meant by "demonstration of control." It should be noted that the indicator, "a curriculum that is centrally defined," does not necessarily mean one solely defined by the board or even the state. The curriculum may be defined by teachers, but ultimately it is adopted *for the system* as a whole. The definition of curriculum does not mean every teacher does his or her own thing *despite the system*. It does stand to reason that a state-imposed curriculum will advance the interests of the state. In some situations, these interests may not be those of the local system or an individual classroom teacher. This condition could also exist if teachers themselves defined a curriculum instead of the state. The minimal pre-conditions that must exist are the creation of objectives as standards *for the system*. How such objectives are created, what they embody, the processes used to define them, and who defines them are not proscribed by the audit.

Curriculum Management Audit Standard Two

The school system has established clear and valid objectives for students.

There are two pre-conditions in this standard. The first pertains to clarity of the objectives. The second involves the validity of the same objectives. Clarity is a matter of specificity. To a very large extent, specificity has been subsumed under the rubric of measurability. If something is measurable, it is considered specific. In reality, what this has meant is that the process of evaluation has become dominant over the process of creating educational objectives. The "behavioral objectives" movement has substituted measurement for specificity. A "behavioral objective" is one that, by definition, is measurable. The process has confused measurability with desirability. Furthermore, "behavioral objectives are not good work statements because they address themselves more towards the outcomes of the work than the work itself" (English, 1987, p. 193).

Furthermore, given current emphasis on constructivist strategies for curriculum development, there is little room for the teacher to create those activities that provide meaning within their individual work context and that may not be anticipated (or even desired) by system officials. The audit does not require, as a pre-condition, the elimination of constructivist concepts of curriculum development in which learners are more active in discovering and applying knowledge than one would typically find in traditional schoolrooms (see Jones et al., 1987). It does require clarity regarding what they might be and where they pertain within the system (for a good example see Hord et al., 1987).

Validity pertains to how and who has determined which objectives are to be employed. When a curriculum is validated, it refers to some logical process that the major stakeholders were or are to be involved in approving the content or objectives contained within a curriculum. This process can be encapsulated in the creation of a simple curriculum validation matrix (see English, 1992, p. 35). Such a matrix provides a vote for each major stakeholder group in approving a curriculum.

Common Indicators for Standard Two

The common indicators for Standard Two are

- a clearly established, systemwide set of goals and objectives adopted by the board of education
- knowledge and use of emerging curriculum trends (validity issues)
- curriculum that addresses the full range of student effectiveness issues, both current and future
- objectives that set the framework for the system and its sense of priorities
- demonstration that the system is contextually responsive to national, state, and other expectations as evidence in local initiatives
- major programmatic initiatives designed to be cohesive
- provision of explicit direction for the superintendent and professional staff
- evidence of comprehensive, detailed, short- and long-range curriculum management planning
- mechanisms that exist for systemic curricular change

The indicators for Standard Two contain the expectations that curriculum development embodies local initiatives *that are reflective* of national and state trends/directives. It retains the locus of control for curriculum development at the local level, however. The indicators revolve around *systemic* as opposed to piecemeal change. The system must ensure that it changes *holistically.*

Curriculum Management Audit Standard Three

The school system demonstrates internal connectivity and rational equity in its program development and implementation.
Standard Three of the curriculum management audit is centered on

moving away from the idea that standardization (equity) is best (the same treatments for all students), to a notion of those children with greater needs receive more resources (equity). A school system must treat different children differently in order to be fair to all of them. The differences within schools and school systems are important variables that impact learning (see Murnane, 1975). Under the idea of equity, such differences are dealt within the audit.

Within this standard, auditors examine resource allocation (how dollars are distributed), financial, programmatic, and racial disparities and inequities that exist within the schools and comment on how they may be both injurious to children and how they should be remedied.

This audit standard also is cognizant of the requirement for cohesiveness and constancy within a school system. Systems that do not demonstrate consistency cannot be improved. They may not be systems at all (see Weick, 1985; Patterson et al., 1986).

The audit assumes that a school system must act like a system even if it isn't one, in order to survive in contemporary governmental/ funding contexts. Rationality is a way of life in public administration. Agencies that are not rational will not do well in efforts to improve their financial standing. It also stands to reason, for an organization to engage in differential allocations of resources that are rational, control is absolutely critical to the success of alternative distributive approaches (see Glatthorn, 1987).

The audit requires supervision of the cohesion of the curriculum within a school and a school system. Such supervision can be of a variety of kinds and types, depending upon the situation (for some characteristics of "positive supervision," see Squires et al., 1983, pp. 24–45).

The Common Indicators of Standard Three

The common indicators for Standard Three are

- documents/sources that reveal internal connections at different levels in the system
- predictable consistency through a coherent rationale for content delineation within the curriculum
- equity of curriculum/course access and opportunity
- allocation of resource flow to areas of identified greatest need
- a curriculum that is clearly explained to members of the teaching staff and building-level administrators and other supervisory personnel

- specific professional development programs to enhance curriculum design and delivery
- a curriculum that is monitored by central office and site supervisory personnel
- teacher and administrator responsiveness to school board policies, currently and over time

Curriculum Management Audit Standard Four

The school system uses the results from system-designed and/or adopted assessment to adjust, improve, or terminate ineffective practices or programs.

It is not enough that the school system as the unit of analysis has the capability to adjust, improve, or terminate programs (also a measure of control), but that it has actually *engaged in these acts.* This curriculum management audit standard is not assessing a pre-condition, but *actions.*

It is within this standard that curriculum management auditors examine the nature and scope of the assessment system, the diversity of assessment strategies, the real use of feedback in decision making, the manner in which the school system reports to its stakeholders, and whether or not the system has engaged in continuous improvement over a specific time period. Of course, the type of evaluation system is linked to system performance objectives (see Levin and Long, 1981). The final link is to see if evaluation results have been linked to subsequent budgetary requests. The use of auditing techniques are beginning to be applied to large case school reform efforts outside of the curriculum management audit (see Quinn et al., 1993, pp. 2–11).

Common Indicators for Standard Four

The common indicators for curriculum management audit Standard Four are

- a formative and summative assessment system linked to a clear rationale in board policy
- knowledge and use of emerging curriculum and program assessment trends
- use of a student and program assessment plan that provides for diverse assessment strategies for multi-purposes at all levels — district, school, and classroom

- a timely and relevant base upon which to analyze important trends in the instructional program
- a way to provide feedback to the teaching and administrative staffs regarding how classroom instruction may be evaluated and subsequently improved
- a vehicle to examine how well specific programs are actually producing desired learner outcomes
- a data base to compare the strengths and weaknesses of various programs and program alternatives, as well as to engage in equity analysis
- a data base to modify or terminate ineffective educational programs
- a method/means to relate to a programmed budget and enable the school system to engage in cost-benefit analysis
- organizational data gathered and used to continually improve system functions

Curriculum Management Audit Standard Five

The school system has improved productivity.
This standard deals with results, costs and benefits, and conditions in which teaching/learning takes place. The standard recognizes that school systems as governmental entities are accountable but do not control all of the variables that determine costs and results.

The audit does not mandate a program budget (for characteristics of a program budget, see Hartman, 1988, pp. 27–29). But it is equally clear that some sort of nontraditional budgeting process is required to track results to programs and engage in informed administrative decision making as a consequence. This audit standard deals with the cost-quality relationship to the extent it can be determined in public school settings. Barriers to determining cost-quality relationships have been identified by Mundt et al., (1982) as an atmosphere of management by crisis, lack of motivation to engage in change, start-up costs, lack of staff to engage in analytical problem solving, and the lack of information about existing productivity levels (pp. 127–128).

Common Indicators for Standard Five

The common indicators for Standard Five are

- planned and actual congruence among curricular objectives, results, and financial costs

- support systems that function in systemic ways
- district and school climate conducive to continual improvement
- specific means that have been selected or modified and implemented to attain better results in the schools over a specified time period
- a planned series of interventions that have raised pupil performance levels over time and maintained those levels within the same cost parameters as in the past
- a financial network that is able to track costs to results, provide sufficient fiduciary control, and is used as a viable data base in making policy and operational decisions
- school facilities that are well kept, sufficient, safe, orderly, that comply with all requirements, and that facilitate delivery of the instructional program

WHAT THE CURRICULUM MANAGEMENT AUDIT DOESN'T ADVOCATE

Perhaps the most serious intellectual criticism that can be leveled at the audit is that it does not advocate social reconstruction. Social reconstructivists begin considering school reform by seeing it as a tool to alter existing and inequitable socio-economic-political relationships (Stanley, 1992, p. 11). The reconstructivists argue that education is not now a neutral institution. It reinforces the socio-economic-political status quo by reproducing it (see English, 1991, pp. 84–104).

While the reconstructivists may be right, it is also a political fact of life that few, if any, existing governmental entities would undertake such a venture that would act directly within the larger society to alter the political power structure. Retribution would be swift and overwhelming. In this respect, the audit is a compromise between the "real" and the "utopian" worlds as they exist. There is much the audit has done to change educational systems for the better. It is true that it has not engaged in recommendations that would intercept or alter socio-political arrangements. The audit has not been a tool to advance *critical pedagogy* (see Giroux, 1983) as it would act directly to remove the state's influence in education. If a local board of education adopted critical pedagogical practices, it would accept and audit them accordingly. But to incorporate in its standards such larger social change would doom it to a largely academic exercise. Perhaps in this respect, the curriculum management audit is not radical enough. Only time will tell.

REFERENCES

Apple, M. W. (1981) "Curricular Form and the Logic of Technical Control," In *Rethinking Curriculum Studies*, L. Barton, R. Meighan and S. Walter (eds.), Lewes, England: Falmer Press.

Brady, J. (1993) "A Feminist Pedagogy of Multiculturalism," In *The International Journal of Education Reform*, 2(2):119–125.

Dearden, J. (1976) *Cost Accounting and Financial Control Systems*. Reading, Massachusetts: Addison-Wesley Publishing Co.

English, F. W. (1987) *Curriculum Management*. Springfield, Illinois: Charles C. Thomas Publisher.

English, F. W. (1988) *Curriculum Auditing*. Lancaster, Pennsylvania: Technomic Publishing Co., Inc.

English, F. W. (1991) "Visual Traces in Schools and the Reproduction of Social Inequities," In *Contemporary Issues in U.S. Education*, K. M. Borman, P. Swami and L. P. Wagstaff, (eds.), Norwood, New Jersey: Ablex Publishing Corporation, pp. 84–104.

English, F. W. (1992) *Deciding What to Teach and Test*. Newbury Park, California: Corwin Press.

Giroux, H. A. (1983) *Theory and Resistance in Education: A Pedagogy for the Opposition*. South Hadley, Massachusetts: Begin & Garvey Publishers, Inc.

Glatthorn, A. A. (1987) *Curriculum Renewal*. Alexandria, Virginia: ASCD.

Hartman, W. T. (1988) *School District Budgeting*. Englewood Cliffs, New Jersey: Prentice-Hall, Inc.

Hord, S. M., W. L. Rutherford, L. Huling-Austin and G. E. Hall. (1987) *Taking Charge of Change*. Alexandria, Virginia: ASCD.

Jones, B. F., A. S. Palincsar, D. S. Ogle and E. G. Carr. (1987) *Strategic Teaching and Learning: Cognitive Instruction in the Content Areas*. Alexandria, Virginia: ASCD.

Kaufman, R. and J. Herman. (1991) *Strategic Planning in Education*. Lancaster, Pennsylvania: Technomic Publishing Co., Inc.

Levin T. and R. Long. (1981) *Effective Instruction*. Alexandria, Virginia: ASCD.

Merriam-Webster. (1972) *Webster's Seventh New Collegiate Dictionary*. Springfield, Massachusetts: G & C Merriam Company, Publishers.

Mundt, B. M., R. T. Olsen and H. I. Steinberg. (1982) *Managing Public Resources*. New York: Peat Marwick International.

Murnane, R. (1975) *The Impact of School Resources on the Learning of Inner City Children*. Cambridge, Massachusetts: Ballinger Publishing Company.

Patterson, J. L., S. C. Purkey and J. V. Parker. (1986) *Productive School Systems For a Nonrational World*. Alexandria, Virginia: ASCD.

Quinn, D. W., M. Stewart and J. Nowakowski. (1993) "An External Evaluation of Systemwide School Reform in Chicago," *The International Journal of Educational Reform*, 2(1):2–11.

Silver, P. (1983) *Educational Administration*. New York: Harper and Row.

Stanley, W. B. (1992) *Curriculum for Utopia*. New York: State University of New York Press.

Squires, D. A., W. G. Huitt and J. K. Segars. (1983) *Effective Schools and Classrooms: A Research Based Perspective.* Alexandria, Virginia: ASCD.

Walker, D. F. and J. F. Soltis. (1986) *Curriculum and Aims.* New York: Teachers College Press.

Weick, K. (1985) "Sources of Order in Underorganized Systems: Themes in Recent Organizational Theory and Inquiry," in *Organizational Theory and Inquiry,* Y. S. Lincoln (ed.), Beverly Hills, California: SAGE Publications, pp. 106–136.

CHAPTER 2

Background and Criticisms of the Curriculum Audit and Total Quality Management

LARRY E. FRASE—*San Diego State University*

TOTAL QUALITY MANAGEMENT

TQM to Japan

TOTAL quality management has emerged as a promising management and leadership strategy for both industry and education. However, unlike many managerial panaceas that have come and gone leaving little substantive improvements in their wake, TQM has a powerful track record. W. Edwards Deming is given credit by both the Japanese and Americans for bringing the Japanese industry from rubble and a reputation of incompetence to the most effective and highest quality system in the world.

Since Deming began work in Japan in 1950, the Japanese economy has become the envy of other nations (Johnson, 1993). In stark contrast to their reputation for producing cheap and shoddy goods in the 1940s, Japan is now heralded for its high-quality products. In a very systematic manner, Japanese industrialists took on corporate giants around the world and emerged as the victor every time. Examples include the American automobile industry; American television, radio, and electronics industries; Xerox; IBM; Harley-Davidson; the Swiss watch industry; and many others. Japan literally stunned the world's corporate giants by winning massive market shares long thought to be sacred holdings of others. They did it by focusing on quality, not profits and market shares. As Deming (1992) asserts, if a high quality product is offered, all else will follow.

Author's note: The effects and debate regarding TQM are evolving very rapidly. The most current information regarding TQM is carried in the news media and has not yet been addressed in professional books and journals. Hence, readers will note the author's use of *The New York Times* as reference material.

Japan, soundly defeated militarily in World War II and reduced to rubble, came back to defeat economically its conquerors, the United States of America and its allies. To add insult to injury, the resourceful Japanese accomplished this with a gift from the United States. The gift was W. Edwards Deming's presence and management philosophy. After helping Japan prepare for their 1951 census, Deming was sent to Japan by General Douglas MacArthur to help an unreliable radio industry build a strong radio communications network. Simply put, MacArthur wanted reliable radios in Japanese homes so that he could communicate directly with them. The radios were to be distributed by the Occupation Forces. This endeavor was a success, and Japanese industry accepted Deming and his management philosophies. Soon, other American management and statistical control experts, such as Juran, Feigenbaum, and Shewart, were invited to Japan. Together, these sensei (teachers), the determination of the Japanese, and the leadership of Iciro Ishikawa, Japan's top industrialist, transformed their country into an industrial giant respected worldwide as the world's leading exporter of high-quality products.

American Resurgence

In keeping with the American spirit, financial, personnel, and technical expertise was given freely to Japan immediately following the war. Japan used it well, and the American economy and pride suffered. Now the gift of TQM has come home and is recognized for its merit. Many American industries have greeted it with cautious, but open arms. These industries, with American drive and ingenuity and demands for strong negotiations for fair economic practices, are staging an economic comeback (Sterngold, 1993). True to the American spirit, many American industries are quickly building their reputation for high-quality workmanship. General Motors' Saturn and Cadillac Projects, Xerox, Harley-Davidson, Ford, and many others have won back respect, a reputation for quality, and, as a result, strong market shares. As Xerox's Paul Allaire, Chairman of the Board and Chief Executive Officer, said, "We will accomplish our objectives by using leadership through quality" (Allaire, 1993). Xerox is back on top. Other American industries once thought to be dead are also regaining respect for quality and reliability. The much maligned Harley-Davidson motorcycle, the Cadillac STS, the Ford Taurus, GM's Saturn, and the Xerox copiers are selling well all over the world. IBM is staging a major comeback with its Thinkpad notebook computers. IBM's Bruce Claflin, General Manager of Mobile Computing, attributes the success to TQM style management, ". . . It [the Thinkpad] would have been smothered by the old management gridlock, and none of what we have today would have happened" (Lohr, 1993).

Confidence in American automobiles has returned to American buyers. Sales in 1993 have exceeded the gains made in 1992. Americans turned to Japanese automobiles in the 1980s because of their quality. Now they are turning to American automobiles for the same reason. Companies such as Chevrolet which took a beating in the '70s and '80s are poised to reclaim their old glory. They are narrowing their focus and stressing quality (Bennet, 1994). President Clinton summed up this trend by declaring that United States car makers are "Winning the Quality Race" (Devon, 1993).

American is doing very well in another important indicator. After lagging far behind Japan in the number of patents filed in America in 1992, three American companies now hold three of the top five spots. IBM regained the number one spot for the U.S., Eastman Kodak is fourth and General Electric is fifth beating out Toshiba and Canon. The significance of this is that patents represent investments in research and a means of protecting them (Pollack, 1994).

This is not to imply that TQM is a panacea. It is not. It is only as good as the people using it. This message is captured in a response from Juran when the Japanese requested his permission to name an award after him, "I did indeed lecture in Japan as reported, and I did bring something new to them—a structured approach to quality. I also did the same thing for many other countries, yet none of these attained the results achieved by the Japanese. So who performed the miracle" (Garvin, 1988, p. 184) (emphasis added). The same could be said of the resurgence of American industry. TQM provided guidelines, but good old American ingenuity, determination, and a sound understanding of theory made it happen. Possibly the best example of this is GM's Saturn Project, which, in competition with all cars, is winning numerous quality awards. It is a result of American ingenuity in management, unifying the roles and purposes of management and labor in a new company. Success has not come from protectionistic trade agreements, it came from quality. Trade agreements have not yet been resolved between the United States and Japan, although slow progress is being made (Anonymous, 1993). The United States has responded with "quality."

Total Quality Management: Not Without Its Critics

Criticism of TQM is varied. During a recent four-day Deming seminar on TQM, one critic decried Deming by stating that it is likely that total quality management worked in Japan solely because it fit the Japanese culture, ethics, etc. (Deming, 1992). This criticism has been negated by the fact that quality management has also been used effectively in the United States and other countries.

Another major criticism is that Deming's focus on "reducing variation" is inhumane and wrong because of the fact that current thinking strongly suggests that creativity and variation in people is needed and desirable. Reducing variation in people is a misinterpretation. The traditional Tayloristic notion is to make people robots in order to gain uniformity on the assembly line. However, as we have learned, this didactic approach reduced variation in workers and resulted in lower morale, reduced creativity, and decreased quality of products, rather than consistent high quality. Deming's intent is to reduce variation in the quality of products—to create and maintain high-quality products. If anything, TQM relies on people to be creative, to engage their workplace and co-workers to be critical of the system and to offer suggestions for improvement with the focus on improving quality.

Total quality management school administrators empower teachers to modify the system to achieve this quality state so that, despite the wide variety of student characteristics, all students attain a high-quality education. The accent is on cooperation rather than competition. Further, TQM embodies applications of post-industrial practices such as transformational leadership (Burns, 1979), reflection (Schon, 1984), and learning organizations (Senge, 1990).

Pallas and Neumann (1993) have questioned nine aspects of what they consider to be TQM assumptions and their applicability to higher education. They comment that the questions are also pertinent to the application of TQM in public education. The nine aspects in question are grouped into three categories: emphasis on tight coupling, assumptions regarding rationality, and reduction of variation. Each category is addressed.

TQM's Emphasis on Tight Coupling

Pallas and Neumann (1993) contend that tight coupling would prevent schools and colleges from ". . . conducting education while simultaneously responding, with credibility to the often conflicting or inappropriate demands of powerful external agents who require responses" (p. 22). Their claim is that loose coupling makes it possible for educational institutions to develop subsystems to respond to various demands.

First, neither Deming (1986, 1992) nor TQM imply that only the chief administrative officer should make decisions. Rather, Deming (1992) is quite clear that everyone in an organization must participate in transforming it to one where all are involved in improving the work environment, the work processes, and the work product. Second, the critics imply that TQM is bureaucratic rationality or mechanical, rather than substantial rationality that is reflective and self-organizing (Morgan, 1986). In essence, they complain that TQM is goal-directed and thereby overemphasizes . . . its concern with coherence, and . . . its attention to linear sequencing of thought and action." TQM does imply rationality and organization, but this author knows of no organization that has succeeded without designating goals and establishing plans to attain them. However, effective organizations do alter plans in order to keep on target. All members of a TQM team must see and know the global picture, actively participate in attaining the ends, and help formulate changes to ensure meeting the ends (Deming, 1993).

The notion that substantial rationality implores everyone to follow their own leads and do what they want anytime they want is nonsense, a near perfect illustration of professorial fuzzy-headedness. Highly successful renegade companies such as Apple Computer Company are examples of the principles of rationality and loose coupling working in concert to attain success.

The notion of constancy of purpose, Deming's first point, is germane here. Many United States companies failed to stick to their areas of expertise in the 1970s and 1980s. They over-diversified and failed. The latest example is Westinghouse's action (Anonymous, 1993) to sell fourteen hotels to gain liquid capital in an attempt to stop massive financial losses. It was smart to sell them. It was foolish to acquire them in the first place. After all, what does Westinghouse know about hotels? The situation could have been avoided had they maintained greater constancy of purpose and stuck to their area of expertise.

With regard to education, it is possible that coupling should be tightened. This may be the most effective way to focus education on a task long enough to accomplish it, rather than changing goals on the political whims of ignorant critics and politicians—those in govern-

ment and those in schools. Pallas and Neumann's extreme views of bureaucratic and substantial rationality appear to offer them the comfort
of continuing not only to determine and implement the best way to get
a job done, but also to determine the job. No legislation offers individual teachers the authority or responsibility to determine the curriculum
and the prescribed means for delivering it. Such a school would be
anarchy and would accomplish little—think, for example, of the
Summerhillian-type schools of the 1960s and 1970s, where the means
became the ends and students learned little.

Questions about TQM's Assumptions Regarding Rationality

Criticism of the principle of rationality is also levied at the curriculum management audit and is addressed in detail later in this chapter.
For this section, however, Pallas and Neumann (1993) claim that the rationality promised by TQM misconstrues the relationship between human thought and action, "expecting thought to produce action rather
than the more liekly reverse" (p. 25). This argument has come and
gone repeatedly, without successfully demonstrating its claims in practice. In response, one has to ask the authors if they wait until they run
out of gas before they fill up. Or do they wait until they are out of
breakfast cereal before they stock up? Are filling up and stocking up
detrimental to people? I don't think so. It simply makes sense, and I
wager the authors practice rationality at home. It is at work that they
resent rationality. If it were their children in question, it is likely they
would want the teacher to have a predetermined curriculum of some
sort. This argument harkens back to the Rousseauian notion of natural
unfoldment, where the teacher makes no assumptions about what
children should know and, instead, waits for the children to unfold and
demonstrate their needs. Rousseau's ideas failed in Europe, and Dewey,
a descendent, failed in the same quest in the United States in the 1920s.
Dewey's followers failed in the 1960s. These arguments about rationality are old and tired. Further, they are self-serving and lack substance.

Questions about Reduction of Variation

Pallas and Neumann (1993) characterize reduction of variation incorrectly. They assume variability refers to differences in workers, that is,
teachers. It does not. Deming (1992, 1993) clearly states that workers
in every organization should be continually involved in making im-

provement in the work systems, expressly to achieve success and experience joy in work. This point, to constantly improve the systems (point number 5), is made very clear in the Red Bead Game that Deming employs in his four-day seminars. In this game, workers are not allowed to communicate and are forced to work with a system that cannot possibly produce desired results, regardless of how hard employees work. Encouraging creativity and diversity for workers is a hallmark of TQM. Improving quality of learning is its aim.

Granted, no one instructional methodology works best for every teacher. TQM calls for groups of employees to continually examine the environment for ways to improve. The requirement to allow for and promote continuous learning is clearly illustrated in the Red Bead Game. It is echoed over and over again in TQM literature; it is Deming's point number 13.

The remainder of the criticisms/questions are variations on the same themes. Pallas and Neumann conclude that "We do not expect our analysis to be terribly persuasive—not because of the lack of merit of our arguments, but because of the tenor of the times" (p. 37). The essences of their criticisms are cognitively wrong and philosophically deranged. Certainly, the tenor of the times will eschew acceptance and so will the merits of their criticisms. They claim one can only perceive TQM and its possibilities for education through their wide lenses. They claim that if TQM is viewed through other lenses, it can only be seen as a panacea. That is quite self aggrandizing; certainly, there is room in education for more than one lens. I know of no one who denies that education has room for improvement, and many agree there is room for much improvement. Rejecting TQM on misapplied theoretical and philosophical principles is malpractice. Learning about it, finding in it that which can bring about improvements, and making adjustments along the way are the practices of professionals. To fully reject an idea which has already demonstrated benefits (Schmoker and Wilson, 1993), while falling back on only moderately successful practices replete with frailties, is not wise. The Pallas and Neumann posture regarding TQM is a perfect misapplication of the reasoning by the King of Hearts after reading the nonsensical poem of the White Rabbit: "If there is no meaning in it, that saves a worth of trouble, you know, as we needn't try to find any" (Lewis Carroll, 1988, p. 102).

No reasonable leadership or management practice sould be discredited based on whim. Likewise, no practice should be transferred "as is" from one company to another, one educational system to another, and certainly not from one country to another. As the companies mentioned in this chapter have done, TQM must be modified to accommodate the talents and needs of people in the organization and its clients. The criticisms of TQM are theoretical and appear defensible. They will be proven or disproven in practice.

THE CURRICULUM MANAGEMENT AUDIT

While TQM has emerged as a promising treatment for corporate America's ills, the curriculum management audit has taken a place front and center for America's educational system. After initial development of the audit, the founder, Fenwick English, centered the audit with the American Association of School Administrators (AASA), which orchestrates the practice of and training for curriculum management audits. As of this writing, over seventy curriculum management audits have been conducted in nineteen states, the District of Columbia, Saudi Arabia, and Bangladesh.

The name *curriculum management audit* belies the audit's broad scope. Contrary to simply reviewing the written curriculum, the audit covers all aspects of a school system that affect design and delivery of the curriculum. The audit offers an objective, third-party review of all data pertaining to the design and delivery of curriculum. Auditors become experts in the process by experiencing an intensive five-and-one-half–day training program and an internship sponsored by AASA.

Two sets of standards govern the curriculum management audit. One set focuses on guiding principles and the other on practice. The first set is: (English, 1988)

- *Objectivity*—Any two auditors using the same standards and data base will reach approximately the same conclusions.
- *Independence*—The auditors will have no vested interest in the outcomes of the audit.
- *Consistency*—The same procedures, techniques, and methods will be followed with each audit.
- *Materiality*—The auditors will have authority to make the distinction between what is important and what is not.
- *Full Disclosure*—The auditors will reveal all information that is important to the users of the audit.

The second set of standards, based on sound management principles and practices, is used by the auditors to assess plans and practices for curriculum design and delivery. These standards (English, 1988) ask that the school system should

- Demonstrate control of its resources, programs, and personnel.
- Establish clear and valid objectives for students.
- Demonstrate internal connectivity and rational equity in its program development and implementation.
- Use the results from district-designed or -adopted assessments to adjust, improve, or terminate ineffective practices or programs.
- Improve its productivity.

The response to the curriculum management audit has been overwhelming (see Chapter 11 of this book by Vertiz). After its curriculum management audit, the Darlington County Schools experienced a twenty-six–point increase on the Stanford Achievement Test (SAT), while state and national scores declined. Prior to the audit, Sunoco Products moved its headquarters to Darlington County and provided the majority of financing for the audit. Director of Community Relations for Sunoco, Jack Westmoreland, said that Sunoco is pleased with their involvement; the audit was a necessary step, and they have seen the district moving toward implementation of audit recommendations: "The curriculum has improved; curriculum chairs have been added; school maintenance has improved; the quality of leadership has been critically reviewed; and staff development has been put into place" (Vertiz, 1992).

Gary Livingston (1992), superintendent of the Topeka Public Schools, characterized the Topeka Schools' curriculum as a "wild animal marauding out of control," prior to the curriculum management audit. The first audit was performed in 1982 by English, then with Peat, Marwick, Mitchell. The audit promised so much that the district commissioned a second or post-audit by English in 1989. The post-audit revealed that many of the recommendations of the first audit had been successfully implemented and the number of design and delivery problems had been greatly reduced. As stated by Livingston (1992), "The original audit provided the bridle and the second audit the bit in our continuing quest to tame the curriculum. The question now is: Will there be a third audit?" (p. 202).

Larry D. Coble (1992) has commissioned curriculum management audits in two North Carolina school districts, first, in 1988, as superintendent of the Durham County Schools and again in 1991 as superintendent of the Winston-Salem/Forsyth County Schools. Coble sees the audit as ". . . one of the best assessment tools available to local school boards and school administrators" (Coble, 1992, p. 190). He credits the audit with providing direction to make profound changes, such as eliminating ability tracking.

As the new superintendent of the Little Rock Public Schools, Mac Bernd (1992) read the recent audit of the school district and said it "provided me with an excellent diagnosis of the district and key insights and direction for reform in the Little Rock Public Schools." Superintendent Bernd was sufficiently impressed with the advanced findings the audit offered him in Little Rock that he required that his contract with his new district, Newport-Mesa School District, Newport California, contain language obligating the board to fund a curriculum management audit. This was a condition of signing the contract to be superintendent of schools (Personal conversation b, 1993).

The curriculum management audit has resulted in major educational improvements. The audit has established itself both in and out of court as the most rigorous process available for an impartial look at school system curriculum, educational programs and outcomes, and their relationship to decision making and budgeting.

The Curriculum Management Audit: Not without Critics

The theory of rationality asserts that a rational system is one in which the people and the activities are directed by goals and objectives. Because the theory of rationality is the foundation for the curriculum management audit, it is not without critics (English, 1992). The critics, argue that "control" is the cornerstone of classical organizational theory (Foster, 1986; Maxcy, 1991a and b). Further, they claim "empowerment" not control, should be the only aim of management and the only means for attaining substantial improvements in productivity (English, 1992). Weick (1985) has asserted that rationality is a myth and that management perpetuates it to conceal the fact that the theory is not rational at all. Organizational theory is seen by many critics as reinforcing central power by legitimating a coercive and repugnant set of Tayloristic practices and beliefs. Domination, rather than emancipation, is claimed to be the operational and philosophical operating style.

The writer's experience provides substantial evidence that these accusations are false. Audits have been used by superintendents and school boards to more clearly identify their mission and to monitor their progress in attaining that mission. Further, unethical practices by those supposedly in power, school boards and school superintendents, have been exposed by audits and then rectified through prescribed channels. For example, in the Little Rock Public Schools, the audit found that a board member was in violation of board policies and generally accepted board practice by abusing staff with verbal assaults and issuing orders to administrators and teachers (American Association of School Administrators, 1990b). This board member resigned his post shortly following the audit.

The audit found that the Washington, D.C., school board was spending 1.25 million dollars on their salaries and personal staff, while at the same time claiming lack of funds for school and program improvements. Further, the audit pointed out that "ghost" employees were on the school payroll and hidden by the personnel office. The audit further found that thousands of evaluations, which were scheduled, never occurred, and a ridiculously low percentage of the D.C. teachers, 0.05%, were considered marginal or unsatisfactory and 22% of the teachers were not evaluated (American Association of School Administrators, 1991; Horwitz, 1992; Anonymous, 1992). The administration was guilty of malpractice in not providing constructive feedback to teachers (Frase and Streshly, 1994).

The audit found that individual members of the Huntsville City School Board (American Association of School Administrators, 1993) were violating board policy and generally accepted board practices by issuing orders and requests for time-consuming reports directly to administrators and teachers. These practices were brought to light in the audit, and the board and superintendent are now working to alleviate these problems.

The audit determined that the superintendent of the Boyd County Schools in Kentucky (American Association of School Administrators, 1990a) practiced nepotism and revealed many examples of malpractice. The superintendent resigned shortly after the audit.

These achievements exonerate the theory of rationality from the critics' contention as being inherently unjust. The critics' accusations are only accurate when leadership is inadequate. The benefits of the theory of rationality, of establishing goals, monitoring progress, and making corrections in course, have been demonstrated. The theory of rationality is also a cornerstone of TQM. The principle of maintaining constance of purpose strongly imply goal setting, monitoring, and redirecting the organization toward the goals.

SUMMARY

This chapter addressed the initial criticisms of TQM in education and criticisms of the curriculum management audit. In summary, the criticisms are theoretical and not based on experience. In fact, experiential evidence strongly indicates that the criticisms are inaccurate. As with every other theoretical debate, the final conclusion lies in practice. Only time will tell.

REFERENCES

Allaire, P. (1993) Presentation to San Diego Count Superintendents and the San Diego County Education Office, February, 14.

American Association of School Administrators. (1990a) A Curriculum Audit of the Boyd County School District. Washington, D.C.: American Association of School Administrators.

American Association of School Administrators. (1990b) A Curriculum Audit of the Little Rock School District. Washington, D.C.: American Association of School Administrators.

American Association of School Administrators. (1991) A Curriculum Audit of the Washington, D.C. Public Schools. Washington, D.C.: American Association of School Administrators.

American Association of School Administrators. (1993) A Curriculum Audit of the Huntsville City School District. Washington, D.C.: American Association of School Administrators.

Anonymous. (1992) New York *Times*. Editorial (February 28).

Anonymous. (1993) New York *Times*. "Money section" (February 10):19.

Bennet, J. (March 16, 1994) "Chevrolet Is Seeking To Reclaim Old Glory," *New York Times*, Vol. CXLII, 49, 637, p. C1.

Bernd, M. (1992) Author's personal communication with Mac Bernd, new superintendent of Little Rock Public Schools.

Bernd, M. (1993) Author's personal conversation with Mac Bernd, superintendent of Newport-Mesa School District.

Brimelow, P. and L. Spencer. (1993) "How the National Education Association Corrupts Our Public Schools," *Forbes*, 151 (12):72–84.

Burns, M. (1979) *Leadership*. New York: Simon and Schuster.

Carroll, L. (1988). *Alice's Adventures in Wonderland*, New York, NY: Tom Doherty Associates.

Coble, L. (1992) "A District's Response to Its Audit Report," *Education*, 113(2):1990-1992.

Deming, W. E. (1986) *Out of the Crisis.* Cambridge Massachusetts: Massachusetts Institute of Technology, Center for Advanced Engineering Study.

Deming, W. E. (1992) Notebook from seminar presentation, *Quality, Productivity, and Competitive Position,* held in St. Louis, Missouri, October 6-9.

Deming, W. E. (1993) *The New Economics.* Cambridge, Massachusetts: Massachusetts Institute of Technology, Center for Advanced Engineering Study.

Devon, L. (1993) New York *Times.* Section C (May 26):4.

English F. (1988) *Curriculum Auditing.* Lancaster, Pennsylvania: Technomic Publishing Company, Inc.

English, F. E. (1992) *Deciding What to Teach and Test.* Newbury Park, California: Corwin Press.

Foster, W. (1986) *Paradigms and Promises.* Buffalo, New York: Prometheus Books.

Frase, L. and W. Streshly. (1994) "Lack of Accuracy, Feedback, and Commitment in Teacher Evaluation," *Journal of Personnel Evaluation in Education,* 1:47-57.

Garvin, D. (1988) *Managing Quality: The Strategic and Competitive Edge.* New York: Free Press.

Horwitz, S. (1992) "New Audit Lambasts D.C. School System," Washington Post (February 19): D 1,5.

Johnson, J. (1993) *Total Quality Management in Education.* Eugene, Oregon: Oregon School Study Council.

Livingston, G. (1992) "Curriculum Control—After an Educational Performance Audit, Are You Really Finished?" *Education,* 113(2):199-202.

Lohr, S. (1993) "Notebooks May Hold Key to I.B.M.'s Revival," *New York Times* (June 23).

Maxcy, S. J. (1991a) *Educational Leadership.* South Hadley, MA: Bergin and Garvey.

Maxcy, S. J. (1991b) "Sources of Order in Underorgainized Systems: Themes in Recent Organizational Theory," in *Organizational Theory.*

Morgan, G. (1986) *Images of Organization.* Beverly Hills, California: Sage.

New York Times (1993) "Stake in 14 Hotels Is Sold to Pay Down Bank Debt," Business Day Section. (July 10):19.

Pallas, A. and A. Neumann. (1993) "Blinded by the Light: The Applicability of Total Quality Management to Educational Organizations," Paper presented at the *Meeting of the American Educational Research Association,* Atlanta, Georgia.

Pollack, A. (March 14, 1994). "U.S. Gains on Japan in Patents," *New York Times,* Vol. CXLIII, 49, 635, p. C-!-2.

Schmoker, M. and R. Wilson. (1993) *Total Quality Education: Professionalization of Schools.* Bloomington, Illinois: Phi Delta Kappan.

Schon, D. (1983) *The Reflective Practitioner: How Professionals Think and Act.* New York: Basic Books.

Schon, D. A. (1984) "Leadership as Reflection in Action," In *Leadership and Organizational Culture,* T. J. Sergiovanni and J. E. Corbally, eds., Urbana, Illinois: University of Illinois Press, pp. 36-63.

Senge, P. (1990) *The Fifth Discipline: The Art and Practice of Learning Organizations.* New York: Doubleday.

Sterngold, J. (1993) "A New Old Trade Policy," *New York Times*, Section C–Business Day, page 1.

Vertiz, V. (1992) "The Curriculum Audit: A Quality Control Vehicle to School Reform," *Education* 113(2):165–167.

Weick, K. E. (1985) "Sources of Order in Underorganized Systems: Themes in Recent Organizational Theory," in *Organizational Theory and Inquiry*, Y. S. Lincoln., ed., Beverly Hills, CA: Sage.

CHAPTER 3

The Quality Fit

CAROLYN J. DOWNEY— *San Diego State University*
VIRGINIA C. VERTIZ — *National Curriculum Audit Center, American Association of School Administrators*

INTRODUCTION

THE word *quality* is sweeping the world of education. Many educators have been quick to label their current programs "quality" without careful examination of the quality movement to determine if their idea or approach fits quality premises. Unfortunately, some exceptionally well thought out ideas on quality, ideas which could help transform education, may be lost by educators who jump on the quality bandwagon without careful study.

The desire to be "in" could destroy a major opportunity for the field of education to transform itself. At the same time, other educators are engaged in appropriate processes and approaches that emerge from quality principles but could be overlooked in the rush for everyone to bring attention to programs that may not fit.

The authors propose that any educational program be examined for its quality fit. They present herein a two-pronged approach as an important first step for the education community to consider. The authors briefly explore some of the basic premises of the quality movement, as synthesized in Downey's Quality Fit Framework (Downey, 1992). The framework incorporates many of the ideas of Dr. W. Edwards Deming, who helped the Japanese to turn their economy around after World War II. He was invited to Japan to teach business leaders about quality; he taught them about a system and how to optimize it. He worked with American industry for decades, and, recently, the educational community began to listen.

The fact that this analysis is a first step only cannot be overemphasized. *Deming's principles and their application emerge from theory and cannot necessarily be copied for successful practice from one institution to another.* To put it in Deming's words, " To copy an example of success, without understanding it with the aid of theory, may lead to disaster" (Deming 1992a, p. 70).

The authors also examine the American Association of School Administrator's (AASA's) curriculum management audit, developed by Fenwick W. English when he was a partner at Peat, Marwick, Mitchell. Dr. English established the National Curriculum Audit Center (NCAC) at AASA in 1988. The audit is now prominent in the educational sector as a vehicle for examining the quality of curriculum management in school systems.

The authors then, in a two-pronged approach, review the audit for quality indicators. First, there is an overlay of the Downey Quality Fit Framework and the standards of the curriculum management audit. Second, there is the overlay of Deming's four areas of Profound Knowledge and his fourteen points with the curriculum management audit. The purpose of this approach is to answer the following question: How do the premises of the curriculum management audit and the ideas of the quality movement relate to one another?

The purpose of the audit is not to look directly at concepts of quality, as presented by Deming and others, but, instead, at the rationality of a system. It should be noted that the curriculum management audit and quality premises have different purposes. Quality premises apply to the design of the work, whereas the curriculum management audit is a descriptive evaluation of the work design and becomes prescriptive only through its recommendations (English, 1992). This chapter offers a particular view of a rational school system as a basis for applying Profound Knowledge and for determining the questions that school personnel must ask themselves as they consider the application of quality to school systems.

Deming defines quality as "the meeting and exceeding of customer's needs—and then continual improvement (of the product or service)" (Deming, 1992g). The authors further define quality as delighting the customer, with the recognition that customer needs change over time (Vertiz and Downey, 1993).

DOWNEY'S QUALITY FIT FRAMEWORK

The first prong of the approach in examination of the curriculum management audit is to use the Quality Fit Framework devised by Downey (1992). A review of the literature on quality reveals both similarities and differences by the major thinkers and gurus of the quality movement. School systems should focus on similarities and not get caught up in debating these differences. There is concern that educators are getting bogged down in debate on the differences and not moving forward in what needs to be a major overhaul of the education system.

There is significant agreement about the many principles that provide ample richness of thought for action. Downey has identified eighteen common core premises providing a framework that a system can use to move toward becoming a full-fledged quality system. These premises incorporate the thinking of Deming (1982, 1991, 1992); Juran (from Deming, 1982); Joiner (1985); Sashkin and Kiser (1991), and other "quality experts."

The premises are structured around three powerful leverage points in every work setting, which Marvin R. Weisbord identified in his book entitled *Productive Workplaces* (1987). The three leverage points that can be used to "turn anxiety into energy are purpose, structure, and relationships" (p. 258). Weisbord states that:

- Purpose or mission is the business we are in. It embodies future vision on which security and meaning depend.
- Structure is defined as "who gets to do what" and this affects self-esteem, dignity, and learning.
- Relationships are defined as the "connections with co-workers that let us feel whole—require cooperation across lines of hierarchy, function, class, race and gender."

The eighteen core premises are interrelated and must be integrated in a systematic way. The Quality Fit Framework and its premises are briefly described as follows.

Purpose

- It focuses on the customer with the aim of the organization built around exceeding both internal and external customers' needs and desires.
- It provides for a meaningful shared mission/aim/purpose that binds people together around a common identity and sense of destiny.
- There is a belief in continual improvement toward the aim of the organization with ever higher standards of benchmarks toward that mission.
- There is a sense of mission, constancy of purpose.

Structure

- The framework believes in and acts as a systemic organizational structure in which organizational relationships are orchestrated.
- It focuses on optimization in the system in which departments or units are encouraged to work together in a cooperative, rather than a competitive, fragmented way.
- This is a rational organization using Profound Knowledge founded on prediction and based on theory and reason.
- It has an integrated webbed structure rather than a hierarchical structure and works on an ad hoc basis rather than a bureaucratic one with integrated cross-functional teams with a collective inquiry strategy.
- There is a focus on the processes and various quality checkpoints, including supply points; incoming quality; process; distribution, and user, to increase quality.
- A data orientation for planning and as feedback to solve problems for continuous improvement of the process toward ever-increasing efficiency and effectiveness is used.
- It has an understanding of variation and uses the information for improvement of processes.

Relationships

- The framework mobilizes the workers to change the process.
- It has workers who collaboratively, cooperatively work in an inter-dependent way to carry out tasks.
- It provides for an organizational culture of shared values and beliefs about how to work together in an environment of fairness, openness, trust, clear standards, and dignity of others.
- There is leadership that understands how people are motivated and that moves employees toward intrinsic motivation.
- It recognizes that most failures are attributable to faults in the system, rather than the employee, and focuses on process improvement rather than individual accountability.
- A community of learners (internal and external customers) and learning teams, who are provided education and training on a continual basis in an attempt to improve the system, is established.

• It provides for constant communication and feedback within and between units of the organization.

DEMING'S PROFOUND KNOWLEDGE

Deming developed a theory of Profound Knowledge, which undergirds his principles about quality management and is comprised of four interacting parts. Profound Knowledge helps us make the shift from our current paradigm to a new one, which is necessary because America cannot increase its productivity within the old paradigms in business and education. The four parts are as follows.

Appreciation of a System

Deming describes a system as "an inter-connected complex of functionally related components that work together to try to accomplish the aim of the system." He states that "management of a system therefore requires knowledge of the interrelationships between all the components within the system and of the people that work in it." He further states that "optimization is a process of orchestrating the efforts of all components toward achievement of the stated aim. For optimization, a system must be managed. Management's responsibility is to strive toward optimization of the system through time" (Deming, 1992a, pp. 62–63).

"The obligation of any component" (of the system), says Deming, "is to contribute its best to the system, not to maximize its own production, profit, or sales, nor any other competitive measure. Some components may operate at a loss to themselves, in order to optimize the whole system, including the components that take a loss" (Deming, 1992a, p. 66).

Knowledge of Psychology

Deming's second critical area of Profound Knowledge is psychology. He says that managers must recognize that people are different from one another and learn in different ways and at different speeds. Managers must optimize the abilities and talents of each individual, while managing the interactions between them. It is also important that they understand how people are motivated, and that they know how to reinforce intrinsic motivation. Monetary and other rewards can destroy intrinsic motivation (Deming, 1991, 1992a).

Knowledge of Variation

Deming illustrates that most variation of a product or a service is attributable to the system in which it is produced. Without knowing the limits of variation, one cannot know if observable differences are predictable or common causes, attributable to the system or special causes, or attributable to an individual situation or person (Deming, 1991, 1992a).

Theory of Knowledge

Deming (1992a, p. 69) states that "management in any form is prediction." Rational prediction is based on theory and builds knowledge as the theory is revised and extended based on a comparison of predictions to results. He told one of the authors, "Experience teaches nothing without theory" (1992b). Without theory, therefore, there is no learning.

DEMING'S FOURTEEN POINTS

Deming's Fourteen Points, or principles for transformation of western management, are based on Profound Knowledge. According to Deming (1992a) they are natural applications of the system of Profound Knowledge and these segments cannot be separated. Variation, psychology, and the theory of knowledge are generic to the transformation of any system. Understanding of a specific system is necessary in order to apply the principles that achieve quality.

Deming's Fourteen Points are as follows (Deming, 1982):

"(1) Create constancy of purpose for improvement of product and service.

(2) Adopt the new philosophy.

(3) Cease dependence on mass inspection to achieve quality.

(4) End the practice of awarding business on the basis of price tag alone. Instead, minimize total cost by working with a single supplier.

(5) Improve constantly and forever every process for planning, production, and service.

(6) Institute training on the job.

(7) Adopt and institute leadership.

(8) Drive out fear.

(9) Break down barriers between staff areas.

(10) Eliminate slogans, exhortations, and targets for the work force.

(11) Eliminate numerical quotas for the work force and numerical goals for management.

(12) Break down barriers that rob people of pride of workmanship. Eliminate the annual rating or merit system.

(13) Institute a vigorous program of training and self-improvement for everyone.

(14) Put everybody in the company to work to accomplish the transformation."

THE CURRICULUM AUDIT

The curriculum management audit, offered through NCAC/AASA in cooperation with Fenwick English, is an objective, third-party examination of the curriculum design and delivery system of a school or school district. Both curriculum policy, and the system in which curriculum functions, are analyzed by the audit team. Specific recommendations are developed to improve those functions and to enhance school effectiveness.

The curriculum management audit is a tool that enables one to look at a school system in terms of its functionally related components as they pertain to the design and delivery of curriculum. Although schools are usually grouped together in what are called "school systems," it has been the authors' experience that they often operate individually, rather than as systems.

The curriculum management audit is governed by similar principles, procedures, and standards as a financial audit. The audit team uses documents, interviews, and site visits as major sources of data to determine the extent to which there is congruence among the written, taught, and tested curricula. The process is probably the single most powerful tool yet created for the improvement of curriculum, student achievement, and school districts, in general.

TABLE 1. The five curriculum management audit standards.

Standard Number	Standard Title	Standard The School System:
One	Control	. . . demonstrates its control of resources, programs, and personnel
Two	Direction	. . . establishes clear and valid objectives for students
Three	Connectivity and Equity	. . . demonstrates internal connectivity and rational equity in its program development and implementation
Four	Feedback	. . . uses the results from district-designed or adopted assessments to adjust, improve, or terminate ineffective practices or programs
Five	Productivity	. . . has improved productivity

The five standards of the curriculum management audit, and the criteria against which schools are evaluated with the audit process, illustrate the relationship of the functionally related components of school systems. Table 1 shows the five standards and corresponding indicators.

A LOGICAL CONNECTION AND
THE OVERLAY OF QUALITY

As school personnel attempt to understand how quality relates to education, it is important that they understand school districts as systems. Both Deming and English offer philosophies of management. How are these philosophies alike and how are they different? The specific questions the authors will raise are:

(1) To what extent do the concepts of the curriculum management audit relate to the Quality Fit Framework?

(2) To what extent do Deming's Profound Knowledge and Fourteen Points relate to the audit standards and their criteria?

(3) What implications might the application of quality management have on the recommendations auditors make to school districts?

FIRST PRONG: QUALITY FIT FRAMEWORK

The first comparison is how the curriculum management audit and quality ideas are aligned with eighteen quality premises outlined earlier, as well as Deming's areas of Profound Knowledge:

- *Customer Focus:* Both bring the concept of customer focus. In the quality movement, the aim of the organization is to meet and exceed the needs of the customer. In the curriculum management audit, Standard Five focuses on the need for increased student productivity as the planned purpose of all interventions in the system. The student is the ultimate customer in public schools; the product of the schools is learning. English (1987) states, "Work measurement in curriculum evaluation consists of two foci: (1) a determination of the results of the work of the clients (learners), and (2) a determination of the results of the work upon the system" (p. 285).
- *Shared Mission:* Both bring the concept of a mission or purpose to the organization. Although the curriculum management audit does not call for a shared mission, it does identify mission as an ingredient of long-range planning.

  Of a shared mission, Senge (1990) states, "If any one idea about leadership has inspired organizations . . . it's the capacity to hold a shared picture of the future we work to create. One is hard pressed to think of any organization that has sustained some measure of greatness in the absence of goals, values, and missions that become deeply shared throughout the organization" (p. 9).
- *Constancy of Purpose:* Both have a belief in constancy of purpose. The first of Deming's Fourteen Points is to create constancy of purpose. He states, "Problems of the future command first and foremost constancy of purpose and dedication to improvement . . . " (Deming, 1982, p. 25).

  English (1987) states, "Breakthroughs do not happen in organizations without purposes . . . and purpose[ful] work design . . . the insights are most powerful in purposive environments because they make a difference and can lead to changes in internal processes and new kinds of outcomes. Organizations without purposes . . . are not in control of themselves" (p. 205).

- *Continual Improvement:* Both Deming and English embrace the concept of continual improvement for increasing efficiency and effectiveness. Deming, in talking about continual improvement, indicates that every worker needs to ask the question every day: "Is there continual improvement in methods to understand better each new customer's needs?" (Deming, 1982, p.50).

English (1992a) states: "At the heart of the curriculum management audit is the idea that quality control should be functional in a school system. That means that there are clear goals or objectives; human activity is directed toward accomplishing them; feedback is gathered about system performance (internal and external); and such data are used to examine current levels of performance in order to change things to subsequently improve performance" (p. 107). English says that when this concept is repeated over time, there should be overall, systematic improvement.

Standard Five of the curriculum management audit includes the concept of continual improvement. "Productivity is simply the relationship between all of the inputs and the cost of obtaining any given level of outputs" (English, 1987, p. 66). "A school district meeting this standard of the audit is able to demonstrate consistent pupil outcomes, even in the face of declining resources. Improved productivity results when a school system is able to create a more consistent level of congruence between the major variables involved in achieving better results and in controlling costs" (p. 132).

Structure

- *Systemic Organizational Structure:* Both are based on the concept of systems thinking. One of Deming's four areas of Profound Knowledge is the appreciation of a system, as described earlier in this chapter. Deming indicates that management must understand systems and orchestrate all the integrated parts toward the aim of the organization.

A premise of the curriculum management audit is that "curriculum has two essential functions. The first is to create a system maximizing resources within that system (articulation and coordination) and thereby maximizing results (student learning)" (English, 1987, p. 285).

• *Optimization:* Both embrace the concept of optimization. Deming indicates that a leader is expected to understand systems and to manage the interaction of the components of the system for its optimization. English (1987) states that an expectation of effective curriculum management is that "the system is behaving as a system, and will be able to optimize its resources through optimal operations" (p. 286).

• *Rational Organization:* Both embrace the concept of rationality. Deming's theory of knowledge has as its underpinnings the idea that the organization should be rational. An organization that is rational requires prediction, observation, and theory. It is management's responsibility to look ahead, predict, change the product, keep the company in operation . . . management in any form is prediction; rational prediction is based on theory and reason (Deming, 1991). In a document on Theory of Knowledge, Deming (1992a) writes, "Any rational plan, however simple, requires prediction concerning conditions, behavior, comparison of performance of each of two procedures or materials" (p. 8).

English states, "A rational system is one in which the people and the activities are directed by goals and objectives (Silver, 1983, p. 77). English also states that "curriculum management audits operate on the premise that there is system rationality present and that it is possible to improve the relationship between internal activities and external performance, however measured" (English, 1992a, p. 106).

English (1988) also says "a rational organization develops goals, translates them into activities that are congruent with the goals, portions its resources based on goal priorities, and translates both into tangible jobs to be performed and subsequently evaluated. Based upon feedback obtained from evaluation, the cycle is repeated until the desired results are obtained at the lowest possible cost" (p. 329).

• *Integrated Webbed Structure:* Only the quality movement has this as a concept. The concept of an integrated webbed structure, rather than a hierarchical structure, is implied by many quality experts when systems thinking is discussed (Senge, 1992). This type of structure often uses cross-functional teams for critical decisions. Individuals bear equal power and authority in such situations.

The curriculum management audit does examine the formal organizational structure, as depicted by a table of organization, but a webbed integrated structure is not an explicit indicator. What is examined is whether the system is functioning well under whatever organizational structure it has and whether or not that structure impedes the system's output.

- *Process Focus:* Both direct the concept of focus on the process, rather than the product, recognizing that improving the process improves the product. One of Deming's four areas of Profound Knowledge is that leaders must have an understanding of variation. This information is useful to determine which sources of variation are caused by the system and which are attributable to a specific situation or person.

  English (1992a) states that "quality control becomes operational when adjustments are made by the worker (to the process) to attain a closer match to the work standard based upon (formative) feedback data. This is the dynamic and fluid part of quality control" (p. 45).

- *Data Orientation:* Both the quality movement and the curriculum management audit are data-oriented. The quality movement has a high profile in the area of using a data orientation to solve problems for continual improvement of the process toward ever-increasing efficiency and effectiveness. Deming's Plan-Do-Study-Act (PDSA) cycle is one example of this emphasis.

  A critical standard in the curriculum management audit is the feedback standard. As English states, "Too often, curriculum management auditors find that school districts are 'data rich' but 'information poor.' Most school systems have more data than they know how to use. Data become information when their utility has been established and someone finds them functional in terms of being useful in decision making based upon them" (English, 1992).

- *Variation:* Both include the concept of variation. One of Deming's four parts of Profound Knowledge is having some knowledge of the theory of variation. He states, "Some understanding of variation, including appreciation of a stable system, and some understanding of special causes and common causes of variation, is essential for management of a system, including leadership of people . . . variation there will always be, between people, in output, in service, in product" (Deming, 1993a).

English (1992b) talks about reducing "in system" sources of variation, which includes aligning curriculum and building consistency into documents that guide the work. He also identifies a third source of variation, the student. The third standard's equity issue focuses resources on areas of greatest need. Effective instruction actually increases variation. Thus, variation, in that respect, should lead to differential resource allocation.

RELATIONSHIPS

- *Mobilization of the Workers:* Only the quality movement explicity describes this as a concept. Joiner (1985) states that in many cases a difficult but expected aspect of quality "is to create an environment of ALL ONE TEAM . . . everyone throughout the organization must work together to improve processes . . . "(p. 5). Deming's (1982, p. 86) fourteenth point is to put everybody in the organization to work to accomplish the transformation.

  There is no explicit expectation in the curriculum management audit regarding the need for all workers to work on the processes. This decision is left to the system. However, there is an implicit standard that everyone should pull together to improve the instructional program.
- *Collaborative Workers:* Only the quality movement has this concept. One of Deming's Fourteen Points is to break down barriers between staff. There are two areas in the curriculum management audit where staff and community are to be involved. First, one ingredient of long-range planning is involvement of stakeholders, and, second, employees must give input to the budget process. Not having involvement, however, would not keep a district from meeting the standard.
- *Shared Values and Beliefs:* Only the quality movement has this concept. Sashkin and Kiser (1991), in writing about the quality movement, indicate that one of the more difficult parts in understanding and applying quality ideas is "creating, nurturing, and sustaining a culture based on the quality movement beliefs

. . . values and beliefs must be embedded and operate with that culture" (pp. 60–61).

There are no direct statements regarding the need for shared values and beliefs in the audit standards. Again, this is an implicit standard and, often, becomes a finding when a system is dysfunctional.

- *Leaders Who Understand People's Motivation:* Only the quality movement has this as an explicit concept. This is one of the points Deming stressed often. It shows up several times in his Fourteen Points: drive out fear; cease dependence on mass inspection; eliminate slogans, exhortations, and targets for the work force; eliminate numerical quotas; and break down barriers that rob people of pride of workmanship.

  Although the audit includes no indicator in this area, during interviews, auditors seek to understand motivation in the context of the audit and its impact on productivity.

- *Most Failures as Faults in the System:* Only the quality movement has this as an explicit premise. Deming (1982) states, "The supposition is prevalent the world over that there would be no problems in production or in service if only our production workers would do their jobs in the way that they were taught. Pleasant dreams. The workers are handicapped by the system, and the system belongs to management. It was Dr. Joseph M. Juran who pointed out long ago that most of the possibilities for improvement lie in actions on the system . . ." (p. 134).

  The audit examines work structures and deals with this concept implicitly (English, 1992). Curriculum audit training articulates the difference between design and delivery problems within a school system. What are usually design or system, problems are usually blamed on delivery, or performance.

- *Community of Learners:* Only the quality movement has this concept. Deming (1982) identifies education and training as vital to the well-being of the employee. This shows up in two of his Fourteen Points.

  The curriculum management audit does examine staff development endeavors as a vehicle for imparting consistency in the delivery of the curriculum under Standard Three. However, a system need not have ongoing staff development efforts to meet the standard if the auditors find no problems in connectivity, consistency, and equity in the system.

• *Ongoing Communication and Feedback:* Both the quality movement and the audit include communication as an explicit expectation. However, with respect to ongoing communication and feedback, the audit has no implicit standard.

Joiner (1985) points out that ongoing communication between managers and workers is critical to improvement of the process. Communication is addressed by the audit in the indication on clear communication of policy. It is also addressed in the third standard indicator which is clearly explaining the curriculum to members of the teaching staff and building-level administrators. An implicit expectation is that communication is built into the system to make it more productive.

SUMMARY OF THE FIRST PRONG ANALYSIS

When the overlay of the audit and quality premises is examined using Downey's framework and Deming's areas of Profound Knowledge, one can see that there is strong alignment in the areas of purpose and structure, and there is little alignment in the area of relationships.

In analyzing the audit with respect to purpose, there are mission expectations, client focus, strong constancy of purpose, and continual improvement beliefs. Less of a match occurs with respect to shared mission.

The strongest match is in the area of structure, especially in the areas of systemic organizational structure, optimization, rationality, and data orientation. There is fairly strong alignment in the areas of process focus and knowledge of variation. The weakest linkage is in the area of integrated webbed structure.

As mentioned earlier, the area where there is least alignment is relationships and Deming's focus on knowledge of psychology. Organizational psychology is implicit throughout the audit. There are a few explicit statements on involvement or participation in some areas of curriculum management and decision making and the need for staff development, which could link to community of learners. For the most part, the audit does not address mobilizing the workers, working in collaborative ways, or fostering shared values and beliefs. There is no explicit alignment in the areas of leadership, understanding people's motivation, and understanding variation as it relates to the failures of systems versus individuals.

SECOND PRONG: DEMING'S PROFOUND KNOWLEDGE AND FOURTEEN POINTS OVERLAY

The second prong of the "quality fit" approach is to compare an approach or strategy to Deming's Profound Knowledge and his Fourteen Points. For ease of understanding, the standards for the audit and their indicators are shown one by one in tabular form in relationship to those of Deming's Fourteen Points that relate to each standard. The tables offer a starting point for discussion, which goes beyond the standards, indicators, and Fourteen Points to the extent the authors are knowledgeable about the audit process and Deming's principles. Sources of information also include conversations with Deming about many of these ideas and a variety of his presentations from 1991 through his final seminar in December 1993.

Standard One: Control

Standard One of the curriculum management audit concerns control. It establishes the framework and responsibility for curriculum design and delivery. The standard concerns the development of policies, the planning function, and the organizational structure of the school system.

According to Deming, "Accountability for quality rests with top management" (1993a–c). Table 2 shows Standard One with its indicators and those of Deming's Fourteen Points that have implications for the standard. Deming's first point, *create constancy of purpose for improvement of product and service,* has implications for the way in which policy is structured and for the relationships within the school system, from the board and superintendent to the classroom teacher. It also relates to curriculum definition and adoption, establishing a mechanism for controlling change, and improving system effectiveness.

Deming's second point, *adopt the new philosophy,* relates to board definition and adoption of curriculum, development of policies, and a mechanism to control change and innovation within the school system. In his book, *Out of the Crisis* (1982), Deming's discussion of this second point includes the stabilization of top-level management. The auditors recommend that a district that has had an extraordinary amount of turnover of superintendents and other key personnel stabilize its top-level management. Stability increases the likelihood of constancy of purpose.

TABLE 2. Standard One: control and Deming's points.

Audit Indicator	Deming's Point
A curriculum that is centrally defined and adopted by the board of education	1. Create constancy of purpose for improvement of product and service 2. Adopt the new philosophy
A clear set of policies that establish an operational framework for management that permits accountability to be ascertained	1. Create constancy of purpose for improvement of product and service 5. Improve constantly and forever every process for planning, production, and service
A clear set of policies that reflect state requirements and local program goals and the necessity to use achievement data to improve school system operations	1. Create constancy of purpose for improvement of product and service 2. Adopt the new philosophy
A functional administrative structure that facilitates the design and delivery of the district's curriculum	7. Adopt and institute leadership
A direct, uninterrupted line of authority from school board, superintendent, and other central office officials to principals and classroom teachers	1. Create constancy of purpose for improvement of product and service
Documentation of school board and central office planning for the attainment of goals over time	5. Improve constantly and forever every process for planning, production, and service 7. Adopt and institute leadership
Organizational development efforts which are focused to improve system effectiveness	1. Create constancy of purpose for improvement of product and service 6. Institute training on the job 13. Institute a vigorous program of training and self improvement for everyone
A clear mechanism to control change and innovation within the school system	1. Create constancy of purpose for improvement of product and service 2. Adopt the new philosophy 5. Improve constancy and forever every process for planning, production, and service 7. Adopt and institute leadership

Deming's fifth point, *improve constantly and forever every process for planning, production, and service,* has implications for the way in which policies might be developed and how a long-range plan might be created. He is very clear about the necessity of long-term planning. "One does not achieve long-term goals by short-term thinking," Deming says (1992b). The curriculum management audit calls for planning as an important aspect of control for the future. The point would further suggest that any district's plan should provide for continual improvement of the system, using the Plan-Do-Study-Act (PDSA) cycle (1992c). This point also relates to another indicator of Standard One, which pertains to a mechanism for change and innovation. That mechanism should not be fixed and static but, rather, should provide for continual improvement.

The sixth point, *institute training on the job,* relates to job-related training as part of organizational development efforts.

The seventh point, *adopt and institute leadership,* means that the job of management is to lead, rather than supervise. In order to do so, leaders must understand curriculum and instruction "and know the work they supervise," Deming tells us (1992a). Often, the auditors find that school principals are building managers, rather than instructional leaders, more concerned with the smooth operation of facilities than with teaching and learning, and this is cited in audit reports.

This point also pertains to the structure of the school system. In his lectures, Deming said that the typical pyramid-shaped table of organization is useful only in illustrating who reports to whom. He also said that the pyramid contributes to fragmentation of the organization. He recommends making a flow diagram of the work, "which is actually an organization chart" (1992d). He says we need to see a "cat-walk" between the elements of the diagram (1992e). The auditors make recommendations concerning a school system's table of organization and/or decision making flow charts, when necessary. Deming's advice would suggest that the auditors recommend flow diagrams to school districts so they might better understand the work.

Although site-based management is not specifically addressed by the standards, the audit bias is concerned with the problem of sub-optimization. Such sub-optimization is "accentuated in organizations where they are decentralized and where central authorities lack the capacity to deal with sub-optimization. As a result, site-based management, if not balanced with a tightly coupled curriculum systemwide, can often become a fragmented system" (English, 1992b). Deming agrees. He discussed the need to ensure that workers, however independent, are working toward the common aim of the system (1993c).

Deming's thirteenth point, *institute a vigorous program of training and self improvement for everyone,* although similar to his sixth point about job training, concerns, instead, ongoing education, rather than job-specific training and would also serve to improve organizational effectiveness.

Standard Two: Direction

Standard Two of the curriculum management audit is called the direction standard. This standard is concerned with written goals and objectives; a clear sense of priorities and record of explicit direction from the board and superintendent; concentration of resources on priority targets; and demonstration of local control (see Table 3).

Deming's first point, *create constancy of purpose for improvement of product and service,* and his second point, *adopt and institute leadership,* relate to all the Standard Two audit indicators. Deming (1992d) says, "Aim at the target every time," and illustrates the need to do so in his funnel experiment. If school systems are clear about their aim or mission, they should not adjust their direction when they see variation in their efforts but, rather, should continue to aim at the target.

Deming's seventh point, *adopt and institute leadership,* relates to five of the nine indicators. Leadership must be assumed at the local level, regardless of state, national, or other conflicting or confounding factors in order for school systems to move forward in efforts to transform.

Deming talks about meeting the needs of the customer, which ties in well with these indicators. Resources are easy to place when one has a clear understanding of mission and continual sense of purpose. If the focus of resources is on the process for reaching the desired mission, Deming's third point, *cease dependence on mass inspection,* could link with this standard as well. Rather than use inspection at the end of the process, grades 3, 9, or 12, to determine effectiveness, ongoing data should be used to assess processes and resources and given quickly to those areas in need before the end inspection. And the process would be unending—constantly improving (fifth point).

TABLE 3. Standard Two: direction and Deming's points.

Audit Indicator	Deming's Point
A clearly established, systemwide set of goals and objectives adopted by the Board of Education	1. Create constancy of purpose for improvement of product and service 7. Adopt and institute leadership
Knowledge and use of emerging curriculum trends (validity issues);	1. Create constancy of purpose for improvement of product and service
Curriculum that addresses the full range of student effectiveness issues, both current and future	1. Create constancy of purpose for improvement of product and service
Objectives which set the framework for operation of the system and its sense of priorities	1. Create constancy of purpose for improvement of product and service 7. Adopt and institute leadership
Demonstration that the system is contextually responsive to national, state, and other expectations as evidenced in local initiatives	1. Create constancy of purpose for improvement of product and service
Major programmatic initiatives designed to be cohesive	1. Create constancy of purpose for improvement of product and service
Provision of explitit direction for the superintendent and professional staff	1. Create constancy of purpose for improvement of product and service 7. Adopt and institute leadership
Evidence of comprehensive, detailed, short- and long-range curriculum management planning; and	1. Create constancy of purpose for improvement of product and service 7. Adopt and institute leadership
Mechanisms that exist for systemic curricular change	1. Create constancy of purpose for improvement of product and service 7. Adopt and institute leadership

Standard Three: Connectivity and Equity

Standard Three, the connectivity and equity standard, concerns the school district's demonstration of internal connectivity, consistency, and rational equity in its program development and implementation. Table 4 shows the Standard Three indicators and the related points of Deming. Although Deming does not have a corresponding point concerning equity, in his lectures he says, "If we don't keep equity in the forefront, we will destroy our society." He also says that "efficiency must be subsumed to equity" (Deming, 1992c).

Deming's first point, *create constancy of purpose for improvement of product and service,* relates to the indicators concerning internal connections in the organization, consistency, allocation of resources, and teacher and administrator responsiveness to board policies. The audit process clearly establishes the linkages that must be present for policy to be connected with what transpires in the classroom.

Deming's second point, *adopt the new philosophy,* relates to allocation of resources to areas of greatest need. Customer focus is at the heart of Deming's philosophy, whether the customers are internal or external to the system. If everyone adopts the new philosophy, then

*TABLE 4. Standard Three: connectivity and equity
and Deming's points.*

Audit Indicator	Deming's Point
Documents/sources that reveal internal connection at different levels in the organization	1. Create constancy of purpose for improvement of product and service
Predictable consistency through a coherent rationale for content delineation within the curriculum	1. Create constancy of purpose for improvement of product and service
Equity of curriculum, course access, and opportunity	*
Allocation of resource flow to areas of greatest need	1. Create constancy of purpose for improvement of product and service 2. Adopt the new philosophy
A curriculum that is clearly explained to members of the teaching staff and building-level administrators	14. Put everybody in the company to work to accomplish the transformation
Specific professional development programs to enhance curriculum implementation	6. Institute training on the job 13. Institute a vigorous program of training and self improvement for everyone
A curriculum that is monitored by central office personnel and building principals	7. Adopt and institute leadership
Teacher and administrator responsiveness to school board policies, currently and over time	1. Create constancy of purpose for improvement of product and service

*No corresponding point; see text.

the system is moving toward assuring quality in its products and services as they pertain to customer needs.

Deming's seventh point, *adopt and institute leadership,* relates to the monitoring of curriculum by central office personnel. In order for there to be consistency from school to school, there must be shared systemwide responsibility.

Deming's sixth and thirteenth points, concerning job training and self-improvement, relate to the indicators for specific training programs to enhance curriculum implementation. Deming stresses the importance of training the worker better to perform the job. The audit proposes focused professional growth experiences as determined by the needs of the school system.

Deming also believes the organization should provide opportunities for ongoing educational experiences for the worker. He says we shouldn't decide what training is inappropriate. "Who knows what study is connected with your work? Nobody knows. There's no such thing; that's nonsense. If someone wants to study the theory of music, help him study it; nobody knows what's connected with the work" (1992a).

Deming's fourteenth point, *put everybody in the company to work to accomplish the transformation,* relates to the criterion for clearly explaining the curriculum to members of the teaching staff and building-level administrators. Only if everyone understands the work can they work together to transform a school system.

Standard Four: Feedback

Standard Four of the curriculum management audit, the feedback standard, provides for the use of assessment data to adjust, improve, or terminate ineffective practices or programs. Table 5 shows the Standard Four indicators and Deming's points.

Deming's point number three, *cease dependence on mass inspection to achieve quality,* coincides with seven of ten indicators. It also coincides with auditor's recommendations to do away with those norm-referenced tests that are not state-mandated. The auditors have not recommended doing away completely with norm-referenced tests, since they do believe the local system must be in compliance with state mandates. However, auditors would encourage districts to lobby to get rid of the tests for the purposes currently used. When asked his opinion about state-mandated tests, Deming said, "Just don't give them." (1992f).

TABLE 5. Standard Four: feedback and Deming's points.

Audit Indicator	Deming's Point
A formative and summative assessment system linked to a clear rationale in board policy	3. Cease dependence on mass inspection to achieve quality 5. Improve constantly and forever every process for planning, production, and service
Knowledge and use of emerging curriculum and program assessment trends	5. Improve constantly and forever every process for planning, production, and service
Use of a student and program assessment plan which provides for diverse assessment strategies for multi-purposes at all levels—district, school, and classroom	5. Improve constantly and forever every process for planning, production, and service
A timely and relevant data base upon which to analyze important trends in the instructional program	3. Cease dependence on mass inspection to achieve quality 5. Improve constantly and forever every process for planning, production, and service
A way to provide feedback to the teaching and administrative staffs regarding how classroom instruction may be evaluated and subsequently improved	3. Cease dependence on mass inspection to achieve quality 5. Improve constantly and forever every process for planning, production, and service
A vehicle to examine how well programs are actually producing desired learner outcomes	3. Cease dependence on mass inspection to achieve quality
A data base to compare the strengths and weaknesses of various programs and program alternatives, as well as to engage in equity analysis	3. Cease dependence on mass inspection to achieve quality
A data base to modify or terminate ineffective educational programs	3. Cease dependence on mass inspection to achieve quality
A method/means to relate to a programmed budget and enable the school system to engage in cost-benefit analysis; and	5. Improve constantly and forever every process for planning, production, and service
Organizational data gathered and used to continually improve system functions	3. Cease dependence on mass inspection to achieve quality 12. Break down barriers that rob people of pride of workmanship. Eliminate the annual rating or merit system

"Ranking people is a farce," Deming says; yet we usually rank students and award those at the top, while punishing those at the bottom. What are thought to be differences in performance are actually attributable to the system in most cases. Deming says, "Only trivial things can be measured. . . . Raw totals and not customer needs is what concerns management" (1992a).

The auditors recommend strongly to school systems to use formative data to improve the system. Daily and weekly diagnostic measures are needed to improve instruction for students. Criterion-referenced tests aligned with curricular objectives are urged by auditors for ongoing feedback. This also relates to Deming's ideas of continual improvement and constancy of purpose, to reduce system variability (Deming, 1992a). Graduate follow-up studies should include questions about customer, or community, satisfaction.

Both the audit and quality perspectives have as a major premise the use of feedback to improve the process, which in turn affects the results (student learning). Audit recommendations often include ongoing diagnostic use of student assessment devices to influence daily instruction. Deming's beliefs on variation are in alignment with this audit standard. Use data to work on the system, not the worker (in this case, the student as well as the teacher).

Finally, Deming's twelfth point, *break down barriers that rob people of pride of workmanship; eliminate the annual rating or merit system,* relates to the use of a database to compare strengths and weakness of various programs and program alternatives. This point also suggests that auditors recommend against teacher rating and ranking, merit pay, and grades for students. Data should be used to improve the program, or system, rather than to differentiate between and among students and staff. This is one of the most difficult points to consider in applying quality principles to schools because of constraints of state laws and public pressure. However, most states allow districts to apply for waivers to state regulations.

Deming does not have an explicit point that relates to the final indicator, which refers to a data base to modify or terminate ineffective educational programs, but it would be safe to assume that, if attention were given at the system, or program level, ineffective programs or practices would be terminated.

Standard Five: Productivity

Standard Five (Table 6) of the curriculum management audit, the

TABLE 6. *Standard Five: productivity and Deming's points.*

Audit Indicator	Deming's Point
Planned and actual congruence among curriculum objectives, results, and financial costs	1. Create constancy of purpose for improvement of product and service 4. End the practice of awarding business on the basis of price tag alone; instead, minimize total cost by working with a single supplier 5. Improve constantly and forever every process for planning, production, and service
Support systems that function in systemic ways	5. Improve constantly and forever every process for planning, production, and service
District and school climate conducive to continual improvement	12. Break down barriers that rob people of pride of workmanship. Eliminate the annual rating or merit system
Specific means that have been selected or modified and implemented to attain better results in the schools over a specified time period	1. Create constancy of purpose for improvement of product and service 4. End the practice of awarding business on the basis of price tag alone; instead, minimize total cost by working with a single supplier 5. Improve constantly and forever every process for planning, production, and service
Demonstration of planned interventions to raise pupil performance over time within the same financial parameters	1. Create constancy of purpose for improvement of product and service 4. End the practice of awarding business on the basis of price tag alone; instead, minimize total cost by working with a single supplier 5. Improve constantly and forever every process for planning, production, and service 14. Put everybody in the company to work to accomplish the transformation

(continued)

TABLE 6. (continued).

Audit Indicator	Deming's Point
A financial network that is able to track costs to results, provide sufficient fiduciary control, and is used as a viable data base in making policy and operational decisions; and	1. Create constancy of purpose for improvement of product and service 4. End the practice of awarding business on the basis of price tag alone; instead, minimize total cost by working with a single supplier 6. Institute training on the job
School facilities that are well-kept, sufficient, safe, orderly, that comply with all requirements, and facilitate delivery of the instructional program	1. Create constancy of purpose for improvement of product and service

productivity standard, refers to the congruence between curriculum outcomes and costs, the means to attain better results over time, and demonstration of planned intervention to raise pupil performance.

Deming's first point, *create constancy of purpose for improvement of product and service,* relates to five of the seven indicators in this standard. Deming advises going upstream to improve quality. The audit sees productivity as the overriding purpose of good curriculum management.

Deming's point number four is *end the practice of awarding business on the basis of price tag alone; instead, minimize total cost by working with a single supplier.* The audit standard is concerned with improving results within existing financial parameters. Deming's advice to work with a single supplier has the potential to actually reduce costs. One of the authors asked Dr. Deming how a school district could get around state laws requiring districts to contract with the lowest bidder. He replied that it isn't necessary to get around the law; rather, that use needs to be calculated into prices, and districts would thereby be able to work with a single supplier. For instance, if a district purchased high-quality tires for its school buses, more costly than those of lesser quality, wear would be calculated into the price, thereby potentially making the higher quality, more expensive ones less expensive to use (1992e).

Point number five, *improve constantly and forever every process for planning, production, and service,* relates to four of the indicators of Standard Five, which has a strong relationship to the quality movement. The purpose of the audit is to increase productivity over time through continual improvement practices.

Point fourteen, *put everybody in the company to work to accomplish the transformation,* relates to the final Standard Five criterion regarding planned interventions to raise pupil performance.

SUMMARY OF THE SECOND PRONG

There is considerable overlap of Deming's principles for system transformation and the curriculum management audit standards and their indicators. Ten of his Fourteen Points relate to audit criteria. Most of these points, as in the first prong of this chapter, pertain to purpose and structure of the organization.

The remaining points, numbers 8, 9, 10 and 11, do not appear to relate to existing curriculum management audit indicators. As with the first prong, these are primarily concerned with the way in which management should relate to workers to achieve maximum intrinsically-motivated results. Were the auditors to use the curriculum management audit as a vehicle to turn a school system into a quality school system, top-level management should:

- *Drive out fear.* That would mean empowering and enabling all those in the system to have input into the decision-making process as it involves student learning without being afraid of doing so. It would also preclude schools from awarding raises based on student test scores.
- *Break down barriers between staff areas.* This would mean creating cross-disciplinary teams and having everyone work together to improve student learning.
- *Eliminate slogans, exhortations, and targets for the work force.* Although the audit teams often see all kinds of slogans and posters—both those that encourage students to do well and those that poke fun at school work, the standards do not address them except to the extent that they are part of the "hidden curriculum," which means they are seen as positive if they are positive and negative if they are negative. Deming's point would suggest that slogans and exhortations imposed from the top do not serve people well.

Were this point applied to the audit process, the auditors

suggest that posters should, rather, explain to everyone what the administration is doing to provide better materials, supplies, maintenance, supervision, and/or statistical aids to improve quality and productivity.

Another significant part of this point refers to targets for the work force. Arbitrary goals do not suggest a method for implementation. Determining teacher raises based on students' test scores also causes fear, as described earlier.

Deming's reference to targets are criteria for staff to meet, while targets in the curriculum management audit concern areas of need as they relate to process, so they are not in disagreement, as they are used in different contexts. These points suggest that school district goals should focus on continual improvement of education.

- *Eliminate numerical quotas for the work force and numerical goals for management.* School systems sometimes award teacher raises based on student scores on norm-referenced, standardized tests, as discussed under Standard Four. The earlier discussion concerns not giving the tests at all. This point suggests not establishing the quotas, regardless of which data were used for comparison.

SUMMARY AND RECOMMENDATIONS

The two-pronged analysis of the curriculum management audit in quality terms revealed that, while there is significant overlap between the curriculum management audit and quality management principles in some areas, there are other areas that are not explicitly addressed but, rather, are implicit in the context of the audit. As auditors suggest changes to schools, they need to be aware of these implicit criteria and their relation to quality principles. When a school district is audited, the audit team creates findings that show where the district falls short of meeting the five standards. Then the auditors make recommendations as to how it might go about meeting them.

The authors found, in their analyses of quality principles posed by Downey's Quality Fit Framework and of Deming's four areas of Profound Knowledge and the Fourteen Points with the audit indicators that, were the audit process to be conducted with quality in mind, there are other criteria and subsequent recommendations that might be considered. The question as to where these indicators might fit into the audit framework deserves further study. Perhaps the indicators under each standard might be expanded; perhaps a new standard might be created. That standard might be called the relationship standard.

Further recommendations the authors pose are a result of numerous lectures and private conversations with Dr. Deming, who provided an understanding of the application of his principles to the education system.

Table 7 shows a summary of those areas where the authors did not

TABLE 7. *Summary of possible criteria to make explict in the curriculum audit.*

Quality Criteria	Prong	Standard
Create a shared sense of mission	1	1
Create an integrated webbed structure	1	1
Mobilize workers	1	1,R
Manage relationships	1,L	R
Encourage collaboration	1	R
Create a sense of shared values and beliefs	1	1,R
Understand what motivates workers	1,L	R,3
Understand that failures are attributable to the system	1,L	4,R
Use the Plan-Do-Study-Act (PDSA) cycle	2,L	4
Create flow diagrams to show how the work is connected	2,L	1,4
Drive out fear	2	R,1,3
Break down barriers between staff areas	2	R,1
Eliminate slogans, exhortations, and targets	2	R,1
Break down barriers that rob people of pride of workmanship; eliminate the annual rating or merit system	2	R
Eliminate numerical quotas and goals, ranking, rating, and grades	2,P	3,4
Institute training and education for everyone	2,L,P	3,R
Eliminate the norm-referenced testing program	2,P	4
Work with a single supplier	2,P	5
Eliminate unnecessary paperwork	2	R
Teach theory to everyone	L,P	1,3
Allow freedom, intrinsic motivation	L	R,3
Optimize system by encouraging cooperation	L	R,1,3
Help students see how their learning fits	L	R,2
Put more effort into early stages of learning; research into theory	L	2
Allow freedom for teachers, students, and staff to learn, create, and innovate	L	R,3

find strong overlap, references the prong where the issue was discussed, and suggests a standard number and/or shows an "R" to indicate it might belong to a new relationship standard or needs to be included explicitly under the existing five standards. When an "L" shows in the prong column, it indicates that the idea came from Dr. Deming's lectures. A "P" refers to private conversations with Dr. Deming during 1992 and 1993. These criteria have not all been discussed in detail in this chapter, but they certainly bear consideration as school personnel begin to understand quality and as proponents of the curriculum audit continue to improve the process of examining school districts.

ACKNOWLEDGEMENTS

The authors are extremely grateful to Dr. W. Edwards Deming and to Dr. Fenwick English for their assistance in helping them understand their theories and for reviewing this manuscript and improving it. They cherished the opportunity to learn from Dr. Deming whose recent death has put an end to an era where he can be asked directly for understanding. Hopefully, the American Education System will contrive to seek understanding of his principles.

REFERENCES

Deming, W. E. (1982) *Out of the Crisis*, Cambridge, Massachusetts: Massachusetts Institute of Technology.

Deming, W. E. (1991) *Seminar on Quality, Productivity, and Competitive Position*, Santa Clara, California.

Deming, W. E. (1992a) *Seminar for Educators*, Washington, D.C.

Deming, W. E. (1992b) Conversation with Virginia Vertiz at Dr. Deming's Home, February 8, 1992.

Deming, W. E. (1992c) *Seminar on Quality, Productivity, and Competitive Position*, Orlando, Florida.

Deming, W. E. (1992d) Remarks in speech to students at Amherst College of the University of Massachusetts, April 22, 1992.

Deming, W. E. (1992e) Remark to a group at the Ritz Carlton Hotel in Arlington, Virginia, February 15, 1992.

Deming, W. E. (1992f) Twenty-Ninth Annual Cosmos Club Award Dinner and Presentation, April 11, 1992.

Deming, W. E. (1992g) Rewritten text in response to request to review this manuscript.

Deming, W. E. (1993a) *Seminar on Quality, Productivity, and Competitive Position*, Maui, Hawaii.

Deming, W. E. (1993b) *Seminar on Instituting Dr. Deming's Methods for Service Agencies,* Washington, D.C.

Deming, W. E. (1993c) *Seminar on Quality, Productivity, and Competitive Position,* Universal City, California.

Downey, C. J. (1992) "Out of the Debate and Into Action: Seventeen Core Premises of the Quality Movement: Let's Use the Quality Fit Framework," Presentation at the Institute San Diego, California.

Downey, C. J. (1994) "Applying the Quality Fit Framework to the Curriculum Management Audit," *Education,* Winter Issue.

English, F. W. (1987) *Curriculum Management for Schools, Colleges, Business.* Springfield, Illinois, Charles C. Thomas.

English, F. W. (1988) *Curriculum Auditing.* Lancaster, Pennsylvania: Technomic Publishing Company, Inc.

English, F. W. (1992a) *Deciding What to Teach and Test.* Newbury Park, California: Corwin Press, Inc.

English, F. W. (1992b) Conversation with Virginia Vertiz and Carolyn Downey in Pueblo, Colorado, November 1, 1992.

Joiner, B. (1985) *Total Quality Leadership vs. Management by Results.* Madison, Wisconsin: Joiner Associates, Inc.

Sashkin, M. and K. Kiser. (1991) *Total Quality Management.* Seabrook, New York: Ducochon Press.

Senge, P. (1990) *The Fifth Discipline: The Art and Practice of the Learning Organization.* New York: Doubleday.

Senge, P. (1992) Keynote Presentation, American Association of School Administrators, San Diego, California.

Silver, P. (1983) *Educational Administration: Theoretical Perspectives.* New York: Harper and Row.

Vertiz, V. C. (1994) "A Look at the Curriculum Management Audit Applying Deming's Principles for System Transformation," *Education,* Winter Issue.

Vertiz, V. C. and C. D. Downey. (1993) The International Quality Standards for Education. Presented at the Governors' Conference on Quality and Education, Denver, Colorado.

Weisbord, M. R. (1987) *Productive Workplaces: Organizing and Managing for Dignity, Meaning, and Community.* San Francisco, California: Jossey-Bass, Inc.

CHAPTER 4

The History and Context of the Curriculum Audit

BETTY E. STEFFY – *University of Kentucky*

INTRODUCTION

THE curriculum management audit is the intellectual progeny of several historic practices in American education. First, the idea of going to the schools and asking them for data upon which to draw conclusions about their operations is at least as old as Horace Mann's questionnaire used to form the basis of his "First Report" to the Massachusetts State Board of Education in 1837 (Messerli, 1972, p. 288).

Later, the School Survey Movement, which sprang from the universities and established research bureaus in emerging schools of education and large city districts, reinforced the traditions of the continuous study of actual school operations as being essential to their improvement (Sears, 1933, pp. 217–262).

The educational performance audit was advocated by Leon Lessinger (1970) in his famous book *Every Kid a Winner*. Lessinger borrowed the idea of an external financial audit as a product and process to restore public confidence in education.

The curriculum management audit was first employed by Fenwick English in Columbus, Ohio, in 1979 (English, 1988). English led a team, mostly business consultants with Peat, Marwick, Mitchell, in a six-month study of one of the nation's largest urban school systems. Audits were then performed in Topeka, Kansas; Bellflower, California; and Long Branch, New Jersey. In 1988, the curriculum management audit was finally centered in the American Association of School Administration (AASA) in Arlington, Virginia. AASA developed training programs for educators to become curriculum management auditors under the direction of Dr. Jerry Melton and later Dr. Virginia Vertiz. AASA not only trained auditors, it performed audits nationally and internationally.

AUDITS AS EXTERNAL-INTERNAL EYES ON SCHOOL SYSTEM MANAGEMENT

It has become firmly implanted in the public's mind that public functions embodied in tax-supported institutions require systematic inspection and supervision. Since Watergate, the high levels of public suspicion about the honesty of elected and appointed officials have escalated. Increasingly, the public is skeptical about expanding levels of support to fund enterprises for which they have come to believe that their tax monies are not being utilized expeditiously.

The financial audit has both an external face and internal process. The external part of the audit is a public report in which an independent account tells the public how much confidence they can place in the records and financial activities of an entity's management. Internally, the accounting profession has evolved a set of standard procedures called GAAP (generally accepted accounting principles) by which they arrive at this public decision.

As its financial cousin, the curriculum management audit consists of a public report and an internal set of standards and procedures by which it observes school systems operation and communicates impressions of the integrity, reliability, and validity of the curricular, instructional, and fiduciary documents of the system.

The standards of the curriculum management audit are not centered on curriculum theory. Rather, the standards of the audit are grouped around organizational theory. The reason is not hard to discern: curriculum theory has not involved system operations; it is not anchored by administrative practices nor engaged in any discussion regarding how an organization can optimize its operations. Secondly, curriculum is designed within a system, and it is delivered by a system. The effectiveness of the design is one measure of the capability of the curriculum to "fit" that system and the capacity for it to implement it. At least, inasmuch as the effective operations of a school system are concerned, organizational theory is an appropriate base upon which to examine its efficacy within an educational system. The standards of the audit are therefore centered on operations and the theoretical base that governs it.

Of course, organizational theory is not value-free, and it contains implicit notions of how the world is and should be. Audit training shows how aspiring auditors can learn to question these assumptions and make auditing a reflective, as well as operational, examination and practice.

SCHOOL ACCOUNTABILITY AND THE AUDIT

The fundamental question addressed in the curriculum management audit revolves around whether the work of the system is resulting in the ability of the organization to continually improve student achievement. The audit assumes that the system, ultimately, is committed to that goal. Unfortunately, what the audit frequently uncovers is documentation that the system is not accomplishing that objective. Still more disconcerting is the realization that, far too often, the system has alternate goals such as being more concerned about satisfying the needs of adult workers rather than fulfilling the educational needs of student clients, maintaining the present political power structure of the system, and finding ways to avoid system and school accountability measures. These alternate goals can, in some instances, become the primary goals of the school district.

The present accountability theme emerges as an analysis of the effectiveness of the system in meeting the educational needs of *all* the children in the system. Districts undergoing curriculum management audits can expect an analysis of the equity of programs for gifted and talented students, learning disabled students, students representing minority populations, and students from all socioeconomic circumstances. The assumption here is that the system has a responsibility to deal with a diverse student population in ways that enable *all* students to achieve high academic standards.

By looking at five interrelated standards (English, 1988), the audit provides an assessment of district and school accountability firmly planted in school effectiveness measured by student achievement. In the past, districts relied heavily on student achievement based on district averages on national standardized tests, the percent of students attending post-secondary education institutions, and district scores on the SAT and ACT. With the evolution of authentic assessment strategies such as performance events, portfolios, open-ended response items and writing prompts, school scores and measures of individual student growth over time will become the accepted barometer of school and district success. Poorly performing schools and subgroups of students will no longer be able to hide behind the district average. As schools struggle to improve over time and document this improvement through demonstrated student competence, districts will be forced into reexamining their priorities to be sure improving student achievement, however the district chooses to assess it, is the primary goal of the system.

Assessing a district's ability to design and deliver programs, procedures, and processes to address the five standards of the curriculum management audit relates directly to the ability of the district to continually improve. The five standards of the audit are as follows (English, 1988, pp. 33–34):

(1) The school district is able to demonstrate its control of resources, programs, and personnel.

(2) The school district has established clear and valid objectives for students.

(3) The school system demonstrates internal consistency and rational equity in its program development and implementation.

(4) The district uses the results from the district-designed or -adopted assessments to adjust, improve, or terminate ineffective programs.

(5) The district has been able to improve productivity.

As more and more state legislatures enact statutes that link school sanctions and rewards to state-mandated authentic assessment systems, the need for third-party reviews of the curriculum management practices of districts will increase.

THE IMPACT OF STATE EQUITY TRENDS

The Constitution of the United States makes states responsible for designing, implementing, and monitoring the public education system. Increasingly, class action equity suits are being filed by local school districts because of the inequitable funding of education across school districts within a state (Kozol, 1991). The idea that a state General Assembly is the accountable body for the effective functioning of the school districts within the state is an emerging concept. Generally, state legislatures have vested local school districts with the autonomy and power to make whatever decisions are necessary to produce an effective school system. If a school district failed or appeared to focus on different goals, the General Assembly regarded that as a decision of the local board and not one that required intervention by the General Assembly.

In Kentucky, the Supreme Court ruled that, even though the legislature had empowered local school boards, the ultimate accountable agent was the General Assembly (*Rose v. Council for Better Education, Inc.*, 1989). Increased accountability of state legislatures has brought increased pressure for monitoring the functions of local school districts for producing accountable systems. In the past, the accountability function resided with state departments of education. It was the state education agency that developed school district monitoring systems. An analysis of the effects of state agency accreditation programs where state officials visited districts and monitored district reports has shown that there was little relationship between the state accreditation function and local district school improvement. There appears to be a growing mistrust regarding the ability of a state education agency to effectively monitor the school improvement capabilities of local districts. This mistrust is resulting in the development of offices of educational accountability apart from the state education agency. Kentucky is an example of such a legislated effort (Steffy, 1993). The Office of Educational Accountability is authorized to monitor the work of the Department of Education, the Commissioner of Education, and the State Board of Elementary and Secondary Education, as well as the functioning of local school districts. The office reports directly to the leadership of the General Assembly. As these emerging offices conduct their investigations, they frequently use procedures similar to the curriculum management audit.

The need for a third-party review, where the third party is not part of the political, educational network, is growing. The general public is becoming more suspect of the ability of educators to solve the problems facing public education in this country. Given a major increase in resources over the past ten years, schools have not been able to document comparable increases in student academic achievement.

STATE AGENCY INVOLVEMENT IN CURRICULUM AUDITING: THE KENTUCKY EXPERIENCE

In the fall of 1988, the Kentucky Department of Education began to pilot the curriculum management audit as a service of the state agency.

The American Association of School Administrators (AASA) conducted the first audit training in July 1988, and three newly hired officials from the Kentucky Department of Education attended the training. During the next three years, seventeen audits were conducted in Kentucky. The practice of using the curriculum management audit as a mechanism for assessing the effectiveness of a school district's curriculum management system ended with the passage of the Kentucky Education Reform Act (KERA) and the reorganization of the Department of Education.

During the first year, the department solicited district volunteers to undergo the audit. Five districts were audited that year, four of which volunteered. The first audit was conducted in a district that had a long history of state intervention. The district had a new superintendent, and he requested the audit in order to have a "blueprint for change." Unfortunately, the district continued to have difficulty and eventually became a district identified for state "takeover." State takeover did not result in removal of school district officers; however, it did result in continuous monitoring of the district activities and the placement of a state department representative in the district. The state official was responsible for monitoring all budgetary decisions of the district.

In January 1989, the state department took official intervention action against two districts, the district that had originally volunteered for the audit and one additional district. As part of the intervention strategy, the State Board of Elementary and Secondary Education authorized a curriculum management audit for the second intervention district. The resulting reports of the audits in these two districts became the basis for the state's intervention strategies.

Apart from the two state intervention districts, three additional districts volunteered for a curriculum management audit. During the second year, audits were performed in five districts that were identified for management assistance. Management assistance was a program that provided state department technical assistance to districts that were typically having severe financial difficulties to the point where they were not able to submit a balanced budget. In addition to the five management assistance districts, two additional districts volunteered for audits during the 1989–1990 school year. During 1990–1991 school year, five additional audits were performed in management assistance districts.

All audits performed in Kentucky were completed by audit teams made up of state department employees and educators from outside the state of Kentucky. The audits were jointly sponsored by the Kentucky Department of Education and the American Association of School Administrators. In each case, the lead auditors, who are responsible for the content of the audit reports, came from outside the state. They edit the work of the audit team and usually present the audit to the district board. Using lead auditors from outside Kentucky increased the credibility of the audit and enhanced the public's confidence in the objectivity of the document.

An analysis of audits completed by the Kentucky Department of Education revealed different patterns among districts where the audit was part of a state takeover or management assistance intervention and districts that requested the audit but were considered to be effective in producing student results (Steffy, 1989, and a survey of all seventeen audits).

The pattern that emerged in districts where some form of state intervention was required revealed a district where there was little evidence of formalized, strategic planning. These districts were frequently devoid of updated school board policies, and there was an almost universal lack of board involvement in long-range goal setting or systematic evaluation of the superintendent. Curriculum guides in these districts were either out-dated or nonexistent. The textbook served as the curriculum guide of preference, and successful implementation of the curriculum was usually related to covering the material in the designated time, as opposed to an assessment of what students knew and were able to do. Teacher lesson plan development was confined to the typical weekly, block plan that specified the pages to be covered in the textbook. Practices for monitoring the instructional program were mixed and often depended on the expertise and motivation of the building principal rather than any concrete direction from central administration. Lack of student success was often explained in terms of the socioeconomic status of students. Classrooms and buildings were often in disrepair, and instructional materials were frequently outdated and scarce. During the time the audits were conducted, the state required the California Test of Basic Skills as the official measure of student achievement. These tests were scored by the state department, and districts were furnished with detailed item analysis data. These data may have been shared with building administrators, but there was little evidence that plans were made to significantly alter the existing instructional program or practices based on the data. In most of these districts, the budget development process operated apart from consideration for significantly improving the instructional program. In general, these districts failed to operate as a system of schools. Also, practices that could be described as politically motivated in relationship to hiring, contracts, bidding, and school facilities improvement tended to be more typical for districts experiencing state intervention. The auditing process identified specific practices that needed to be improved and concrete recommendations that the administration needed to implement to enable more students to be successful learners.

In districts that requested the audit and that were generally deemed to be producing results, the audit frequently revealed that the design for improvement was often in place. What seemed to need improvement in these districts was closer monitoring of whether the curriculum management design was being delivered. These districts generally had some semblance of a strategic plan and board policies that were more current, and there was greater evidence of board involvement in long-range planning, goal setting, and evaluation of the superintendent. These districts frequently had curriculum guides that were periodically updated although there was generally not strong evidence of teachers' use of the guides for instructional planning. Problems relating to equity and consistency among buildings were typical for most districts undergoing an audit. Higher performing districts had greater evidence that test results were used for some form of feedback to teachers and modification of the instructional program. These districts also tended to show evidence of budget development related to efforts to improve the instructional program.

The patterns that emerged from an analysis of the seventeen audits performed in Kentucky clearly showed differences between districts that could be categorized as involved in some form of state department intervention and districts that requested the audit as a mechanism for improving a good district.

Under the direction of the new commissioner of education in Kentucky, superintendents in two of the state intervention districts that were audited have been removed from office. Another superintendent retired under pressure from the state, which included charges of misconduct and neglect of duty (Pack, 1991). While formalized audits using the AASA process are not currently being conducted in Kentucky, many of the reports being prepared by the Office of Educational Accountability contain similar patterns.

What Was Learned

The use of the curriculum management audit by a state education agency is a labor-intensive activity. Whether the audit is used to document the status of the district or as the basis for monitoring improvement over time, there is an expectation that the state department will assist the district in implementing the audit recommendations.

One of the patterns that emerged from conducting audits in state intervention districts was the realization that district and school administrators needed extensive professional development in the concepts and practices of curriculum management. These administrators could more typically be characterized as managers rather than instructional leaders. Pointing out the curriculum management deficiencies of the district was simply the beginning.

Likewise, the curriculum management expertise of most state department employees is limited. State departments have historically been oversight, regulatory agencies rather than technical assistance agencies. Even though personnel could be trained to conduct curriculum management audits, providing the follow-up technical assistance demanded by the audited districts proved difficult. In order for a state agency to provide the technical expertise to assist districts in implementing the recommendations, additional staff, trained in curriculum management procedures, would be required. Since most state agencies are downsizing their staff, the prospects of state agencies using the audit are dim.

Another pattern that developed with increased state agency involvement in a district was the transfer of ownership for solving the district's problems from the district to the state. As long as state personnel were involved in a district, administrators, board members, and teachers tended to expect state personnel to "fix" whatever was wrong. It was not unusual for state department personnel assigned to a district to be blamed for lack of progress.

State agency involvement in the affairs of a local school district tends to become a media event. Once the intervention begins, all parties can expect continued coverage for as long as the state agency is involved. Subgroups in the community often use this media coverage to project and debate issues. These activities can actually impede the progress of the district.

Since the problems facing most of these districts evolved over a long period of time, they are not solved quickly. State agency involvement could be required for several years. Most state agencies are not in a position to sustain long-term local district support.

Future of the Audit by State Agencies

Rather than using the audit as a mechanism to document local school district deficiencies, state agencies may want to consider using audit training as a mechanism for professional development for practicing school administrators at the district and school level. Administrators completing this training could have one school year to implement programs designed to meet the five standards of the audit. A year after training was completed, a curriculum management audit could be conducted to assess whether the administrators of the district had been successful in designing and implementing a curriculum management program for the district. Continued certification as a school district administrator would be dependent on the results of the audit. The audit would become the performance event to document the curriculum management competence of a district's administrators. Using the audit in this way is in keeping with the current authentic assessment trend. Unless practicing school administrators in districts identified for state intervention are held accountable for the continuous instructional improvement of the schools and districts they lead, it is doubtful that these administrators will learn the skills and implement the changes required.

Currently, there appears to be a movement toward teacher empowerment and school site accountability as the solution for poor performing schools and districts. It is the opinion of this author that this trend, by itself, will be ineffective. Certainly, teachers should be involved in decisions that affect them and the school as the unit of accountability has merit. However, schools operate within the context of a larger system, namely, the school district. Teachers are first and foremost teachers, not administrators. They generally do not have sufficient time to devote to administrative functions in addition to a full-time teaching load, nor are they properly trained in curriculum management techniques. The simple act of electing teachers to serve on school councils does not adequately prepare them to design, monitor, and evaluate the effectiveness of the instructional program. In some ways, it enables school and district administrators to transfer ultimate accountability for the effectiveness of the system to the teachers rather than utilizing teachers to assist the administrators in improving the system. From my point of view, it is the school and district administrators who must accept ultimate accountability for effective instructional leadership.

NATIONAL AND INTERNATIONAL USE OF THE AUDIT

By January 1992, over sixty audits had been conducted in nineteen states, the District of Columbia, Saudi Arabia, and Bangladesh (Vertiz, 1992). The American Association of School Administrators through the Curriculum Audit Center continues to train curriculum management auditors from school districts all over the country. Training sessions are usually held four times a year.

CHALLENGES FOR SECOND GENERATION AUDITS

The Paradox of Site-Based Management

One of the fundamental questions addressed by the audit is whether the school system is in control of itself. With the growing emphasis on school-based decision making, questions have been raised as to whether the school district should remain as the accountable agency of the state or whether school councils should ultimately become the accountable, independent authority of the school. Advocates of school-based decision making are quick to point out advantages to involving staff in decision making (Bailey, 1991). These benefits can include increased worked satisfaction, less resistance to change, higher motivation, and better communication (Lawler, 1987). What seems sometimes to get lost in the dialogue is the fact that school-based decision making is not an end in itself. Rather it can be a better means to the end of improving student achievement. Research has yet to document a clear relationship between school based decision making and improved academic achievement for students.

It is the position of this author that the audit is an appropriate process to assess the effectiveness of the curriculum management system of a school district with or without school-based decision making. Most of the decision areas assigned to school councils deal with the day-to-day decisions about instructional delivery. Materials selection, use of school time, choice of instructional strategies, discipline codes, fund raising activities, and parent communication systems are often areas where school councils and individual classroom teachers utilize their decision-making authority. These decisions must be made within the parameters of union contracts, district budgets, and local board policy. Statutorily, local boards of education are the accountable agents of the state in assuring that the district is operating within state statute and with a balanced budget, and is conducting business according to the open meetings laws. School councils should be a mechanism to enable districts to achieve district goals more effectively. The standards of the audit can be applied at both the district and school levels. For instance, Standard One states that the district is in control of resources, programs, and personnel. A district operating with school councils and allocating money to purchase materials to the building level would still be able to document control of resources. The locus of decision making could be the building or the district. The important point is whether the decision to expend resources is connected to a logical analysis of how best to meet the educational needs of students. Similarly, allowing a school council to make the decision about which principal candidate will be recommended to the board for hiring does not mean that there is not an approved, systematic process for filling a principal vacancy.

Still, there is growing conflict between teacher autonomy vested in school councils and the school boards' statutory authority. Until this tension gets resolved, questions will be raised about the authority of the system versus the authority of the teacher.

Selecting the Curriculum—Teacher vs. District

Present trends in curriculum are moving away from subject-oriented, knowledge-focused content to integrated, concept- and skill-focused content and process. At the same time there is a movement toward inclusionary instruction as opposed to pull-out or specialized programs. In addition, multi-age, multi-ability grouping is becoming more popular, as well as instructional practices that enable students to work collaboratively.

In the future, Standard Two, dealing with whether the district has established direction in the form of curriculum guides that are useable and used, will probably expand from analyzing the mathematics program of a district in isolation from the science program to include an analysis of the mathematics program as it is integrated with the science program, the music program, and, perhaps, the computer technology program. The standard will remain; however, the focal point of the analysis will be broadened to include curricular integration.

These changes will require the development of sophisticated student management systems to enable teachers and parents to assess the growth of students. There will also be a need to broaden the parameters of what is meant by successful achievement of curricular objectives as schools become more sensitive to the diverse needs of students in our pluralistic society. Recent information released by the Census Bureau indicates that, by the year 2050, only 53% of the population in the United States will be white (Vobejda, 1992). Hispanics, Blacks, and Asians will make up 48% of the population. In addition, the Immigration Act of 1990 increased by nearly 40% the number of immigrants entering the country (Vobejda, 1992, p. A-6). The ability of local schools to meet the curricular needs of this increasingly diverse student population will produce a greater diversity in the implementation strategies. However, it will be even more important that the district has identified the curricular ends the system is striving for.

As these changes in practice take place, the analysis of data relative to the standards will also change. In the future, this analysis may take place at several levels: the district, the school, and programs within the school. There will still be a need to assess whether the district has designed clearly established curricular goals and objectives. How these goals and objectives are delivered to diverse groups of students in schools with diverse student populations will require a more sophisticated analysis of Standard Two and Three.

The march toward a unified, national set of curriculum standards that can be the basis for a national assessment is moving ahead as the National Assessment Governing Board considers proposals for national assessments in reading and writing (Rothman, 1992). In 1990, National Assessment of Educational Progress (NEAP) results were reported at grades 4, 8, and 12, which compared student achievement against agreed-upon standards (Rothman, 1992, p. 13). Even though the process used for setting the standards was sharply criticized by the National Academy of Education, the National Center for Education Statistics, and the General Accounting Office, the movement toward national curriculum standards and national assessment continues to gain momentum.

Changes in Tests—From Memory to Application

The authentic assessment movement is quickly sweeping across the country (Herman et al., 1992). This movement has generated an expanded variety of assessment practices to determine whether students have achieved the goals and objects of the curriculum. With authentic assessment, there has been an expanded use of performance events, portfolios, and problem critique and analysis assessment strategies.

Performance events are commonly conducted as group activities that not only assess the members' knowledge of facts, but also the group's ability to work effectively together and use the collective knowledge of the group to analyze problems, create models, or defend positions. Scoring these events requires the development of strategies to assess partial responses and strategies to deal with a variety of responses that may all be considered correct.

Portfolios are flourishing in a variety of content areas. Kentucky currently requires students in grades 4, 8, and 12 to develop official portfolios in the areas of math and writing. Within the next two years, students will be required to keep portfolios in math, writing, science, and social studies. Vermont uses portfolios to assess student mathematics and writing skills at grades 4 and 8 (Forseth, 1992). As the movement toward integrated curriculum continues, it is expected that one day students may be required to keep an integrated portfolio that represents the student's academic achievement in all content areas. An assessment of student portfolios may become part of the college acceptance process or may be used to meet graduation requirements from high school or advancement from one level of schooling to another (from primary school to fourth grade or from middle school to high school).

At the same time, the nature of standardized achievement tests appears to be changing. These assessments are beginning to include more open-ended response items and writing prompts requiring students to demonstrate higher level thinking skills in addition to the typical standardized multiple choice items. As these new assessment systems evolve and become required as the basis for school accountability, student assessment reporting systems will undergo significant change. During this period of transition, it may be difficult to track student achievement data over time using consistent measures of achievement. While the types of measures may change, the process of student assessment will continue. Standard Four assesses whether a district and the schools within the district use student assessment data to make decisions about the development and modification of the instructional program. The data sources may change, but the standard will remain.

THE FUTURE OF THE CURRICULUM AUDIT

The fifth standard of the audit relates to whether a school system is continuing to improve over time. The idea of continuous improvement, embodied in the Japanese concept of kaizen (Imai, 1986) closely parallels this standard. It is also included as one of the principles for Total Quality Management. Increasingly, the objectives toward which school districts are striving are international ones. Most school districts are no longer content to measure their effectiveness by comparing student achievement results on standardized tests with the district next door. Rather, the evolving curriculum standards and assessment measures appear to involve whether high school graduates are internationally competitive. These international comparisons will undoubtedly become more important in the future. Comparing student achievement from different countries is not an easy task. It is common to give the same test to students from different countries and then compare the results. In these comparisons, the United States is typically found near the bottom, suggesting that our students do not know as much as the students from competing countries. However, these data may simply mean that the typical curriculum delivered in most U.S. schools is not aligned with the curriculum that is assessed on these tests. This was the conclusion reached by Ian Westbury (1992) in his recent analysis of U.S. and Japanese student achievement on the Second International Mathematics Study (SIMS). He concluded that, "Where the American curriculum is comparable to both the curriculum of the test and the curriculum of Japan, . . . U.S. achievement is similar to that of Japan." His analysis suggests that where there is a relationship among the goals and objectives of the instructional program, what teachers teach in classrooms, and what is assessed, students achieve. This concept of curriculum alignment is the foundation upon which the curriculum management audit is based. As we struggle to set national and international standards, deliver instruction to an increasingly diverse student population, and assess our ability to improve continuously over time, certain trends will emerge. First, the curriculum management audit will become an integral part of our analysis of our ability to achieve the high curriculum standards that are evolving internationally. Second, this analysis will take place at the district, program, and school level. Third, there will be a movement away from looking at consistency of teacher, principal, and school implementation strategies toward analyzing consistency of student outcomes. Finally, the standards of the curriculum management audit and the procedures necessary to implement these standards will become integrated into teacher and administrator training programs at the preservice and inservice level.

The ability of our public educational system to improve over time, given limited resources, will mandate these changes. If the public education system, as it is presently configured, cannot rise to this challenge, we are likely to see a variety of alternate models to the public system arise. The New American School project that emerged out of the Bush administration is likely to continue, albeit with a Clintonized mask. The concept of charter schools being piloted in Minnesota and Philadelphia is gaining popularity. Projects designed to privatize public education continue to emerge, such as Chris Whittle's Edison Schools. All of these efforts are focused on expanding the numbers of "successful students" produced from our schools. While the design of these programs may not address the language of the curriculum management audit, they all address the fundamental principles upon which the audit is established.

REFERENCES

Bailey, W. (1991) *School-Site Management Applied.* Lancaster, Pennsylvania: Technomic Publishing Co., Inc.

English, F. (1988) *Curriculum Auditing.* Lancaster, Pennsylvania: Technomic Publishing Co., Inc.

Forseth, C. (1992) "Portfolio Assessment: In the Hands of Teachers," *The School Administrator* (December):24–28.

Herman, J., P. Aschbacher and L. Winter. (1992) *A Practical Guide to Alternative Assessment.* Alexandria, Virginia: Association for Curriculum and Supervision.

Imai, M. (1986) *Kaizen.* New York: McGraw-Hill Publishing Company.

Kozol, J. (1991) *Savage Inequalities.* New York: Crown Publishers, Inc.

Lawler, E. (1987) *High Involvement Management.* San Francisco: Jossey-Bass.

Lessinger, L. (1970) *Every Kid a Winner.* New York: Simon and Schuster.

Messerli, J. (1972) *Horace Mann.* New York: Alfred Knopf.

Pack, T. (1991) "Donta Says He'll Resign as Boyd School Chief," *Lexington Herald Leader* (October 26):A-1, 12.

Rose v. Council for Better Education, Inc., Kentucky. (1989) 790 S.W. 2d 186.

Rothman, R. (1992) "NEAP Weighing 1st Standards for Reading, Writing," *Education Week* (November 25):1.

Sears, J. B. (1933) "The School Survey Movement," In *Modern School Administration*, J. C. Almack (ed.), Boston: Houghton Mifflin Company.

Steffy, B. (1989) "Curriculum Auditing as a State Agency Tool in Takeovers," *National Forum of Applied Educational Research*, 3(1)5–16.

Steffy, B. (1993) *Kentucky Education Reform: Lessons for America*. Lancaster, Pennsylvania: Technomic Publishing Co., Inc.

Vertiz, V. (1992) "The Curriculum Audit: A Quality Control Vehicle to School Reform," unpublished document.

Vobejda, B. (1992) "Census Bureau Projects Ethnic Profile to Make Dramatic Shift," *Lexington Herald Leader* (December 4):A-1, 6.

Westbury, I. (1993 June–July) "Comparing American and Japanese Achievement to the United States," 21(5):18–24.

PART II

CURRICULUM MANAGEMENT AUDIT STANDARDS AND PROCEDURES

CHAPTER 5

Standard One: The Control Standard

CAROLYN J. DOWNEY – *San Diego State University*
LARRY E. FRASE – *San Diego State University*

INTRODUCTION

A school system that is in control of itself is a rational organization, that is, one that can systematically bring about increased productivity. Therefore, many consider the Control Standard, the first Curriculum Audit Standard (English, 1992), to be the most powerful. If an organization is not in control, the likelihood of it being able to accomplish its mission is diluted. In education, there is a major need to restructure in order to increase the ability to be in control, thereby enhancing the curriculum and the learning of students.

In school systems, learning is the product, and the student is the ultimate customer. As a child goes through the school system, each moment must be designed to increase learning (Downey, 1992). Organizations that meet Standard One of the audit are more likely to be able to make a difference in student learning.

This chapter first defines Standard One and presents its criteria; then, three primary audit foci of this standard (policy, administrative structure, and planning) are described. For each of these three foci, the following data are presented:

- introduction of the area's indicators
- rationale for the area as it relates to control
- specific criteria used in the audit to determine the quality of the design and steps for implementation
- the auditor's role in examining the design and delivery of the area along with data sources used as well as reporting and charting of findings
- typical findings in school systems and frequent recommendations given in audits related to the area

In addition to the three primary foci of Standard One, additional areas frequently examined by auditors are briefly addressed.

STANDARD ONE DEFINED

The first standard of the curriculum management audit is known as the Control Standard. A school system meets Standard One when it "is able to demonstrate its control of resources, programs, and personnel" (English, 1988, p. 33). The description of the standard as presented in the Curriculum Audit Training Workshop (English, 1992, p. 2) is as follows).

Quality control is the fundamental element of a well-managed educational program. It is one of the major premises of local educational control within any state's educational system. The critical premise involved is that via the will of the electorate, a local board of education establishes local priorities within state law and regulations.

A school district's accountability rests with the school board and the public. Through policy development, a local school board provides the focus for the operation of a school system, and implementation of policy is delegated to administrative staff. In this way, the expression of popular will is assured, enabling the district to be responsive to its clients and patrons. This process also enables the system to assess and use student learning as a critical factor in determining its success.

Educational program control and accountability are often shared among different components of a school system; however, "fundamental control of, and responsibility for, a district and its operations rests with the school board and top-level management staff" (English, 1992, p. 2).

A school system meeting Standard One would be able to demonstrate its control of resources, programs, personnel by such indicators as:

- a curriculum that is centrally defined and adopted by the board of education
- a clear set of policies that establish an operational framework for management that permits accountability
- a clear set of policies that reflect state requirements and local program goals and the necessity to use achievement data to improve school system operations
- a functional administrative structure that facilitates the design and delivery of the district's curriculum
- a direct, uninterrupted line of authority from school board/superintendent and other central office officials to principals and classroom teachers

- documentation of school board and central office planning for the attainment of goals, objectives, and mission over time, and
- a clear mechanism to define and divert change and innovation which the school system to permit maximization of its resources or priority goals, objectives, and mission

The audit uses five standards against which to compare, verify, and comment upon the school system's existing curricular management practices. The standards reflect working characteristics that any complex organization should possess for being responsive and responsible to its customers (English, 1992, p. 22).

POLICY FOCUS: THE FIRST STEP TOWARD CONTROL

Three of the seven criteria for Standard One are related to the design and implementation of a school system's policy. The three indicators (English, 1992) are:

- a curriculum that is centrally defined and adopted by the board of education
- a clear set of policies that establish an operational framework for management, that permits accountability
- a clear set of policies that reflect state requirements and local program goals and the necessity to use achievement data to improve school system operations

Rationale for Policy

The audit is built on the premise that the first and foremost aspect of control is that the board have clear and strong curriculum management policies to direct the actions of staff. The official "Beliefs and Policies of the National School Boards Association" (Selection book) indicates that a "school board should adopt clearly defined written policies based on a thorough understanding of the education process. . . . The power to make ultimate determinations of policy is vested in the board, and it is the board's duty to exercise this power and not to delegate it to others" (NSBA, 1982, p. 9).

Audit expectations call for an integrated, approach toward both the design and delivery of the curriculum to allow a system to move rationally toward continuous improvement of its learner outcomes. The

Arizona School Board Association sample board manual (Kyrene School District, 1990) states that "policy development in a forward-looking school system is a dynamic ongoing process" (p. 1). Well-delineated curriculum management policies are critical to providing fundamental control over the focus of the system. There are several reasons for having such policies as follows.

Establish Direction

Policies set the framework for control and establish the direction of organizational energy and resources toward accomplishing the mission of the organization. Policies are "principles adopted by the Board to chart a course of action" (Kyrene School District, 1990, p. 4). The audit is built on the premise that the organization must be tightly coupled with respect to the curriculum to avoid a propensity toward being dysfunctional. To be responsive and to increase productivity, systems need to become "tighter" in their curriculum connections.

NSBA beliefs include statements that written policies are the chief means by which the school board governs the schools; regulations (or "procedures" or "rules") are one means by which the superintendent sees to it that board policies are carried out.

. . . If school boards are to govern and administrators are to manage, it is important that board members and administrators know what the policies are—all the policies. . . . It provides everyone with "must-know" information.—(NSBA, 1982, p. 10)

Determine Decision-Making Structure

The audit expects the board's role to involve itself in curriculum to the extent of meta-management. The board needs to establish processes and structures by which individual decisions are made by administrative and other staff. Adopting a rationale for the philosophy of the curriculum, including learner outcomes and assessment tools, is a role the board must not delegate. When administration and staff engage in decision making within board policy, this is considered micro-management, which fulfills their role with respect to the curriculum.

Specific policy in the area of curriculum management provides the framework for the premises of the curriculum; sets goals and a focus for the curriculum; and determines the degree of alignment between the written, taught, and tested curriculum. It can guide both the adequate design of the curriculum and its effective delivery. The National School Board Association (NSBA, 1982) states that "policies are guidelines adopted by the board to chart a course of action" (p. 10).

Provide for Local Control

One of the major reasons that boards should build their own set of policies around effective curriculum management is to provide for local control. Many school systems allow their curriculum to be externally directed—usually by state or federal perspectives. In order to be responsive to their own community, boards need to establish "tighter" connections to what the community wants students to learn. Such written policies also "establish a legal record, as well as a legal basis for many actions" (Van Loozen, 1982, p. 63). Certainly, the board needs to consider federal and state expectations but should integrate these directives into their own perspective.

Establish Equity of Access

In order for the board to ensure that all students exiting the school system have had equitable access to the curriculum, the curriculum needs to be determined at the system level. This is not to imply an audit bias against site-based decision groups. How the system organizes itself for the delivery of the curriculum can vary greatly and still meet Standard One criteria relevant to policy; however, learner outcomes need to be derived and ensured systemwide.

Provide for Long-Term Impact

Adopting policies in the area of curriculum management results in long-term decisions. If adequate policies are in place, it can use these policies to recall past decisions on similar issues. Thereby, when an issue comes before the board, the board can avoid making decisions that contradict policy or react to pressure groups without logically assessing the issues. Van Loozen (1982) indicates that when the board is "armed with a set of well-defined policies, the following types of 'board malpractice' are less likely to occur . . . instant policy making . . . dictatorial policy making . . . illegal policy making . . . sloppy policy making . . . contradictory policy making" (pp. 63–64). He further asserts that well-written policy fosters stability and continuity and "helps assure smooth transitions when organizational or staff changes occur" (p. 63).

One document provided to new board members by the National School Board Association states:

> If there were a physician who specialized in school board service, he would surely prescribe policy making as the penicillin to cure most ills that afflict a board and its administration. . . . When a board and its chief administrator are confused about roles and authority, or are plagued with misunderstandings, board policy is a likely remedy. It serves to clarify board and superintendent functions. Ambiguity, confusion, and trouble are voiced when policies are adopted and published. Clearly written policies that reflect through research, sound judgment and careful planning stave off the maiming accusations of uninformed critics. (Van Loozen, 1982, p. 63)

Provide for Accountability

If policies are well delineated, they will guide staff actions and can serve as the framework for evaluation of a board member, superintendent, or staff practice (Van Loozen, 1982). As stated by the NSBA (1982), policies "set guidelines for staff action. . . . They bring into practice good procedures and approaches. . . . What the employer wants is to get the organization's work done, done well, and according to proper procedure. Good policies, well implemented, serve that purpose" (p. 9). The more specific the policy, the higher the likelihood that its implementation will eventually increase productivity of learning.

Characteristics of Strong Curriculum Management Policies

For a policy framework to be an effective guide for making decisions at all levels in the organization, it must be specific enough that at least inclusion/exclusion decisions can be made by referencing it. Inclusion/exclusion decisions pertain to whether a possible administrative decision is addressed by an existing policy. If board policies are not specific, they are not useful to administrators or teachers; if they do not guide practice, they are not useful in providing control and direction for decision making.

Too often, curriculum policies are "we believes" (English, 1988). Such policies often include nebulous or diplomatic language, which does not guide organizational direction. Adequate policies need specific language that all can understand and interpret in a similar way.

Strong curriculum policies provide specific guidance on all five standard audits—control, direction, connectivity, feedback, and productivity. Policies should focus on both the design and delivery of the curriculum as well as the concept of alignment of the written, taught, and tested curriculum. The audit specifies twenty-one subcriteria that result in strong curriculum management policies. They are presented in Table 1.

In addition to the criteria for strong policies, a second set of eight

Table 1. Policy criteria: characteristics of strong curriculum management policies.

Written Directive Statements—policies that

1. Provide for **Control**—require
   - an aligned written, tested, and taught curriculum
   - statements on curriculum framework approach (e.g., outcome-based, competency-based)
   - board adoption of the curriculum
   - accountability through roles and responsibilities
   - long-range planning

2. Provide for **Direction**—require
   - written curriculum for all subject/learning areas
   - periodic review of the curriculum
   - textbook/resource adoption by the Board
   - content area emphasis

3. Provide for **Connectivity and Equity**—require
   - predictability of the written curriculum from one level to another
   - vertical articulation and horizontal coordination
   - training for staff in the delivery of the curriculum
   - delivery of the curriculum
   - monitoring of the delivery of the curriculum
   - equitable access to the curriculum

4. Provide for **Feedback**—require
   - an assessment program which is multifaceted
   - use of data from assessment to determine program/curriculum effectiveness and efficiency
   - reports to the board about program effectiveness

5. Provide for **Productivity**—require
   - program-centered budget
   - resource allocation tied to curriculum priorities
   - environment to support curriculum delivery
   - data driven decisions for the purpose of increasing student learning

---

Source: English, 1992.

Table 2. Well-written policy criteria.

Well-written policies are
1. Within the scope of the board's authority
2. Consistent with local, state, federal, and constitutional law
3. Supportive of the system's goals or objectives
4. Consistent across policies
5. Directive rather than descriptive in language
6. Easily understood and transferable—free of excessive verbiage but have a proper level of explanation—when education language is used it is defined
7. In a bullet-type format if possible
8. Referenced to other policy and law

Source: Downey, 1992.

subcriteria are used to determine whether the policy is well written. These criteria are listed in Table 2.

The Arizona School Board Association (Kyrene School District, 1990) states that policies should "tell what is wanted and may include also why and how much. They are broad enough to indicate a line of action to be taken by the administration in meeting a number of day-to-day problems; they need to be narrow enough to give the administration clear guidance" (p. 4).

Audit Team's Role/Data Sources/Exhibits

The audit team's role when examining policy is threefold:

(1) Auditors must determine what curriculum management policies, exist. (Design)

(2) If policies exist, are they strong (twenty-two characteristics) and well-written (eight subcriteria). These two issues deal with design—do policies exist, and are they of high quality? (Design)

(3) It is the responsibility of the audit team to ascertain whether personnel implement prevailing policies. This is an issue of delivery—are policies used as opposed to design? (Delivery) This is often called the "so what" question. (Delivery)

The following sections delineate the methods used by the audit team to make these determinations.

To discern the existence of relevant policies, the team requests copies of all policies, regulations, and other board-adopted documents related to any aspect of curriculum, including instructional, facility, and fiscal considerations. Auditors often find it difficult to obtain such policies.

If there are few to be found, auditors seek linkage documents such as administrative regulations or minutes of board meetings to locate data discrepancies. Normally, policies are sent to the lead auditor prior to the site visit to be reviewed by all audit team members as a framework for understanding the system with respect to control. The policies are then taken to the site and used by the team throughout the site visit.

The audit team prepares a list of those documents represented as a comprehensive set of policies/regulations available on curriculum management policy characteristics. The list includes any policy/regulation number, title, and date of adoption. Table 3 displays an example of a policy scope exhibit. All policies identified anywhere throughout the audit report are to be listed in this table.

If policies are in place, the audit team's next role is to examine them to determine which of the subcriteria for strong curriculum management policies have been met. The auditors carefully review all policies and supporting documents and regulations to discern presence or absence of the twenty-one characteristics. Policies are considered adequate or strong if at least 70% of the criteria have been met. Usually, a chart indicating the adequacy level for each characteristic is provided. Charts may utilize three measures (adequate, partially adequate, and inadequate) or only two (adequate and inadequate). Table 4 partially illustrates a two-measure chart. The percent of characteristics that are judged adequate is presented in the narrative of the findings section of the report, along with a synthesis of the findings regarding the strength of each policy.

All relevant policies are listed next to appropriate characteristics and determination made as to adequacy or the characteristic. After all policies have been reviewed, the criteria met by the policies are totaled. If no policies are available for a criterion, word "none" is placed in the column.

With respect to the second set of subcriteria, which deal with how well-written the policies are, the auditors examine the policies as they are reviewed and make judgments regarding style of writing and consistency. This information is usually presented in a narrative form. An example from a recent audit is shown in Table 5.

To answer the third question on policy (use), the audit team most often utilizes interviews, although linkage documents showing implementation are also examined. All board members and the superintendent and his/her staff are questioned about policies—their existence, quality, and use. Other employees are also asked about policies and their use, although this is usually undertaken to validate statements

Table 3. Policy scope example (sample public school board policies, 1992).

Policy	Description	Date Adopted
AE	School District Goals and Objectives	June 1981
AFC	Evaluation of Professional Staff Members	September 1977
CCA-E	Table of Organization	July 1990
CUR-GIDL	Guidelines for Writing of Curriculum	January 1992
DB	Annual Operating Budget, November 1970	
DBD	Budget Planning	December 1972
GCL	Professional Staff Development	April 1985
IFB	Pilot Projects	April 1975
IFD	Curriculum Adoption	November 1966
IFD-E	Procedure for the Development, Implementation, and Evaluation of Curriculum	April 1981
IFD-R	Curriculum Guides and Course Outlines	March 1977
IGA-E	Basic Instructional Program	June 1981
IGAE	AIDS	June 1989
IGBA	Special Education	October 1973
IHB-R	Class Size	November 1976
IHC-E	Scheduling for Instruction, February 1984	
IHC-R	Instructional Time	April 1988
IHC-R-1	Scheduling for Instruction, September 1984	
IIAA/IIAB	Textbook Supplemental Materials Selection and Adoption	April 1975
IIAA-R/IIAB-R	Procedures for Textbook Selection	April 1975
IIAC	Library/Media Materials Selection	March 1991
IIBG	Computer Asst. Inst.	October 1985
IICA	Field Trips	September 1976
IKA-R	Grading Systems	March 1977
IKAA	High School Exams	February 1978
IKB	Homework	January 1976
IKB-R	Homework (Revised)	January 1987
IKE	Promotion and Retention of Students	No Month 1972
IKF	Graduation Requirements, May 1984	
IM	Evaluation of Inst. Programs	June 1975
IM-R	Evaluation of Inst. Programs	November 1970
INA-R	Teaching Methods	November 1976
JB	Equal Educational Opportunities	April 1985
JCAP	Equity/Multi-Cultured Education	September 1991
JECD	Assignment of Students to Classes	November 1966

Table 4. Sample policy characteristics exhibit (characteristics of good policies for curriculum management and auditors' assessment).

Criteria	Policies	Individual Policies Met	Individual Policies Not Met	Criterion Met	Criterion Not Met
1. *Provides for Control*—requires					
A. Aligned written, tested, and taught curriculum	CUR-GIDL	X		X	
	IIAA/IIAB		X		
	IIAA-R		X		
	IM		X		
B. Philosophical statement of curriculum approach (e.g. outcome-based, competency-based)	IGA-E	X		X	
C. Board adoption of the curriculum	IFD	X		X	
D. Accountability through roles and responsibilities	None				X
E. Long range planning	None				X
2. *Provides for Direction*—requires					
A. Written curriculum for all subject areas	IFD-E	X		X	

95

Table 5. Example of narrative on writing quality of policy.

The system policies are adequate in most of the characteristics of strong policy statements. Policies are within the scope of the board's authority and consistent with local, state, federal, and constitutional law. However, the policies were often descriptive rather than directive in tone as well as vague in intent. Key ideas are often lost in long narrative prose.

made by systemwide administrators and board members. Results are usually reported in narrative prose as depicted in Table 6.

Typical Findings and Recommendations

In most audits, policies on curriculum management are lacking, incomplete, inadequate, or in some cases, nonexistent. Policies are frequently outdated. In a few cases, two sets of contradictory policies have been found. Auditors have been quite generous in their descriptions of policies that attempt to provide some type of quality control in curriculum management since so few policies found are of any quality at all.

Auditors have seldom seen evidence of effective use of policy. Most board members do not assume major responsibility for board policy. They rely heavily on the staff to submit policy for board consideration and tend not to concern themselves with any type of curriculum policy. Most board members interviewed in audits are not familiar with policy. In fact, auditors typically find that board members are unaware of the process used to create, adopt, and periodically review policies.

In most cases, recommendations made by auditors relate to the improvement of policies. Recommendations are generally quite comprehensive, suggesting, for example, that boards develop, adopt, and implement a set of board policies to direct curriculum management and

Table 6. Example of narrative on policy use.

When asked about policies on various topics, most board members said they did not know if they existed. Most board members interviewed were not familiar with any plan for evaluating or revising policies. The board lacks a plan for evaluating and revising policies. Board involvement in these activities is inadequate. Moreover, of those staff members interviewed about board policy, most indicated that policies were not used. Most administrators interviewed were not able to locate the policy manual in their offices.

ensure quality control. Recommendations often take the form of proposing changes in existing policies to resolve contradictions, ensure alignment among policies, or provide more substance. Table 7 illustrates this concept.

Recommendations about specific policies only occur when there are substantive policies in place. Usually, more simplistic actions are proposed. Examples of these recommended actions follow:

- a policy that establishes the vision for the curriculum and programs of the district
- a policy that sets minimum goals and objectives for all student learning outcomes
- a policy that requires congruence and harmony among the curriculum goals and objectives, teacher delivery techniques and strategies, and districtwide testing programs and assessment
- a policy that requires curriculum content and activities to be aligned with the state and school system's curriculum outcomes
- a policy that outlines a clear procedure for the development of curriculum, including additions, deletions, and the adoption, evaluation, and termination/continuation of pilot programs
- a policy that requires equity and coordination across schools in

Table 7. Sample recommendation narrative on specific policies.

The following actions are recommended for existing policies:

- All documents used as board policy by administrators should first be approved by the board. This has not occurred for "Strategic Planning Report, 1991" (see Finding 1.1).
- If the previous action is completed, the board should consider rescinding policy IGA-E to avoid the existence of conflicting policies.
- Policy IFD should be revised to include direction for dealing with "undersized classes."
- Policies IFD-R, IIAA, and IIAA-R should be enforced by the superintendent.
- Policy IKB-R should be revised to include directions for deciding how homework should be used in determining grades and how and under what conditions homework should be reviewed by teachers.
- The evaluation components of policies IM and IM-R should be enforced by the superintendent.
- Policy INA-R should be revised to include directions for the content of lesson plans, who should monitor lesson plans, and how they should be monitored.

curriculum outcomes, offerings, and activities, including policy guidelines for determining school-based modifications
- a policy that assigns curriculum development and monitoring responsibilities to specific administrative staff positions
- a policy that requires a comprehensive criterion-referenced testing program, which can measure curriculum outcomes for all students in all areas of the curriculum and which provides assessment information to the board and superintendent
- a policy that requires test results to be disaggregated to help improve individual and group instruction and achievement
- a policy that requires at least one goal in each school's annual improvement plan to be directly related to assessment data and student achievement
- a policy that establishes a sequential linkage among data gathering, planning, goal development, curriculum development, and budgeting
- a policy that requires the board to use the achievement data in their goal-setting process

A sample Curriculum Development and Management Policy and Regulation is provided at the end of this chapter. It is often included as an appendix in audits, in which recommendations regarding policy development are made (see page 122).

ADMINISTRATIVE STRUCTURE FOCUS: PROVIDING FOR CONTROL (TABLE OF ORGANIZATION/JOB DESCRIPTIONS/STABILITY)

A second major focus of Standard One (English, 1988) is to examine the administrative structure for quality control features. Two of the seven indicators (English, 1988, p. 199) of Standard One relate to this focus:
- a functional administrative structure that facilitates the design and delivery of the district's curriculum
- a direct, uninterrupted line of authority from school board/superintendent and other central office officials to principals and classroom teachers

Administrative Functionality Rationale

A strong, functional administrative structure is needed to enhance the management of the curriculum and to focus the direction of the organization. To assist in the assessment of these criteria, auditors minimally examine the table of organizational structure, job descriptions, and board/administrator stability. How decisions are made in the school district is critical. If an organization is unclear about how decisions are made or who makes them, confusion can often paralyze the system. This part of the audit is one of the more sensitive because it deals with relationships as a perceived power.

Administrative Structure Criteria

Job Descriptions

Job descriptions are important tools for creating administrative structures that result in the work of the system being accomplished. The value of job descriptions is described by NSBA (1982). Written job descriptions are indispensable tools for effective school administration. All of the many decisions made by school managers and supervisors either influence or are influenced by determinations about how work is divided into jobs and about how jobs are to be accomplished (p. 37).

The usefulness of job descriptions may be viewed in terms of three primary activities that involve school leaders—organizational planning, budgeting, and personnel administration. The job description is the basic resource for "planning the ways and means by which a job will be done. It can bring to light poorly defined authority and overlapping or duplication of efforts" (NSBA, 1982, p. 37).

With respect to budgeting, the job description is the basic resource for "controlling operations to ensure that each job is done efficiently. A job description program furnishes standard nomenclature for compiling meaningful statements of jobs and provides logical functional groupings upon which compensation schedules can be based" (NSBA, 1982, p. 37).

The third important area is personnel administration. A job description is the "basic resource for selecting and developing the person or people who will do a job. Job descriptions set standards that extend from the employment interview to final separation. They are useful in placement, promotion, and transfer procedures" (NSBA, 1982, p. 37).

The NSBA (1982, p. 37) identified thirteen uses of job descriptions. They can

- provide the basis for recruiting and interviewing job candidates and for personnel planning and budgeting
- clarify employee duties and responsibilities

- help a staff member see his role and contribution in relation to those of other employees
- help a staff member see how his job relates to the school system's overall goals and objectives
- help set fair and objective standards for supervising and evaluating job performance
- help maintain equity in the job classification program
- provide data for wage and salary administration
- serve as guides for part-time help and substitutes
- indicate inconsistencies, inefficiencies, ambiguity, and overload in job assignments and work flow
- clarify lines of authority and communication
- provide guides for the orderly expansion or contraction of the work force
- provide the board and the public information about what school team members actually do
- provide legal safeguards for dealing in a just manner in cases of employee termination

Job descriptions provide a guide for the work to be accomplished in the organization. It is critical, therefore, that the descriptions are aligned to the written, tested, and taught curriculum. In order for this to be accomplished, the job description must be current and present an accurate picture of the job functions.

Personnel Stability

Perhaps the greatest contributor to an effective administrative structure is the stability of those involved in the organization. In many organizations, the board members change often and the superintendency even more frequently. For organizations to make significant change over time, these individuals must remain in the organization for an appropriate period of time. Moreover, the relationships must be positive. Effective relationships among the board, superintendent, other administrators, staff, and parents are essential in a climate conducive to change. Relationships which are at odds create a climate of dysfunction.

No school district is expected to achieve a zero turnover rate; however, a reasonable degree of stability is needed to ensure constancy of purpose and predictable utilization of resources in the organization.

Auditors have found numerous situations where turnover, especially at the superintendent level, was so rapid that it precluded meeting minimal productivity levels. For example, one district employed four superintendents in four years. In another district consisting of one high school, one junior high school, and four elementary schools, the governing board employed seven superintendents, nine principals, thirteen assistant principals, and twenty-one principals for a grand total of fifty appointments for seven positions in a year period. These turnover rates are excessively unreasonable.

Interviews with teachers, parents, and other community members in this district revealed the following perceptions:

- "Constant, unneeded change."
- "This administrator, too, will pass."
- "Nothing is ever finished around here."

When programs and test data were analyzed, the auditors also learned that efforts to improve educational programs were weak and that productivity was very low.

Following are examples of recommendations for a district experiencing high administrative turnover rates:

- Establish administrative stability and integrity in management functioning.
- Establish administrative stability and effective board/superintendent working roles and responsibilities.

Characteristics of "Strong" Administrative Structures

Two areas in this portion of the audit have more detailed sub-criteria—the table of organization and job descriptions.

Auditors use six principles of sound organizational management to critique the table of organization. These are described in Table 8.

For job descriptions, auditors use the eight ingredients identified by the NSBA (1982), as well as a ninth criterion tied to curriculum alignment. Table 9 describes the first eight criteria. In addition, the auditors examine the job descriptions for statements regarding the alignment of the curriculum and expectations regarding the design and delivery of the curriculum. Ratings used are shown in Table 10.

When reviewing job descriptions, auditors also seek a philosophy which includes (NSBA, 1982, p. 38)

Table 8. Principles of sound organizational management.

Principle	Description
1. Span of Control	The span of control for effective day-to-day supervision requires direct responsibility for no more than 12 employees.
2. Chain of Command	No employee should have more than one supervisor.
3. Logical Grouping of Functions	Tasks of similar nature should be grouped together.
4. Separation of Line and Staff Positions	Line and staff positions (principals, teachers, secretaries, custodians, etc.) should be separate from curriculum design and program assessment functions.
5. Scalar Relationships	All positions at the same level must have similar responsibilities, authority, and compensation.
6. Full Inclusion	All central functions, particularly functions that facilitate quality control, are included in the organizational structure.

Source: English, 1992.

Table 9. Job description ingredients.

1. Job title
2. Job qualifications—knowledge, skills, abilities required
3. Immediate links in the chain of command
4. Job goal—how job fits into the aim of the organization
5. Major functions, duties, and responsibilities of the job
6. Terms of employment and reference to evaluation approach
7 Length of contract and salary schedule
8 When job description was reviewed last and who approved

Table 10. Adequacy ratings used for assessing job descriptions for alignment with curriculum design and delivery functions.

Ratings	Descriptions
Missing	No statement made
Inadequate	Present but missing basic ingredients
Adequate	A clear statement but weak in curriculum quality control statements
Strong	A clear statement that includes several aspects of curriculum quality control statements
Exemplary	A clear statement that includes curriculum quality control statements of alignment, design, and delivery of the curriculum coordination

- authority for decision making as near to the task as possible
- responsibility flow through a chain of command
- only one person acting as the immediate supervisor whenever possible
- accountability by the superintendent for all activities and personnel in the school system

The Audit Team's Role/Data Sources/Exhibits

The audit team's role is similar to that described in their examination of policy. Three questions are asked regarding the table of organization:

(1) Is there a table of organization? (Existence-Design)
(2) What is its level of quality based on the six subcriteria? (Quality-Design)
(3) Is the table of organization used? Is it functional? (Delivery)

Three similar questions relate to job descriptions:

(1) Are there job descriptions for all major positions tied to curriculum management? (Scope)
(2) What is the quality of the job descriptions—as determined by the nine subcriteria? (Design)
(3) Are the job descriptions used? (Delivery)

As with the case for policy, auditors explore scope, design, and delivery, that is, what exists, what its quality is, and whether it is used.

Typically, auditors present three tables of organization in the audit. First, they examine the formal written table of organization. This is usually found as an illustration in the board's policy. Sometimes the superintendent will provide it as a linkage document to policy. The illustration is examined for the quality criteria. In addition, board and staff are interviewed to determine the actual table of organization as well as the informal arrangements among staff. Based upon this review of what actually takes place, a proposed table of organization is built unless the formal and informal organizational structure meets the criteria and is functional.

In addition, in many recent reports for systems who are into shared team decision making, a flow of team decisions chart is included. In most cases, cross-function teams using an advocacy approach are recommended.

Job descriptions are reviewed for those positions related in some way to curriculum and instruction. A scope chart that lists position and date of adoption is prepared. Table 11 illustrates an example. The auditors then prepare a job description quality chart. Five rating possibilities, similar to the alignment characteristics, are used. In some cases, not all of the nine criteria are used, but alignment to the curriculum is always included. Table 12 uses four criteria.

Stability is determined by examining the length of service of board members, superintendent, and staff. Auditors look for degree of turn-over and in which positions. Length of service is not the sole determiner of stability, but it becomes a data source when coupled with remarks about the relationships among board, superintendent, and staff. For instance, stability can be maintained between superintendents if there is a smooth transition and the second superintendent carries on the agenda begun by the previous administration. This is more likely to occur when long-range planning is in place within the system. If stability is reported as a finding, it is usually presented in a narrative description of the data obtained by the auditors.

Table 11. Sample job description scope exhibit (list of job descriptions and adoption dates).

Job Position	Date Adopted
Teacher	June 1989
Reading and Language Arts Consultant	March 1991
Library/Media Specialist	October 1990
School Counselor	October 1990
School Psychologist	October 1990
Speech and Hearing Clinician	October 1990
Computer Education Resource Teacher	October 1990
School Nurse	October 1990
Department Chairperson	March 1990
Assistant Principal	June 1989
Principal	June 1989
Supervisor	June 1989
Assistant Supt. for Instruction and Staff Development	July 1989
Assistant Supt. of Schools	May 1970
Superintendent	April 1971

Table 12. Sample job description quality exhibit (quality of job descriptions by job title in sample school district).

Title	Qualifications	Link to Chain of Command	Expectations re: Responsibilities	Alignment/ Curriculum
Teacher	Missing	Strong	Strong	Inadequate
Reading Consultant	Missing	Strong	Strong	Inadequate
Library/ Media Spec.	Missing	Missing	Strong	Adequate
School Counselor	Missing	Inadequate	Strong	Inadequate
Speech Clinician	Missing	Strong	Strong	Adequate
Computer Ed. Res. Tchr.	Missing	Missing	Strong	Inadequate
Department Chairperson	Missing	Strong	Strong	Inadequate
Principal	Missing	Strong	Strong	Inadequate
Assistant Principal	Missing	Strong	Strong	Inadequate
Asst. Supt. of Schools	Adequate	Strong	Strong	Adequate
Supt.	Adequate	Strong	Strong	Adequate

Typical Findings and Recommendations

Findings relative to control and the administrative structure are discussed in audits more frequently than not; however, they generally address table of organization. In about half of the cases, auditors find a dysfunctional table of organization. Their most common findings are linked to the following:

- Formal structure does not portray the actual operational structure.
- Span of control of the superintendent is excessive.
- Principals often have no real supervisor since they report to the superintendent, who typically has too large a span of control.
- There are illogical groupings of functions, typically in the

regular and special instructional areas and often in noninstructional areas.

- Separation of line and staff positions and scalar relationships are often confused on the written table of organization.
- Many staff are confused about the organizational structure and are not sure how to impact decision making.

In those cases where the auditors find problems in the table of organization, typically, there are job description problems worthy of report. The most frequent findings in this area are that job descriptions are incomplete and often fail to link with the curriculum alignment criteria.

Stability of the organizational structure is reported in less than half of the audits as a problem in the organizations. Superintendent turnover is one of the most frequently reported problems, along with board/superintendent relationships.

Therefore, the recommendations in most audits are tied to updating the table of organizations and job descriptions and to revamping tables of organization to be more functional and deal directly with stability and/or board/superintendent/staff relationships.

If job descriptions are identified as deficient, auditors generally attribute the problems to descriptions that are incomplete or fail to link with the curriculum alignment criteria. Insufficient stability in the organizational structure is reported in less than half of the audits. Superintendent turnover and board/superintendent relationships are the most frequently reported problems.

In summary, most audits recommend revising the table of organization to ensure that it is current, functional, and designed to deal directly with stability and/or board/superintendent/staff relationships. Updating job descriptions is also a frequent recommendation.

PLANNING FOCUS: A THIRD STEP TOWARD CONTROL

A third major focus of Standard One (English, 1992) is to examine the system for long-term planning activities. Two of the seven criteria of Standard One relate to this focus:

- documentation of school board and central office planning for the attainment of goals, objectives, and mission over time
- a clear mechanism to define and divert change and innovation

within the school system to permit maximization of its
resources on priority goals, objectives and mission

The audit adheres to no particular planning strategy. The key is to
determine whether the system has a plan and a commitment to planning. Rationality is the major issue.

Rationale for Planning

Planning for change is critical to the continuous attainment of goals.
For a system to be rational, it must change its focus from "fire fighting
and crisis management" to a "process by which the guiding members of
an organization envision its future and develop the necessary procedures and operations to achieve that future" (Pfeiffer, 1986, pp. 1-2).
   Most planning processes are poorly conceptualized and even more
poorly executed. They rarely impact the day-to-day decisions made in
school systems. Often, planning is a top-management exercise that has
little to do with the actual running of the organization (Pfeiffer, 1986).
A successful plan must provide criteria for making day-to-day decisions and against which decisions can be evaluated.
   An important component of effective planning is "down-board thinking." This concept involves considering and planning for the possible
implications of a decision, making difficult choices, and basing additional plans on these implications (Pfeiffer, 1986).

Effective Planning Criteria

Eleven elements have been identified as possible criteria for effective
planning:

(1) *Mission:* General beliefs and educational goals of a school or-
    ganization. The mission is the foundation upon which all educa-
    tional programs and services are built. It describes the reason a
    district exists. Highly successful organizations (private and pub-
    lic) have a clearly defined and communicated mission.

(2) *Critical Analysis:* Collection and analysis of vital data about all
    facets of the internal and external environments of the school or-
    ganization. It defines the status of a school organization and
    describes the future by combining forecasting results with status-
    check results.

(3) *Assumptions:* Predictions of the events and conditions that are

likely to influence the performance of a school organization, division, or key individuals. Preparing planning assumptions is a form of forecasting. Assumptions are concerned with what the future will look like and help bridge the gap between needs and action goals in the planning process. This is also called "environmental scanning."

(4) *Components:* Means of grouping goals for the purposes of communication and management. All goals will be assigned to a component, and each component will consist of one or more goals.

(5) *Objectives:* Statements of results that are measurable and that have time limitations. They describe the condition(s) a school organization wants to improve. The desired improvements are then translated into goals. Objectives are written for each goal. As objectives are met, goals are accomplished.

(6) *Evaluation:* Statements of conditions that show evidence that an objective is satisfactorily achieved and procedures developed for completing the evaluation. Each objective should be evaluated, and the evaluation procedures should be developed at the time the objective is written.

(7) *Action Plans:* Actions that will help achieve objectives. Each objective will have one or more activities. A due date, responsible person(s), and cost are significant parts of each activity.

(8) *Integrated Functional Plans:* Each of the functional plans are integrated with one another in terms of resources (human, funds, time). Managers in charge of plans have agreement to integration of resources. Feasibility within budget parameters is clear.

(9) *Monitoring:* System for assessing the status of activities, analyzing the results, and reporting outcomes.

(10) *Stakeholder's Involvement:* All stakeholders in a system (community, board, administrators, staff, and possibly students) are represented in the plan development.

(11) *Linkage Documents:* All documents in a system are aligned to the plan.

The Audit Team's Role/Data Sources/Exhibits

The audit team's role is similar to that described in the previous focus. Three questions are asked regarding the planning activities of the system.

(1) Is there a plan? (Existence-Design)

(2) Is it based on the element of effective planning? (Quality of Design)

(3) Is the plan used? Is it functional? (Delivery)

The question of whether plans exist poses an interesting problem for auditors. Strategic plans are often found, as well as plans developed, prior to the strategic planning process. Auditors may also discover that plans differ among departments within the system. Often multiple plans are found. The interview process is critical to locating all organizational plans, and it is often necessary for auditors to spend several hours interviewing staff to accomplish this task. It is particularly valuable to question personnel who have been employed in the district for an extensive period of time, since auditors have found that long-term employees may be utilizing plans that others are not aware exist.

All plans, regardless of form, are requested by auditors. Plans may be found in policies, regulations, or other documents adopted by the board, or they may be located in stand-alone documents such as memoranda or reports. Materials are normally forwarded to the lead auditor prior to the site visit for review by all audit team members. This initial review provides a framework for understanding the system with respect to planning; however, the documentation is utilized throughout the site visit.

The audit team prepares a list of all plans and the dates they were formulated. A quality check is then performed using the eleven criteria for effective planning. A chart indicating the level of quality in each area is prepared (see Table 13) and a narrative is provided for each cri-

Table 13. Sample quality check on plans using adequacy of planning ingredients.

Planning Ingredients	Adequacy	
	Adequate	Inadequate
1. Mission	X	
2. Critical Analysis		X
3. Assumptions		X
4. Components	X	
5. Objectives	X	
6. Evaluation		X
7. Action Plans	X	
8. Integrated Functional Plans		X
9. Monitoring		X
10. Stakeholders Involvement		X
11. Linkage Documents		X

terion. Interviews are then held with board members, administrators, and other staff, and linkage documents are examined to determine whether and how plans are used. Findings related to use are usually reported in a narrative form.

Typical Findings and Recommendations

Audit results associated with planning are quite mixed. In about half of the cases, plans of varying quality are found. In more recent audits, strategic planning is often evident. Usually in such cases, previous plans are also in existence. Seldom have these previous plans been merged or eliminated.

Areas most often missing in plans were the criteria or environmental scanning and functional integration of plans. Feasibility to implement the plans based on design often was in question—too many goals, too soon, too fragmented.

In almost all audits, when plans, often adequate in design, were in place, they were not being implemented in a rational way. Well-designed plans usually met most of the eleven planning criteria of the audit. However, auditors typically found that, overall, the system was not using the plan in an orchestrated, focused way. Established plans are often not communicated well to various stakeholders, and the processes for implementing them are not encouraged or monitored.

In those cases where little or no planning is found, auditors make comprehensive recommendations, which include some of the following points:

- Develop a plan, which determines organizational readiness; develops commitment from stakeholders, especially the board and superintendent; identifies the planning team; establishes realistic time expectations; and educates the planning team.
- Conduct a values audit to examine the organization's operating philosophy, and analyze its culture and stakeholders.
- Formulate a system mission statement and subsequent internal and external customer mission statements.
- Provide visionary experiences to change the mental models or current paradigms.
- Define the strategic profile, establish critical success indicators and targets, and describe how indicators will be achieved.
- Conduct a performance audit using the SWOT approach—an

internal audit of strengths and weaknesses and an external audit of opportunities and threats.

- Conduct a gap analysis between current and desired future situations.
- Plan for contingencies—what actions will be taken when an event not considered for in the formal planning process takes place.
- Integrate functional plans into the organization structure.
- Implement and monitor the plan.

In those cases where several plans contradict one another, auditors recommend integrating all plans into a comprehensive long-range plan. For example, in a recent audit conducted by the authors, the system had developed a new mission statement without rescinding the previous statement. To establish a clear direction for the organization, it is important to eliminate the fragmentation created by a variety of plans.

Previous planning efforts should not be completely discarded however. Despite recent approaches that advocate planning "from scratch," many important ideas for change can be found by examining and incorporating data from earlier planning documents.

OTHER CRITICAL ASPECTS OF STANDARD ONE

The topic of control is expansive and cannot be limited to policy, administrative structure, and planning. Based on the principle of materiality discussed earlier, auditors must reveal any situation that inhibits the organization from increasing productivity. Among these control topics are employment contracts, quality of administration and instruction, and quality of board practices. This section examines each of these areas.

Employment Contracts

Sound employment contracts are needed to protect employees and the organization as it attempts to fulfill its mission. Auditors have evaluated districts in which contracts provided insufficient salaries to recruit or retain teachers. In contrast, some contracts prohibit the governing board and administration from exercising the power needed to achieve reasonable productivity levels.

In one district, the auditors found that the teachers' work day was limited to six hours and nine minutes, inclusive of teaching, planning, and lunch. Meetings of professional staff were limited to one per month. Class size was inequitable and excessively low. Teachers had full authority to determine teaching techniques. A basic assumption of the curriculum management audit is a collaborative approach to ensure high-quality instruction; however, observations revealed poor and outdated instructional techniques. The board and administration was too generous delegating its authority in the management of teaching practices and the school day. This created a restrictive and detrimental environment for curriculum quality control. The negotiations process provided undue constraints on the elected board to represent the public and achieve their desired education results.

The following are two examples of recommendations regarding employment contracts:

- Purge the professional negotiation agreement of provisions that unduly limit board control of key educational programs and practices.
- Exercise responsibility to set and carry out timely employment contract agreements.

Quality of Administration and Instruction

The most productive form of personnel evaluation has been a subject of debate for years, but most agree that *constructive feedback* is crucial to improving job performance. In essence, people want to know how they are doing and how to improve. They can do so if given accurate feedback, constructive ideas, and resource assistance. Auditors have found that many school districts are failing to provide this essential information (Frase and Streshly, in press).

Integral parts of the curriculum management audit include reviewing the distribution of evaluation rating and analyzing the quality of supervisor training and provision of feedback and resource assistance to staff. The results of audits strongly support the many complaints about teacher evaluation made by teachers, administrators, and the lay public (Wise et al., 1985; Scriven, 1981; Poston and Manatt, 1992).

In one district of approximately 80,000 students, 89% of teachers received very good or outstanding ratings, while only 0.3% received conditional or unsatisfactory ratings. Further, over a three-year period in this district, 4,728 teacher evaluations, which should have taken place, according to board policy and administrative procedures, were not conducted (Frase, 1992). Similar findings were made in six other districts (see Figure 1).

Research (Langlois and Colarusso, 1988 and White, 1990) and teacher observations in these districts indicate that teachers' ratings are greatly inflated (Frase, 1992). Failing to conduct evaluations only exacerbates the problem. Research findings (Feistritzer, 1986) demonstrate that teachers want to do a good job. Feedback is necessary to help them do so to achieve professional growth and success, which results in the satisfaction they desire. Administrators can misuse humanistic philosophies and the abundance mentality (Covey, 1991) to rationalize their failure to give constructive feedback, but they cannot justify it. This is particularly true when instructional competency is of foremost importance.

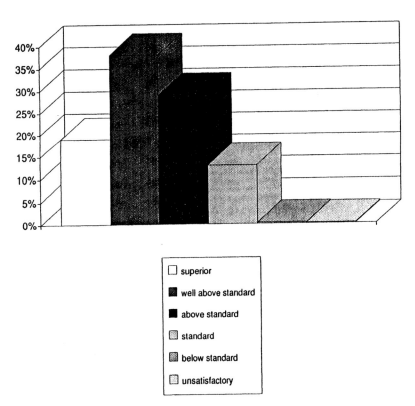

FIGURE 1 Distribution of teacher evaluation ratings in six school districts.

This is not to imply that the fault lies totally with the administrators in charge of conducting teacher evaluations. In one district, the auditors learned that five years had passed since training in teacher observation and instruction had been provided. Review of documents and interviews with administrators revealed that principals were not only confused about what to look for in observations, they were greatly confused about the procedures required by the evaluation policy.

The most powerful element in a child's formal education is the teacher. The failure of school administrators to fulfill their obligation to provide constructive feedback to teachers or to establish mechanisms such as peer coaching to enable teachers to provide feedback for each other greatly limits teachers' success in classrooms. Without high-quality teaching and administration, there can be no assurance of curriculum quality control.

The following are examples of recommendations regarding the quality of teaching and personnel evaluations:

- Clarify the value of personnel evaluation and appropriate procedures and change the focus of plans for assistance.
- Conduct intensive leadership and supervision training for administrators.
- Develop and provide teacher evaluation training.
- Redefine the purposes of teacher evaluation and conduct appropriate training.

Quality of Board Practices

School boards have come under much fire recently for failing to produce high-quality schools. Specifically, they have been charged with spending too much time trying to do the work of the superintendent (Streshly and Frase, 1993). The practice of micro-management by school boards is also rebuked in recent reports (Danzberger, 1992; Danzberger et al., 1992). Without effective working relationships, school boards cannot, with or without the expertise of superintendents, establish control mechanisms to ensure curriculum quality control.

Auditors frequently find board members to be ineffective in carrying out their role. This ineffectiveness ranges from near total lack of involvement to excessive and improper involvement. In the remainder of this chapter, audit findings related to improper board member behaviors and failure to attend to school board duties will be addressed.

Improper Board Member Behaviors

In two districts audited, board members sent requests for reports directly to administrators at all levels. During the seven months audited in one district, sixty-five requests were submitted. Few were substantive and most were frivolous. They represented attempts to respond to a small segment of their constituency or to "second guess" administrators. The majority of these requests only served the political interests and needs of individual board members and were made with board authorization. No policy for processing requests for information was in place in the district. These requests required hundreds of hours of administrator time and yielded little benefit to the district.

Unfortunately, official board policy statements regarding proper board behavior are not effective. In another district, the board had policies in place that carried the following quotations regarding board and board member behavior:

> Individual members as well as the Board *have no status as, and should not attempt to act as, administrators* of the district. [Policy 100-2, emphasis added]

> The board members' right to full information extends to the duty to listen to complaints that citizens bring them. *This right and duty to listen does not convey any right or duty to make any comment whatsoever* in response to such complaints, *except that it will be conveyed to the district superintendent.* [Policy 100-2]

> [Individual board members] shall *avoid making any personal commitments that may tend to hamper or embarrass the board* or prejudice the decision when matters come before it for action. [Policy 100-1P]

The auditors' review of documents and interviews with personnel revealed that board members had not acted in accordance with their policies. Individual board members had crossed the line between macro- and micro-management on numerous occasions in personnel and facilities management. These are illustrated by the following quotations from teachers, administrators, and community members:

- "Board members ask for specific tasks without going through the superintendent. They certainly do that."

- "If a board member comes out and I tell them [sic] about problems, they get them taken care of."
- "One board member disciplined a staff member."
- "They really get into administrative decisions on facilities."
- "The board is into day-to-day operations."
- "We get lots of calls from board members for information."
- "Yes, the parents go through the board."
- "When I need something, chairs, lights, tables, desks, etc., our board member will get it for us."

The fact that some of these quotations appear well-intended, and even effective, in delivering needed furniture to schools sheds light on an important problem. First, the administrative procedures designed to supply the schools with needed furniture is not functioning properly. If this is the case, the administration is at fault. Second, if finances are lacking and a plan is in place to alleviate such needs, the board members are disrupting the plan and possibly denying schools that have even greater needs. This was found to be the case, particularly in districts where board members are elected by an area within the school district, rather than by the school district as a whole.

The following board members' responses to auditors' questions further illustrate the degree to which individual members of this board misused their position to violate the line and staff arrangement of the table of organization.

Question: Do you address problems through administrators or directly with parents?

Answer: "Yes, I meet with parents who have complaints and resolve their problem and then talk to the principal and superintendent."

Question: How do you give a message to principals that things needed to be done?

Answer: "I told them to do it."

Question: How did that teacher transfer occur?

Answer: "I have a meeting with (personnel director) to address this."

Question: How did the school repair occur?

Answer: "I tell principals to put in work orders."

The following responses were given by board members to auditors' questions regarding how the board members select their areas of activity as board members. These answers represent violations of board policies.

Question: How do you determine what you can ask for?
Answer: "Each board member sets standards for what is an appropriate request."
Question: How does the board determine what each member will advocate?
Answer: "Individual choice!"

Further, in violation of board policy, board members demonstrated behaviors that were embarrassing to individual board members, the board, and staff. Many of these behaviors are distasteful and hampered the conduct of school board business. These are illustrated by the following quotations.

- "I'm going to get that sorry son of a bitch" (reference to associate superintendent).
- "She is a PR disaster. Don't let her out in the schools, on TV, or in the newspapers" (reference to the superintendent).
- "She is incompetent" (reference to an administrator).
- "She has skinny little lips and shouldn't be on [sic] the media" (reference to the superintendent).
- "The administration has not really studied this, they do no planning."

Such disrespectful statements obviously have no benefit for the school district. Instead, they lead to divisiveness and further distract the district from its duty to provide high-quality education.

Failure to Attend to School Board Duties

In the majority of audits, the auditors found school boards spending little time performing their number one job—macro-management to ensure curriculum quality control. Board meeting agendas are regularly analyzed to determine the topics addressed by the board. As shown in Figure 2, only 21 of 347 agenda items, or 6.7% were curriculum or curriculum-related topics. The remainder dealt with administrative matters such as

- bids

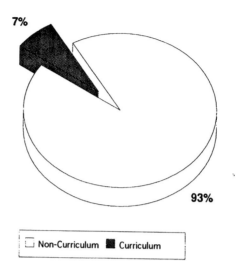

FIGURE 2 Percent of board meeting agenda items dealing with curriculum issues.

- facility agreements
- gifts to schools
- human resource reports
- field trips
- certification of expenditures
- bid recisions
- resolutions
- minutes
- board meeting schedules

This division of topics is in stark contrast to recent recommendations made by national reports (Danzberger, et al., 1992; Danzberger, 1992). These reports state that school board should not

- preside over student or employee grievances
- approve all contracts and purchase order bids competitively
- approve specific payment of expenditure items in approved budgets
- approve construction change orders unless they have a major impact on board policy
- hire, fire, or promote specific personnel, except for the superintendent and a few top-level administrators
- approve detailed items such as field trips, staff-development activities, and bus routes

As shown in Figure 3, 201 of the 347 items (58%) included in the twenty board agendas reviewed by the auditors are not recommended by the national reports. Inclusion of these topics in board agendas prevents school boards from spending sufficient time with macro-management: policy development, curriculum, and long-range planning, all Standard One or "Control" topics. The board behaviors stated in this chapter and the topics included in board agendas preclude efficient and effective board governance.

The following recommendations regarding board behaviors and performance have been made in national and international audits. The goal of these recommendations is to provide direction to the district, which will lead them to more productive and efficient management.

- Develop a system for focusing board energies on matters appropriate for the board of education.
- Establish administrative stability and effective board/superintendent working roles and responsibilities.
- Adopt and follow a policy for improved board governance.
- Establish management stability and integrity.
- Adopt and follow a policy for improved board governance.

SUMMARY

As stated in the introduction to this chapter, Standard One, the Control Standard, represents the backbone of a school district, and reflects

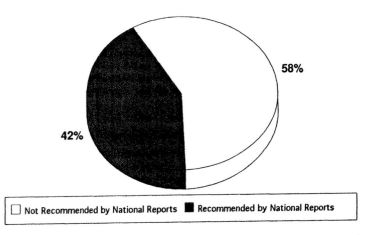

FIGURE 3 Percent of board meeting agenda items not recommended by national reports.

its application of the principle of rationality. Without adequate policies and effective execution, a district's ability to organize district personnel, standardize job descriptions, and monitor the progress of its school district in achieving the mission is greatly diminished.

REFERENCES

Covey, S. R. (1991) *Principle-Centered Leadership.* New York, New York: Simon and Schuster, Inc.

Danzberger, J. (1992) *Facing the Challenge.* New York: The Twentieth Century Fund Press.

Danzberger, J., M. Krist and M. Usdan. (eds.). (1992) *Governing Public Schools: New Times New Requirements.* Washington, D.C.: The Institute for Educational Leadership.

Downey, C. (1992) "Out of the Debate and Into Action: Seventeen Core Premises of the Quality Movement: Let's Use The Quality Fit Framework," Article submitted for publication. Presentation at the Institute San Diego, California, Palo Verde Associates.

English, F. (1988) *Curriculum Auditing.* Lancaster, Pennsylvania: Technomic Publishing Co., Inc.

English, F. (1992) *Curriculum Audit Participant's Manual.* Arlington, Virginia: American Association of School Administrators.

Feistritzer, C. E. (1986) *Profile of Teachers in the U.S.* Washington, D.C.: National Center for Education Information.

Frase, L. (1992) "Constructive Feedback on Teaching Is Missing," *Education,* 113(2).

Frase, L. and W. Streshly. (in press) "Lack of Accuracy, Feedback, and Commitment in Teacher Evaluation," *Journal of Personnel Evaluation in Education.*

Joiner, B. (1985) *Total Quality Leadership vs. Management by Results.* Madison, Wisconsin: Joiner Associates Inc.

Kyrene School District. (1990) *Policy and Regulations Manual.* Tempe, Arizona: Kyrene School District.

Langlois, D. and M. Colarusso. (1988) "Improving Teacher Evaluation," *Education Digest,* 54:13–15.

NSBA. (1982) *The School Personnel Management System.* Alexandria, Virginia: National School Board Association.

Pfeiffer, J. W., L. D. Goodstein and T. M. Nolan. (1986) *Applied Strategic Planning: A How to Do It Guide,* San Diego, California: University Associates Inc.

Poston, W. and R. Manatt. (1992) "Principals as Evaluators: Delimiting Effects on School Reform," *International Journal of Educational Reform,* 2:41–48

Scriven, M. (1981) "Summative Teacher Evaluation," In *Handbook on Teacher Evaluation,* J. Millman and L. Darling-Hammond (eds.), Beverly Hills, California: Sage Publications.

Streshly, W. and L. Frase. (1993) "The Missing Piece of the Reform Pie," *The International Journal of Educational Reform,* 2(2):140–143.

Von Loozen, L. (ed.). (1982) *Becoming a Better Board Member.* Alexandria, Virginia: National School Board Association.

White, B. (1990) "Nearly Every Georgia Teacher Merits a Raise," *The Atlanta Journal and Constitution,* (September 13):

Wise, A., L. Darling-Hammond, M. McLaughlin and H. Bernstein. (1985) "Teacher Evaluation: A Study of Effective Practices," *The Elementary School Journal,* 86:61–121.

The following is the sample referred to on page 98.

Appendix

CURRICULUM DEVELOPMENT AND IMPLEMENTATION

Curriculum Development and Review

The need for and value of a systematic, ongoing program of curriculum development and evaluation involving students, parents, teachers, and administrators are recognized. The design and implementation of the curriculum will be consistent with the Board's stated curriculum goals and objectives. The Board deems it essential that the school system continually develop and modify its curriculum to meet changing needs. The Board authorizes the Superintendent to cooperatively develop the curriculum for the school system and to organize committees to review the curriculum. Staff contributions to curriculum development will be provided through curriculum committees. Whenever possible, efforts will be made to involve the Tempe Union High School District in the curriculum development and review process so that the curricula of both districts will be more closely aligned.

It shall be the responsibility of the Superintendent to develop proposals relating to curriculum modifications and additions that, in the opinion of the Board, the staff, and consultants, are essential to the maintenance of a high-quality program of education from kindergarten through grade eight (8).

While instructional differentiation is expected to occur to address the unique needs of specific students, that instruction will be derived from a curriculum that is common to all students and all levels of that curriculum, and supplementary resource materials shall be available to all students and staff members regardless of grade assignment. A primary consideration in all curriculum development, modification, review, and implementation shall be the establishment of an integrated, multidisciplinary curriculum that conveys multiple learnings simultaneously in order to maximize the educational benefits of a limited and precious instructional time.

The Planned and Written Curriculum

It is the expectation of the District that learning will be enhanced by adherence to an integrated curriculum that promotes continuity and cumulative acquisition of skills and knowledge from grade to grade and from school to school. The curriculum should reflect the best knowledge of the growth and development of learners, the content of the various content disciplines of man, and the needs of learners based on the nature of society and the desires of the

122

residents and taxpayers of the District. The curriculum is designed to provide teachers and students with the District's expectations of what children and young people are to learn. Teachers are expected to follow the curriculum teaching assignments.

The Taught Curriculum

The design and implementation of the curriculum will be aligned with the planned and written curriculum as presented in the curriculum guide, the taught curriculum as presented to students by the teachers, and the tested curriculum as determined by student assessments. Each of these three components of the curriculum shall be matched to bring about a high degree of consistency, except where planned otherwise (e.g., national/state norm-referenced test).

All curriculum, including but not limited to elimination of programs and courses and extensive content alteration will be subject to Board approval. Curricular proposals from the certificated staff may be presented to the Superintendent, who will be responsible for disclosing and making recommendations to the Board on such matters.

Curriculum guides shall be provided for the various subject areas or interdisciplinary offerings. These guides shall present at least a minimal outline for instruction and a basis for further development of the particular area.

The guides will reflect alignment to the state essential skills and shall be designed to assist all users in strengthening and clarifying their philosophy regarding the teaching of a learning, and will, when possible, suggest a variety of possibilities for instruction, patterns of individualization, variations of approaches, and materials.

The Superintendent will formulate procedures for the development and use of curriculum guides.

The Tested Curriculum – Evaluation

The District will establish models for determining the effectiveness of instructional programming at District, school, and classroom levels. Evaluations will focus on determining the extent to which students are achieving and maintaining their mastery of appropriate specific learning outcomes and the extent to which instructors are displaying effective conveyance of curriculum in the classrooms.

Adopted: date of manual adoption

LEGAL REF.: A.R.S.   15-203(15)(16)(17)(19)
15-341(A)(7)
15-701
15-701.01
15-721(A)
15-722(A)

CURRICULUM DEVELOPMENT AND MANAGEMENT

The design and implementation of the curriculum will be consistent with the Board's stated curriculum goals and objectives. The curriculum will include provisions of the state laws and regulations established by the State Department of Education. The curriculum will be planned and coordinated to provide a common direction of action for all instruction in the District. There will be one core curriculum with equal access for all students regardless of program or funding source. The Superintendent will recommend all new and revised curriculum to the Board for its approval.

The Board shall officially adopt curriculum at a regularly scheduled meeting. Adoption dates shall be stated on the cover of each guide.

The curriculum will be taken to the Board for adoption after it has been reviewed by at least two external experts/scholars (whenever possible) who attest to its content validity. The opinion of the experts shall be affixed to each guide as it is being considered for adoption.

Every effort will be made to coordinate the process with the Tempe Elementary School District and the Tempe Union High School District.

Curriculum Philosophy

The purpose of education is primarily the imparting of basic skills, knowledge, processes, and attitudes necessary for the student to successfully function in society. Education also recognizes the characteristics unique to each individual and provides a process for development and expression of each student's innate potentiality and talents.

To assure that students leaving schools will possess the skills and knowledge to have successful experiences in higher education and in the work-place, an outcome-based, continuous-progress model shall be used for the students of the District.

The curriculum is to be designed and delivered using an outcome-based continuous-progress approach. Such an approach is based on the following premises:

- All students are capable of achieving excellence in learning the essentials of formal schooling.
- Success influences self-concept; self-concept influences learning and behavior.
- The instructional process can be adapted to improve learning.
- Schools can maximize the learning conditions for all students through clearly stated outcomes, high expectations for all students, and continuous, "authentic" assessment of student learning.
- Successful, "authentic" student learning must be based on providing appropriate educational experiences at the appropriate level of challenge in order to ensure maximum student achievement.

The District subscribes to an outcome-based approach to curriculum and instruction that focuses and organizes all of the District's efforts around the exit outcomes.

The exit outcomes are the goals from which all subject-area curriculum development efforts are derived during the curriculum development process.

The District has the following exit outcomes based on life-related skills:

- develop a commitment to the process of learning; acquire the necessary skills to promote continued learning and assume responsibility for self-directed learning
- develop an appreciation of the intrinsic value of education and its necessity in a democratic society
- demonstrate mastery of reading, writing, speaking/listening (communication), and mathematical skills sufficient for daily living and for effective, efficient functioning in a complex society
- demonstrate knowledge of basic historical, geographical, political, and economic literacy; demonstrate application of skills and knowledge to the solution of human problems
- demonstrate knowledge of science and its processes in day-to-day decisions
- demonstrate the skills of creative and disciplined thinking; identify needs and problems, locate and analyze information from all appropriate sources for meaning and/or action, and apply problem-solving strategies
- appreciate and understand cultural diversity, the arts and humanities, current events, and ways to predict and influence future events
- identify and establish a common, mutually acceptable set of moral standards, values, and ethics to ensure the continuation of an advanced society
- establish effective, supportive, and cooperative interpersonal relationships, good citizenship, and a sense of social responsibility
- demonstrate self-respect, self-esteem, and self-understanding; demonstrate respect for others and an awareness of their needs and potential
- demonstrate how to live a physically, mentally, and emotionally balanced life
- develop an appreciation for the importance of each individual's unique contribution and value in the workplace and in the community

Planned and Written Curriculum

The components of the written curriculum will include belief statements and five "layers" of outcomes in order to achieve total alignment through the level of teacher lesson delivery. The components are:

- *Belief statements* for each discipline area, which are broad statements reflecting current research, expert opinion, and teacher experience in a field of study.
- *Learning exit outcomes* for all students, which are broad life-related skills and characteristics that students should have at the end of the 12th grade, incorporating likely future trends that will impact on the lives of students and to which they will be expected to make moral, ethical, financial, or civic decisions.
- *Program outcomes*, which are derived from the exit outcomes, describing in broad terms what students will know or be able to do, or attitudes they will hold after completing an entire program of study.
- *Level/course outcomes*, which are derived from program outcomes and are District objectives describing in specific terms what students will be able to do at the end of a year/semester in a particular area.
- *Unit outcomes*, which are teacher-prepared subobjectives that are tied to a particular theme or instructional unit and are necessary to achieve a level/course outcome. (Note: In some special curriculum efforts these may be District developed.)
- *Lesson outcomes*, which are teacher-prepared objectives for specific daily lessons related to unit outcomes. (Note: In some special curriculum efforts these may be District developed.)

Subject-area *written curriculum guides* shall be developed locally for all grade levels or interdisciplinary subjects in the District. These guides shall be logically derivative of the District's philosophy and beliefs and shall represent tangible operational bridges to and from them. The guides shall be revised and readopted by the Board every six years, or sooner as necessary. The guides shall contain the following components:

- mission statement of the District
- curriculum philosophy of the District
- belief statements related to the subject area and linked to appropriate exit outcomes
- program outcomes for the subject area with expected emphasis
- a scope-and-sequence chart for use in designing instruction at the appropriate level of difficulty for all learners
- level/course learner outcomes derived from the program outcomes, for the subject area at all instructional levels, which identify the specific content skills, attitudes, and processes to be taught
- correlation of learner outcomes to the state essential skills and District criterion-referenced tests as well as standardized tests and state tests
- correlation of outcomes to available instructional resources, adopted texts, and other supplemental materials

- relevant modifications and enrichment learner outcomes and strategies as well as interdisciplinary approaches, when appropriate
- recommended time allocations for curriculum areas and time range for outcomes
- progress report procedures
- homework guidelines

There is an expectation that all curriculum will be documented in writing, that the planned courses will be updated at least once every six (6) years, that teachers will have copies of planned guides and use them to develop daily lesson plans, and that administrators will work with teachers to maintain consistency between curriculum design (written curriculum) and curriculum delivery (what is actually taught).

Copies of the curriculum guides in complete sets shall be available to all teachers and the public, in each school media center, for review and reference.

Instructional resources such as textbooks, software, and other materials shall be selected based upon their alignment with the written outcomes.

A focused staff development plan will be designed and implemented to prepare staff members to teach the designed curriculum.

The Taught Curriculum

The District has several expectations toward the teaching process. Teachers have a right to expect that their teaching efforts are part of a broad plan of quality education. There is to be assurance that teachers and their colleagues are working toward a common goal. All faculty members have a responsibility not only to contribute to the refinements of written curriculum study, but also to teach the curriculum. The principal, department heads, or other supervisors shall see that optimum use is made of available curriculum guides.

Curriculum guides are to serve as a framework from which a teacher will develop units of study, individual lesson plans, and approaches to instruction that will serve the students' particular needs at a particular time. The guides shall be used to map the logical sequence of instruction. Teachers will adhere to the guides.

In addition to consistent delivery of the learning outcomes in the curriculum, it is expected that instructional delivery will be based on sound teaching principles grounded in education research. Instructional supervision efforts are to focus on these sound teaching principles.

A systematic process is to be in place for planning and providing instruction appropriate for each student and for engaging the student until learning outcomes are attained. This systematic process is to include:

- establishing a school climate that continually affirms the worth and diversity of all students
- expecting that all students will perform at high levels of learning
- ensuring that all students experience opportunities for personal success
- varying the time for learning according to the needs of each student and the complexity of the task
- having both staff members and students take responsibility for successful learning outcomes
- assessing current student skills/learning for instructional assignment
- analyzing the content of each objective so that instructional strategies match content and assessment
- when appropriate, sequencing tasks into a hierarchy of learning skills to maximize the effectiveness of instructional delivery
- orienting students to the objective(s) to be learned
- initial teaching to the objective(s) that provides varied approaches, adequate practice time, and multiple opportunities for learning and success
- assessing student mastery of the objective(s) to determine the need for movement to a new instructional objective, extension/enrichment, or correctives
- for those who attain mastery, progressing to the next objective or offering extension/enrichment
- for those who do not attain mastery, providing correctives and/or using different teaching strategies until outcomes are attained

The District staff-development program for teachers shall include a research-based approach to teaching to provide teachers with alternative ways to view the teaching act so that they may be as effective as possible.

Tested Curriculum

The District staff is to design and use a variety of assessment approaches in determining the effectiveness of the planned and written curriculum as well as the taught curriculum. The Superintendent shall develop a set of administrators' guidelines in the area of program evaluation.

The "tested" curriculum is to include the following components:

- a criterion-referenced assessment system that documents, records, reports, and awards credit for student skill attainment
- district-level criterion-referenced tests for selected core objectives across all levels
- a criterion-referenced information-management system at the classroom and building levels for coordinating timely instructional

planning, student assessment and placement, instructional delivery, and program evaluation

- assessment strategies for teachers to diagnose and determine instructional assignments of student learning
- an evaluation system that allows students to demonstrate and receive credit for mastery at any time
- an assessment approach using state/local norm-referenced tests to evaluate the status of students from a national perspective and for curriculum revision as well as program design
- a program-evaluation component that guides curriculum redesign and instructional planning, with the learning outcomes based on program graduates and the performance demands of postschool roles

It is expected that teachers will conduct frequent diagnosis of students on the curriculum objectives. Teacher-made tests as well as criterion-referenced and standardized tests, will be used to determine patterns of student achievement. The teachers and supervisors are to use test results to assess the status of individual student achievement, to continuously regroup students for instruction, to identify general achievement trends of various groups of students, and to modify curriculum and/or instruction as warranted by assessment results.

Principals are to review teacher-made tests to help teachers ensure that tests are congruent with the written curriculum and with what is being taught.

Role Responsibilities

Superintendent and District staff members. The Superintendent is responsible for the implementation of the policy and these regulations. The Superintendent is to serve as the prime mover of the management system. Appropriate District staff members are to serve as technical advisors to principals and to establish the management pace. They assist principals in implementation of the plan, and they look for ways to keep the practices functional and effective.

Principals. The building principal is the key to the monitoring and implementation of the curriculum. The principal must translate this importance to staff members on a daily basis. The principal will observe classes, monitor lessons, and evaluate teacher-made tests. Principals are to use, as a minimum, the following three basic strategies to monitor curriculum:

- full-period classroom observations when possible
- twenty-minute classroom observations
- walk-through observations
- interviews and conferences
- child study team observations

The supervisor of the principal is to evaluate the principal's records of classroom monitoring of instruction. This evaluation consists of analyzing the quantity and quality of observations.

Teachers. Teachers are to carry out several responsibilities that reflect their role in the curriculum management process. Teachers are responsible for teaching to the planned curriculum and for testing their teaching.

Budget

It is the intent of the administration to move the District's budget toward a document that reflects funding decisions based on the organization's educational goals and priorities—the type of document commonly referred to as a program-driven budget. The budget development process will ensure that goals and priorities are considered in the preparation of budget proposals and that any decisions related to reduction or increase in funding levels can be addressed in those terms. The format used in preparation will reflect these considerations, and the public document eventually developed will be an interpretive document that communicates the budget to the public in consideration of the goals and priorities. The expected results of proposed expenditures will be clearly explained in the public document as well as in the proposal-preparation documents.

Curriculum Development Cycle

The curriculum administrator shall ensure that a master long-range plan is in place for District curriculum development, program assessment, and testing. All K–8 curriculum areas are to undergo internal development/ redevelopment cycles on a rotating basis. (*Note:* On a continuous progress model the outcome levels will be prekindergarten through level 10.) The purpose of such an ongoing review is to lend a concentrated focus to a given curriculum area. This procedure will provide a formal means by which all planned courses are revised and kept up to date.

The Superintendent shall take steps, whenever possible, to conduct a curriculum review each year. The Superintendent shall organize a report/presentation to the Board that demonstrates how the policy and regulations are being implemented and to present such recommendations as may be necessary for the improvement of student growth as may be required. It shall candidly point out strengths and weaknesses and form the base for later budget development.

The Board report process shall include a statement of instructional goals by grade level, assessment on testing trends data as may be relevant, important new trends that are to be incorporated into the curriculum, recommended instructional resources (e.g., textbooks) in the curriculum, and input from administrators and the teaching staff. The Superintendent shall, whenever possible, employ one or more curriculum experts to critique the proposed or existing curriculum in light of available knowledge regarding appropriate curriculum in the areas being reviewed, and such reports/critiques shall be appended to the Board report.

When a subject area is undergoing a development/redevelopment review, a K–8 task force will be established composed of teachers, principals, District administrators, parents, and students when appropriate. The task force will be used to provide input into the development cycle. The Superintendent or designee is to establish the procedures for such task forces.

The development cycle will include three phases:

- Phase I—Review and planning
- Phase II—Development of curriculum components
- Phase III—Pilot

This entire process usually will take a two-to-three-year time frame, depending upon the complexity of the task and current status of the curriculum.

Exhibit IFAA*-E illustrates the development/redevelopment cycle. It is recognized that not all of the components of the curriculum may be designed during this period, but it is the expectation of the Board that staff members will move as quickly as possible toward the accomplishment of the development and redevelopment curriculum cycle as resources are made available and as needed.

The "Manual for Curriculum Developers in the Kyrene School District" describes in detail the process and tasks to be accomplished in each phase, reference to relevant Board policy and District administrative directives, and specific directions for curriculum guide development.

CHAPTER 6

Standard Two: The Curriculum Standard

SUE GREENE—*Assistant Superintendent, University Place School District, Tacoma, Washington*

INTRODUCTION

QUALITY control has as its fundamental premise the intent "to improve human performance in human institutions, whether it is involved with the production of goods or the rendering of services" (English, 1987). For quality control assurance, a school system must provide the linkages internally that connect intent to implementation and evaluation. These internal connections are critical to "produce a desired and consistent set of pupil learning outcomes over time" (English and Steffy, 1983). The quality control ingredients are outlined clearly as a tri-part relationship in Fenwick English's *Quality Control in Curriculum Development* (1978): the written, taught, and tested curricula. They incorporate both curriculum and instruction "in delineating goals and objectives and in tying means to ends" (English, 1980).

The written curriculum becomes the work plan and guides the instruction (the taught curriculum or, in industrial terms, the work), the results of which are assessed as the tested curriculum (or the evaluated outputs or results). An instructional system's design and communication of the prescribed curriculum or intended curriculum is critical in achieving alignment of the plan and the work; only then will the assessment of those provide accurate and valid data.

As the "statement of work to be done in the organization," the curriculum reflects "attitudes, assumptions, and dominant modes of believing and doing things" in the organization (English, 1987). When curriculum guides and other vehicles of communicating the work to be done fail to be specific enough to guide delivery and assure continuity, the quality of results is diminished.

Standard Two of the curriculum management audit, having clear and valid objectives for students, focuses on *direction* for the curriculum.

133

It assesses the follow-up steps of translating the policy, planning, and organizational control of Standard One into adequate design of the work plan and effective delivery of the educational program.

STANDARD TWO CRITERIA

Several expectations are considered in reviewing a curriculum system against Standard Two:

- a clearly established, systemwide set of goals and objectives adopted by the board of education
- evidence of comprehensive, detailed, short- and long-range planning
- objectives that set the framework for operation of the district and its sense of priorities
- provision of explicit direction for the superintendent and professional staff
- demonstration of local control

Clearly Established Goals and Objectives

In looking for documentation of clearly established goals and objectives, auditors start with communication of intent expressed in a mission statement or similar broad statement of purpose formally adopted by the board. They look for policy or other board-level statements of educational goals/expectations for the school district's educational program. From there various documents are reviewed as vehicles for the dissemination of instructional or learning goals and objectives that support and/or are consistent with the broader mission and goals statements. These are seen through a trail of documents ranging from curriculum guides and/or teaching guides, through implementation memoranda, and into classroom lesson plans.

What the goals and objectives look like varies among school systems. Many school districts use skill- and content-related statements of goals and objectives that become more discreet as the documents become closer to actual classroom teacher guides. Those districts that have chosen outcome-based curricula will demonstrate a series of outcome statements that move from broad to more specific as the reader proceeds from the general program statements into content areas of instruction.

A hypothetical board-level goal statement regarding curriculum designed with skill- and content-related statements of goals and objectives might be: Students will know how to participate constructively in their local, state, and national governmental processes. A curriculum document objective tied to that goal could be: (9th grade) Students will learn the basic organizational features, processes, and requirements of citizens in Milltown City and Westman county.

One can see a clear, understandable statement of the broad educational program goals in the policy statement. That *control* from the board is translated into *direction* to staff through curriculum objectives like the above example related to grade 9 social studies content.

Auditors might see the same type of control-into-direction information in outcome statements. These range from the broad educational outcome statements to the more discreet outcomes of the curriculum program areas. For example, the University Place School District (Tacoma, Washington) adopted seven broad learning outcomes for the school district. One of those is: *Proficiency in basic skills* – Basic skills are communications (reading, writing, speaking and listening), computation, adaptation, accessing and processing information, and effective interpersonal relations (University Place School District, 1991 and 1992). The curriculum program area outcomes found in the district's curriculum guides are linked to the broad outcomes but are more discreet. The following excerpts from the curriculum guide for the science program area for grade level 5 are linked to *proficiency in basic skills*:

Information processing

Given teacher guidance, the learner will demonstrate ability to apply the steps of the scientific method *by* using the method with teacher direction.

Given teacher instruction, the learner will demonstrate ability to understand the skill of interpreting data *by* explaining in his/her own words an interpretation of given set of facts.

Physical Science

Given teacher instruction, the learner will demonstrate the ability to understand simple atomic structure *by* accurately drawing and explaining the parts of an atom in his/her own words.

Given teacher instruction, the learner will demonstrate the ability to understand nuclear force/energy *by* explaining simple principles. (University Place School District, 1991)

In examining a district's documents with outcome or goal/objective statements, auditors would determine through board meeting minutes whether the board formally adopted the goals/outcomes. The Standard Two alignment assessment looks at systematic adoption of directive information from the board policies through curriculum guides and/or instructional notebooks.

Evidence of Comprehensive, Detailed, Short-and Long-Range Planning

The curriculum management audit looks at planning from a perspective of *direction* under Standard 2. It looks not only for a comprehensive districtwide plan, as sought under the *control* lens of Standard 1, but also for evidence within that plan of detailed and well-developed action plans targeted for specific time frames. Where these are directly related to the curriculum and to classroom instruction, the linkage that carries the plan into action should be capable of being traced from the board adoption of the plan to the guidance and direction provided teachers and other professional staff who will be accountable for the plan implementation.

Auditors look specifically for indications of the plan tasks being assigned to specific staff and communicated in writing as clear expectations. They also seek evidence of meetings, conferences, and/or training related to the communication of specific directions based on the plan details. In this review, the auditors look particularly for evidence that the long-term plan and the short-range planning are clearly linked and specific enough for both staff direction and resource allocations to be developed efficiently.

Direction to both the organization and the individual staff within the district will be more focused and usually more clearly communicated when a clear long-range plan and appropriately detailed short-range plans are in existence.

Objectives That Set the Framework for Operation of the District and Its Sense of Priorities

In reviewing the objectives that support the board's goals for the school district, auditors seek statements that communicate broad expectations for the operation of the educational enterprise. The statements might be explicitly prioritized. Alternatively, they might be communicated in terms of annually revised objectives in support of continuing goals. Statements about funding expectations may provide messages about priorities.

To illustrate this type of board-level information, consider this hypothetical example:

Board Goal Statement:

#3 To provide an educational program that responds to and builds upon students' individuality and diversity of interests, backgrounds, skill levels, and learning styles

Board Objectives for Goal #3 with Supporting Discussion:

(A) The school district will organize its instructional program and student placement system in such a way as to meet the diverse learning needs of students

Discussion: The placement practices will not include "tracking" by "student ability." Mastery of skills and outcomes/expectations will be major considerations in assessing student achievement for the purpose of advancement in the educational program. The implementation of student placement will further provide for the maximum possible individualized instructional attention and cooperative learning activities, with minor emphasis on lecture-style instruction. Multi-grade grouping of students is an option available to the schools' staffs.

(B) The school district will allocate a minimum of 0.3% of its annual operating budget for each of the fiscal years 1991 through 1993 to staff development.

Discussion: Staff development will be provided for teachers and administrators to improve professional skills in the following areas, ranked in order of priority:

(1) Outcomes-based education
(2) Alignment of instruction with the curriculum and the district/state student achievement assessment program
(3) The new state-mandated basic course of study for mathematics K–12
(4) Understanding multi-cultural and diversity of socioeconomic backgrounds represented in the district
(5) Cooperative learning
(6) Identifying and teaching for diverse learning styles

The example shows two objectives and the summary of board intention for each of the sample objectives that support the broader goal statement (#3). The example communicates the expectation and direction of the board; moreover, it further communicates a *sense of priorities*. Auditors reviewing documents for these types of expectations and priorities are looking for linkage that demonstrates responsiveness of the educational program to the direction provided in the governance goal and priority statements.

Provision of Explicit Direction for the Superintendent and Professional Staff

A perpetual debate exists over the question of how specific the direction from a governing board to its chief executive officer ought to be. Some camps advocate very general, broad policy guidance from the board. Others call for clear and specific expectations, especially when those exist informally anyway, as they most frequently do.

The curriculum management audit promotes the communication of clear and explicit direction when addressing the curriculum since the educational program is the very soul and purpose of a school district's existence. Further, from a practical standpoint, observations of school systems over time suggest that most boards have some expectations (spoken or unspoken) of what they want the superintendent and staff to do in managing the community's educational operations. In all fairness to the professional staff and to establish clarity of focus, these expectations need to be communicated clearly and openly to support district direction toward achievement of goals.

An example of *explicit direction* similar to those found in policy statements of many school districts follows:

The superintendent will ensure that an annual report on student achievement assessment is given to the board at the end of the school year. The report should provide information to the board on the following:

- districtwide results on criterion-referenced and norm referenced testing per the adopted assessment program
- comparative analysis of local performance on state and national norm-referenced tests
- all testing results broken down into categories by gender, race, and grade levels across the district and by schools

- information on current state assessment requirements
- nontesting feedback and recommendations for modifications to improve the assessment program

In addition to receiving copies of this report, principals are also to be given breakdowns of results by teachers and test items for follow-up use in modification of curriculum and/or instruction. Teachers will use testing feedback for specific reteaching, student assistance, and related instructional planning, as well as for guidance in their professional improvement efforts.

The policy information in the example leaves little room for doubt as to what the expectation of the board is in regard to reporting to them on student achievement assessment and use of testing and other assessment data.

A look at three hypothetical examples of board direction (or policy) statements, with varying degrees of specificity, illustrates the range of direction observed in policy documents in audit situations. The examples demonstrate: (1) a statement of direction that could have seemed explicit to the board when developed, but that has some vaguenesss to it in the mind of the superintendent as reflected in the question found after the examples; (2) a statement on the same subject that steps too specifically into the executive role of carrying out the intent; and (3) a model statement of expectation that more appropriately meets the criterion under Standard Two of the curriculum management audit.

(1) The textbooks adopted by the school district will be appropriate to the adopted curriculum goals and objectives.

(2) The textbooks adopted by the school district will be aligned with the curriculum goals and objectives. Textbook review meetings will occur in October, January, and March of each year and will address the curriculum disciplines in the following order of rotation: Language arts, social sciences, math, science, and other disciplines. The superintendent, director of curriculum, principals, and discipline representatives of each school will participate in these meetings.

(3) The superintendent and staff will develop a plan for adopting textbook/instructional materials that includes the following:

- correlation of outcomes/learning objectives of the curriculum with instructional resources proposed for adoption

- correlation of materials proposed for adoption with local and state testing programs
- a systematic method for keeping pace with state requirements in the process of scheduling local reviews and adoption of instructional materials
- participation in review committees by representatives of the Office of Curriculum and Instruction, principals, assistant principals, and teachers from both the discipline under review and at least two other discipline areas

A superintendent reviewing Policy Statement (1) for implementation planning would ask at least three questions:

(1) What does the board mean by *appropriate*?
(2) Do they intend other instructional materials to be included with textbooks?
(3) Does this policy direction mean that there must be a textbook for every course taught?

Policy Statement (2) indicates an awareness that there should probably be some expectations stated regarding participation, but it leaves no flexibility for appropriate superintendent delegation, scheduling of meetings, and timing of disciplines according to various factors (including external influences such as state mandates). The statement attempts to administer rather than to set guidelines or communicate expectations.

Policy Statement (3) more clearly and appropriately states the basic expectation—curriculum driving materials selection, systematic procedures, and participatory decisions in the recommendation process. Details are left to the administrative staff, but they know what to do and what to produce.

Auditors look for clarity of intent and basic expectations, but without policymaker intrusion into management roles and duties, in the policy directions to the administration.

Demonstration of Local Control

An audit team considering this criterion will look for evidence that the local school system has developed statements of goals and objectives in response to its own students' needs and congruent with its own adopted curriculum. For example, when reviewing the curriculum documents in states where statewide curricula have been adopted, auditors particularly seek evidence that the school district has developed modifications of the state-developed materials to ensure appropriateness to the local curriculum, priorities, and classroom instruction.

In one such school system, the local curriculum guides reflect a modification that places one segment of math instruction at grade 3, which does not appear in the state guide until grade 4. This change was made rationally in response to historical data showing the sequence to have been appropriate locally, judging from the student achievement success indicated in test data.

Another district in the same state made a nearly opposite choice by placing a set of instructional objectives in a grade level later than the level suggested in the state guide and tested on the statewide assessment instrument. Even though the board knew the students would perform poorly on state test items covering that set of objectives when tested before their local curriculum sequence included it, they based their decision on the recommendations of the local professional staff as supported by assessment feedback and reputable research on mathematics instruction. That decision reflected a *rational* basis and demonstrated local control of the implementation of statewide expectations.

QUESTIONS UNDERLYING STANDARD TWO ANALYSIS

When auditors begin an analysis of a school district's compliance with Standard Two, they are posing three primary questions:

(1) Does the system have clear and valid objectives for students? (i.e., Note where these appear and in what forms — e.g., instructional objectives and outcome statements.)
(2) Are they (in their current format) adequate to provide direction to the system for implementation of the curriculum? (i.e., What is their design quality?)
(3) Are the guides used? (i.e., What is their effectiveness? How are they implemented?)

Does the System Have Clear and Valid Objectives for Students?

As the earlier discussion of goals/objectives and outcomes mentions, these statements may vary in form but will meet the Standard Two criteria if they communicate clearly what students are expected to learn. These statements will most appropriately appear in documents labeled *curriculum guides* or *teaching guides* or *classroom curriculum guides*. In response to this question, the auditors are assessing the scope of the expected curriculum for which curriculum guides are provided. The review is reported and summarized by a table that designates the discipline areas and grade levels taught in the school system. For example, if no adopted objectives are communicated to teachers in curriculum guides for language arts and social studies, auditors determine the percentage of the expected curriculum coverage left *uncovered* and report that in terms of *scope of coverage*. Table 1 demonstrates that determination. This type of table provides the data summary that auditors discuss in writing the finding narrative on the scope of curriculum covered by guides.

After having compiled the summary table on scope of coverage, auditors discuss the discrepancies. They might, for example, note that

TABLE 1. Scope of curriculum coverage in curriculum guides presented by the school district.

Curriculum Area	K	1	2	3	4	5	6	7	8	9	10	11	12	Total
Language Arts	X	X	X	X	X	X	X	X	X	X	X	X	X	13
Mathematics	X	X	X	X	X	X	X	X	X	X	X	X	X	13
Social Studies	X	X	X	X	X	X	X	O	O	X	X	X	X	11
Science	X	X	X	X	X	X	X	X	X	X	X	O	O	11
Foreign Language					X	X	X	X	X	X	X	X	O	8
Music	X	X	X	X	X	X	X	X	X	X	X	O	O	11
Art	O	O	O	O	X	X	X	X	X	X	X	O	O	7
Computer Education			#	#	#	#	#	X	X	X	X	X	X	6
Physical Education	#	#	X	X	X	X	X	X	X	X	X	#	#	9
Miscellaneous														
Health Issues	#	#	#	#	X	X	X	X	X	X	X	X	X	9
Drama											X	X	X	3
Community						X	X	O	O	X	X	X	X	6
Areas taught	6	6	7	7	9	10	10	11	11	11	12	11	11	122
Areas covered	5	5	6	6	9	10	10	10	10	10	11	8	7	107

Percentage of taught curriculum covered in curriculum guides: **87.7%**

Note: Blank spaces in the grid represent areas that the auditors did not expect to find guides because the levels or areas/courses are not presently offered.
X = guide available, grade level covered.
O = guide unavailable, grade level not addressed in guide.
# = guide expected to be available because of state mandate but area not taught locally and guide not available.

the computer education guides to address the state mandate for grades 2 through 6 and the community objectives for grades 7 and 8 are currently in the developmental stage. They would further comment on the areas of the curriculum missing direction and note the percentage of the total program not covered.

Are the Objectives in Their Current Format Adequate to Provide Direction to the System for Implementation of the Curriculum?

The adequacy or quality of the available guides is assessed by auditors in light of the ability of the document to guide and direct instruction. The primary focus, therefore, is on *design*. A set of five criteria with subsets of four levels of adequacy standards provides the basis for rating the guides. Auditors use a standard form in reviewing, rating, and then ranking the district's guides in order of their design quality. That form is reproduced in Figure 1.

Before auditors begin formal analysis of the guides, a process to ensure inter-rater reliability is conducted by the lead auditor with the auditor(s) assigned the curriculum guide analysis tasks. Lead auditors typically use a set of guides other than the ones in audit for this procedure but may choose three or four of the guides from the current client district to critique.

Each of the five criteria has a range of four degrees of compliance with expectations and corresponding points for scoring the auditors' evaluation. The total points achieved by a guide are determined, as well as the rating for each of the five criteria. A maximum of fifteen points is possible; guides achieving a rating of twelve or more points are considered *strong* or *adequate* for Standard 2 criteria measuring *direction*.

Criterion 1, "Clarity and Validity of Objectives," can be described in its optimum as providing a teacher with all the information on the typical expectations of time needed for instruction related to the particular objectives (or outcomes) and specifically, in the case of objectives, when the instruction might appropriately occur (e.g., where in a sequence or at what grade level). If the system uses outcome-based statements, the guides are not penalized in the rating for an absence of specific grade level or for having rationally chosen to sequence the statements without reference to grade levels. However, the total curriculum system and its documents must reflect a consistent design of outcome-based communication to be considered *rationally determined* and to meet the spirit of this criterion.

Curriculum Guides as Management Tools

Curriculum Guide/Discipline _____ Date

Grades/Levels Included _____

Criteria	3	2	1	0	Total
Clarity and Validity of Objectives	—	—	—	—	—

0. no goals/objectives present
1. vague delineation of goals/objectives
2. states tasks to be performed or skills to be learned
3. what, when, how actual standard is to be performed, and amount of time to be spent learning each objective

	3	2	1	0	Total
Congruity of the Curriculum to the Testing/Evaluation Process	—	—	—	—	—

0. no evaluation approach stated
1. some approach of evaluation stated
2. skill, knowledge, concepts which will be assessed
3. objectives are keyed to performance evaluation and district tests in use

	3	2	1	0	Total
Delineation by Grade of the Essential Skills, Knowledge, and Attitudes	—	—	—	—	—

0. no mention of required skills
1. prior general experienced needed
2. prior general experience needed in grade level
3. specific documented prerequisite *or* description of discrete skills required

	3	2	1	0	Total
Delineation of the Major Instructional Tools	—	—	—	—	—

0. no mention of textbook or instructional materials
1. names textbook (or basic instructional materials)
2. names basic text or instructional materials *and* supplementary materials to be used
3. "match" between textbook or basic instructional materials and curriculum, objective by objective

	3	2	1	0	Total
Clear Linkages for Classroom Utilization	—	—	—	—	—

0. no linkages cited for classroom utilization
1. overall, vague statement on linkage for approach subject
2. general suggestions on approach
3. specific examples on how to approach key concepts/skills in classroom

TOTAL POINTS _____

FIGURE 1 Evaluation form used by auditors in evaluating curriculum guides as management tools.

144

The criterion addressing "Congruity of the Curriculum to the Testing/Evaluation Process" can also measure quality of either performance objective-centered or outcome-based curriculum statements of expectation. Regardless of what testing instruments are used by the school district, there should be alignment between the written objectives (or outcomes and objectives) and the student performance evaluation instruments.

Criterion 3 requires "Delineation by Grade of the Essential Skills, Knowledge, and Attitudes." Optimally, there will be specific and documented prerequisites *or* statements describing discrete skills needed for each grade level. If auditors are analyzing an outcome-based curriculum system, attention is given to essential prerequisites for various instructional components since grade levels are rarely addressed in the outcome-based framework. Again, in scoring such guides, the documents are not penalized for the absence of grade-level reference if the system in which they reside is a rationally based, outcomes-driven system.

The fourth criterion, "Delineation of the Major Instructional Tools," expects a clear matching of curriculum and instructional materials (textbook or other materials) on an objective-by-objective basis. A teacher should be able to know what resources to use for each objective.

The final criterion calls for "Clear Linkages for Classroom Utilization" of the curriculum guides. The highest expectation in the range is that there will be specific examples in the guide that show how to approach the key instructional concepts or learning skills in the classroom. Generally, if auditors see any examples, the guide is given a rating of 3 on this criterion; ideally, they want to see numerous examples.

Once the auditors have rated all guides, the results are tabulated and exhibited in a format that provides both criterion-by-criterion scores for each guide and rank-ordered display of the total scores. Table 2 presents an example of this type of data display.

Readers of the sample table can determine several things about the quality of the guides assessed in this audit. For example, the strengths in the greatest number of guides lie in the areas of providing objectives and linkage for classroom use. Weakness shows up consistently in the criteria requiring congruity of the curriculum with testing, delineation of essential skills, and delineation of major instructional tools. The strongest guide developed and used in this school district as judged by the five criteria is the mathematics guide, the only guide to achieve

TABLE 2. Evaluation of the curriculum guides of the school district as curriculum management tools.

Guide	Levels	Year	Criteria 1	2	3	4	5	Total
Mathematic	K–12	1990	3	2	2	3	3	13
Language Arts	K–12	1988	2	2	2	2	3	11
Community	5, 6, 9–12	1991	2	2	1	1	1	7
Computer Education	7–12	1991	2	1	1	2	1	7
Health Issues	4–12	1989	1	1	1	2	2	7
Social Studies	K–8, 11, 12	1986	2	1	1	1	2	7
Science	K–10	1987	2	1	1	1	1	6
Music	K–10	1990	1	2	1	0	1	5
Art	4–10	1990	1	0	1	0	1	3
Foreign Language	4–11	1985	0	0	1	2	0	3
Physical Education	K–10	1989	1	0	1	0	1	3
Drama	10–12	1983	0	0	1	0	0	1
Average score by criterion:			1.4	1	1.2	1.2	1.3	
Overall average score of guides: **6.1**								

enough points (twelve or more) to be considered adequate for the pur-. poses of curriculum management and direction.

Are the Guides Used?

This question brings the auditors' focus onto both design (how the system for ensuring use and implementation is set up) and delivery (how extensively and effectively the guides are used, how helpful they are to the intended users). To determine the use and effectiveness of curriculum guides, auditors look for memoranda of instruction regarding dissemination and implementation of the guides. They seek memoranda to principals from the central office (usually a superintendent or an assistant superintendent for curriculum and instruction) subsequent to school board adoption, and from principals to teachers. Several persons must be interviewed to verify availability, use, and related aspects of implementation. Typically, interviews with principals and teachers are most critical in addressing the effectiveness factor.

DATA SOURCES FOR STANDARD TWO ANALYSIS

Data sources used in the application of Standard Two include documents, interviews, and site visits. As the preceding discussion of Standard Two criteria suggests, the primary data source for Standard Two analysis is documents. Guidance, or direction, is found in mission statements (publicized with long-range or strategic plans or separately), board-adopted goal statements in policy or goals publications, curriculum and/or teacher guides (externally or internally developed), and other documents reflecting implementation of learning expectations. This document collection might also include such papers as course syllabi or courses-of-study documents from individual schools. In some cases, school districts have stated that "the textbook is our curriculum for grades 6–8" or in similar ways have referenced a guide other than the typical locally adopted guides.

Interviews reveal awareness of guides, information about where guides are located, how they are (or are not) used, and what problems they are perceived to have (e.g., usefulness, congruity with current standards in a discipline). Interviews with classroom teachers may also reveal other sources used to direct instruction besides the adopted or approved guides.

Site visits help validate the presence in schools of documents communicating student learning objectives and expectations. Additionally, these auditor walk-throughs can provide opportunities for observation of the actual use of guides or reference to them in the classrooms.

ISSUES AND VARIABLES RELATED TO STANDARD TWO ANALYSIS

As outcome-based curricula become increasingly prevalent in school systems requesting curriculum audits, one variable taken into consideration by auditors is the differences in what "evidence" looks like in outcomes-driven curriculum systems compared with performance-based goals/objectives communicated curricula. While there is no less validity in application of the audit standards to an outcomes-based curriculum than to objectives-focused programs, auditors undertake some different considerations on specific criteria when addressing outcomes-based formats. (Those differences were discussed in the narrative regarding the curriculum guides evaluation.)

Another inquiry relates to the relationship between curriculum guides in a *site-based management* system compared with a more centralized system. The audit bias favors districtwide curriculum goals and objectives, with rational flexibility among schools for implementation if that has been selected by the board as one of the operational options for site-based decisions. This means that a school district would distribute board-adopted guides but that school staffs could determine some of the timing, sequences, supplementary instructional materials, and instructional methods to be used in carrying out the prescribed instructional program. Consistent expectations would exist, however, regarding the goals (or outcomes) and objectives to be included for all students.

Inevitably, someone raises a question about the apparent rigidity of expectation 4 under the criterion "Clarity and Validity of Objectives." They ask, "How can we prescribe exactly how much time each student will take to learn certain objectives or information or skills? Don't we really want to see individualization of the pacing of instruction?" The key consideration of auditors in looking at this criterion is that there is some estimation about what might be expected as necessary time for the *typical* student. With that estimation, at least the teacher has some guidance for planning purposes and can make appropriate modifications for individual students as required for his or her particular class(es).

In general, the spirit of the Standard Two criteria supports clear direction for implementing the adopted curriculum in the classroom. Keeping that focus in mind, trained and experienced auditors incorporate variables such as these discussed here without compromising the consistency and integrity of the curriculum management audit standards and criteria.

TYPICAL FINDINGS IN STANDARD TWO ANALYSIS

Auditors see a variety of school organizations, and the degree to which they measure up to the expectations of Standard Two varies greatly. However, it is common to find school systems that have incomplete curriculum coverage by guides and related documents or guides that are inadequate to direct the implementation of the curriculum. One such finding follows.

Finding 2.2: Existing Curriculum Guides Available in ["Example"] City School District Are Inadequate to Direct Instruction

A written curriculum guide provides direction for instruction from the Board and a blueprint for teachers to follow. The guide should communicate to teachers the instructional goals or objectives, time allocations, evaluation means, instructional materials, and instructional suggestions to truly guide the instruction process. The lack of a curriculum guide for any course or curriculum area forces teachers to rely on other resources for guidance in planning and delivering instruction. These may not be in alignment with the instruction intent of the district or provide for educational consistency across grades and schools. In addition, curriculum guides should be "user friendly." A teacher should be able to understand and use them without any additional information.

Exhibit 2.1 [client-specific version of Table 2 in this chapter] shows the auditors' ratings of the 44 available curriculum guides. Each guide was rated 0–3 on each of [the] five criteria . . . .

The [Example] City Schools have abdicated their curriculum development responsibilities to the State. Curriculum in the district is driven primarily by the minimum standards set forth in the various [state] syllabi and textbooks. Since those guides all follow the same format, they were rated by the auditors by curriculum area rather than individual grade levels or courses. . . . Those rankings appear in Exhibit 2.1.1 [not reproduced here].

The [ratings] of the guides ranged from a high of 12 to a low of 1. The mode [rating] (i.e., the ranking that occurred most frequently) was 6.

Criterion 1. While all of the guides clearly specified goals or objectives, only a few of the guides stated the amount of time [suggested] to be spent on each objective; therefore, the guides received an average rating of 2.02 on the first criterion.

Criterion 2. Most of the guides included a reference to some approach to evaluating student performance on the stated objectives. The mean rating for criterion 2 was .93. The guides which were rated 1 on this criterion did not explain the skill, knowledge, or concepts to be assessed; neither did the guides which were rated 2. All but one of the guides were rated 2 or below because they were weak in identifying methods of assessing student learning of the objectives.

Criterion 3. The mean rating for the third criterion, delineation by grade level of skills, knowledge, and attitudes, was .48. The only reference to prerequisite skills or knowledge for any of the guides is a scope and sequence chart indicating the order of some courses which follow a sequence such as English I, II, III, IV.

Otherwise no description of prerequisite courses or skills for those courses is made. [Exhibit 2.1.1 is presented here in the report.]

Criterion 4. Delineation of major instructional tools was identified as the weakest area with a mean rating of .30. With the exception of one guide, textbooks and instructional tools are not even specified, let alone cross-referenced to specific objectives.

Criterion 5. The rating for clear linkages for classroom utilization reflects the extent to which instructional suggestions are specified. Since a number of guides contained no suggestions for instruction, the mean rating was 1.8. In the vocational areas, Technology Learning Activities offer an excellent example of linking the objectives to classroom instruction.

The majority of state curriculum guides, as they exist, do not contain enough information to provide teachers with a complete and comprehensive work plan to guide their teaching. Again, this was not the intent of the State when developing them.

Related findings are represented in the following headings from other audits performed in recent years:

- Finding 2.2: Curriculum Guides Exist for Almost All Curriculum Areas
- Finding 2.1: Current Curriculum Guides Are Ineffective Instructional and Management Tools
- Finding 2.2: Curriculum Guides in Most Content Areas Are Inadequate to Direct Instruction

RECOMMENDATIONS TO ENHANCE STANDARD TWO PERFORMANCE

When auditors declare a finding reflecting gaps between the Standard Two criteria and an organization's actual performance, they also provide recommendations of specific steps the system can take to improve. The selected recommendations focus on the weakest areas of performance identified in Standard Two analysis and offer direction that is practical and pointed toward changes that will meet the standard's criteria. It is common for the recommendations to respond to more than one finding with a comprehensive set of proposed actions. Such an example is the following recommendation from an audit report to the "Sample" School System.

Recommendation 2.1: Develop Serviceable Curriculum Guides

The auditors recommend that the school district expand upon the state curriculum guides to develop useful tools for instructional purposes. A curriculum guide is supposed to provide direction for instruction so that the objectives of the courses can be accomplished. Unless the curriculum guide communicates to the teacher vital information concerning goals, time allocations, evaluation means, instructional materials, and instructional suggestions, the curriculum guides will be virtually useless. Effective guides also help ensure congruence among the written curriculum, what is taught in the classroom, and the measurement of student's learning related to the stated goals.

A complete set of curriculum guides should exist for all areas of the curriculum. The guides should state objectives which are matched to the major instructional tools used in the system and should be keyed to the testing/evaluation process. The guides should be developed so that they provide clear linkages from grade level to grade level and from course to course. The guides should also be comprehensive yet functional and "user friendly."

To carry out this recommendation:
–Develop system guidelines for writing curriculum guides for all courses offered in [Sample] County Schools;
–Evaluate the state curriculum guides and handbooks in relationship to local needs and modify them [as necessary] to meet the local needs and curriculum guide standards;
–Review all course offerings for [Sample] County Schools and determine which courses lack curriculum guides and which courses need to be revised to meet the criteria set forth in the state curriculum guides;
–Develop [content] evaluation criteria for reviewing all of the system's curriculum guides and determine appropriate individuals [to be] responsible for this activity;
–Establish a timetable for evaluating and revising all curriculum guides in the system; and
–Establish policies and procedural guidelines for formal Board of Education review and adoption of all curriculum guides for [Sample] County Schools.

It is common for auditors to recommend the establishment of systemwide guidelines and procedures to ensure that curriculum documents are consistent with district goals, mission statements, and learning objectives and/or outcomes adopted by the school board; to address all curriculum actually taught in the schools; and to provide the information necessary for effective classroom teaching of the curriculum. The criteria listed on the evaluation sheets also provide assistance to school personnel when they are striving to improve curriculum guides.

Other recommendations often seen in reports link the needs of Standard Two with others related to Standards Three and Four, where connectivity among other school district functions and decisions and the assessment activities of the district must align with the written and taught curriculum in order to establish quality control and achieve desired results.

SUMMARY

Standard Two addresses the ways in which the curriculum management system provides direction to the implementation of the policies, goals, and priorities established by the school district in the design and delivery of its educational program. The criteria for Standard Two expect clear and valid learning objectives for students as well as policy objectives that provide a clear framework for managing the school district's operation of its program. The criteria seek guiding documents that enhance the ability of the system to manage and deliver its curriculum and evidence of the system's exercise of local control. In meeting these criteria, a school district gives direction to the system in its pursuit of student achievement.

Auditors report on findings linked to the Standard Two criteria, looking first at the presence of curriculum documents communicating direction for the educational program and operations of the curriculum delivery system. They examine the scope of the taught curriculum covered in curriculum guides and assess the quality of the guides as tools for effective curriculum management. Evaluations are based on criteria used nationally for evaluation of curriculum guides.

Recommendations made to help the school district meet Standard Two are the result of findings identified in the specific district and are designed to help move the client toward compliance with the standard as rapidly and practically as possible.

REFERENCES

English, F. W. (1978) *Quality Control in Curriculum Development*. Arlington, Virginia: American Association of School Administrators.

English, F. W. (1980) *Improving Curriculum Management in the Schools*. Washington, D.C.: Council for Basic Education.

English, F. W. (1987) *Curriculum Management for Schools, Colleges, Business*. Springfield, Illinois: Charles C. Thomas, Publisher.

English, F. W. and B. E. Steffy. (1983) "Differentiating Between Design and Delivery Problems in Achieving Quality Control in School Curriculum Management," *Educational Technology* (February):29–32.

University Place School District. (1992) *Learning in University Place Intermediate Schools, The Curriculum Grades 5.7.* Tacoma, Washington: University Place School District.

University Place School District. (1991) *Curriculum Notebook*. Tacoma, Washington: University Place School District.

CHAPTER 7

Standard Three: The Connectivity and Equity Standard

William K. Poston, Jr. —*Iowa State University*

For as the body is one and has many members, but all the members of that one body, being many, are one body. (*1 Corinthians 12:12*)

INTRODUCTION

A smoothly functioning school system is not unlike a healthy human body. The body is made up of many individual parts and components, with each part having an important task to perform. These individual tasks make a contribution to the well-being of the total body, thereby aiding the body in accomplishing its purpose and work. The body, in turn, provides support and nourishment to each individual part so it can work properly. The parts and interdependent relationships among all parts provide the framework for the overall quality of the body.

So it is within a healthy school system. Each system is made up of many components or operations—with an interdependency among them (Deming, 1982). No one part can predominate over the others if the body is to benefit or succeed as a whole. If each part is functioning well in relationship to the others, the overall system is enabled to operate smoothly, to reach its goals, and to fulfill its purpose effectively. However, if the various parts of a system are not working together in harmony, or if some parts are not receiving optimal support and direction, the total system will suffer. No system can successfully operate if its parts are in conflict, if proper support is missing, or if some parts are benefitted at the expense of others. In other words, the total body is not only the sum but also the product of its parts. As a whole, it is more effective than the sum of its parts (English, 1989).

The interrelationships of organizational components needed for quality control will be addressed in this chapter, which explores Standard Three (connectivity and equity) of the Curriculum Management Audit. Standard Three is designed to examine how a school system demonstrates internal connectivity and rational equity in its program development and implementation. To satisfy this standard, a school system must be able to document how its programs, services, and activities are focused toward the improvement of learning of its students based on measures of growth and principles of effective leadership.

This chapter first defines Standard Three and presents the criteria for its subordinate parts. The fundamental elements of this standard are described, including presentation of the following information:

- introduction of each Standard Three component and its characteristics
- rationale for each component and its relationship to quality precepts of connectivity and equity
- specific subcriteria used in the audit to determine the extent of congruence with the standard by a system
- the auditor's role in determining and reporting findings
- examples of typical findings and frequent recommendations given in audits under Standard Three

Additional aspects of the elements of Standard Three will be illustrated in this chapter.

STANDARD THREE DEFINED

The Connectivity and Equity Standard is known as the third standard in the curriculum management audit. A school system meeting Standard Three would be able to demonstrate its connectivity and equity by showing how its programs have been developed, implemented and conducted, and by demonstrating a curriculum (English, 1988) that is, (or):

- centrally defined and adopted by the board
- clearly explained to principals and teachers (and that is) visible
- accompanied by specific training programs to enhance implementation
- monitored by central office staff and principals

The description of connectivity, as presented in the Curriculum Management Audit itself provides more specific terms of what the auditors would expect to find in a school system under Standard Three. "A school system meeting this curriculum audit standard is able to show how its program has been created as the result of a systematic identification of deficiencies in the achievement and growth of its students compared to measurable standards of pupil learning. In addition, a school system meeting this standard is able to demonstrate that it possesses a focused and coherent approach toward defining curriculum, and that as a whole, it is more effective than the sum of its parts. . . ." (English, 1989).

Specific Connectivity Subcriteria in Quality Management

In an actual curriculum management audit, the auditors would expect to find a highly developed, articulated, and coordinated curriculum in the school system that is effectively monitored by the administrative and supervisory staffs at the central and site levels. Such a system would have the following attributes:

- documents/sources that reveal internal connectivity at different levels in the system
- predictable consistency through a coherent rationale for content delineation within the curriculum
- equity of curriculum/course access and opportunity
- allocation of resource flow to areas of greatest need
- a curriculum that is clearly explained to members of the teaching staff, building-level administrators, and other supervisory personnel
- specific staff development programs to enhance curricular design and delivery
- a curriculum that is monitored by central office and site supervisory personnel
- teacher and administrator responsiveness to school board policies, currently and over time

Relationship to Quality Improvement

Quality improvement demands consideration of the total system. The components and relationships must be congruent with one another for delivery of quality from the system. The characteristics of a quality system under Standard Three represent those aspects of an effective organization that are derived from the relationships and integrity of organizational elements. Given appropriate control, direction, feedback, and productivity, a system needs more—it needs healthy relationships and attention to its interdependent nature.

One example of how interconnections affect quality is in the realization that the best curriculum in the world would be useless if teachers and administrators weren't trained in its use. Another example is in uneven opportunities for clients of a system, which means that all clients suffer, since all are a part of the total or aggregate group. Still another example is in providing a curriculum without monitoring its use, which makes little sense if the organization wishes to connect its efforts with its goals. Consequently, Standard Three provides a framework for organizational effectiveness in getting and keeping quality in overall performance.

CONNECTIVITY AND CONSISTENCY

A valid curriculum will have clear focus and coherency, expressed with manifestations of connectivity. Connectivity deals with "consistency" in school system operations. Connectivity is a manifestation of a complete chain of events and activities within the system—each being consistent, or congruent, with the others. For example, if a school board has defined policies properly and direction has been established for the teachers and learners, then it would be consistent to find administrators monitoring the implementation of such policy and direction. If the administrators are not monitoring delivery of the curriculum, its chances of successful or effective implementation are reduced. An unbroken, linked relationship must be evident between intention and implementation for consistency. Consistency helps foster coherence and collaborative connections within the system, and in turn, advances quality of the system as a whole.

Connectivity may be demonstrated. For example, it would be possible to predict what might happen at any given level of the system by examination of the levels above. This "predictability" of organizational relationships and functions is one element of connectivity. Moreover, if the system is in control of itself and the chain of relationships is working, connections would be observed as present and functioning effectively.

Internal Consistency

A major or important dimension of connectivity is that of internal curriculum consistency. Basically, internal consistency is the measure of the extent to which any curriculum is a specific product of the goals from which it was derived. Looking at this graphically, one might picture this relationship like a set of related boxes or aspects, arranged like stairs (see Figure 1).

Given internal consistency, any change in one level could be predicted by the level below. If the prediction is not true, then the relationships are inconsistent, and connectivity is diminished. For example, suppose a board of education established an expectation for its system that called for students to be "competent problem solvers and skilled in critical thinking." Then, it would be reasonable to expect the curriculum to reflect activities with higher level thinking skills in courses of study and curriculum materials. Objectives could be classified according to *Bloom's Taxonomy*, at the level of thinking addressed (Bloom, 1956). In this analysis, all six levels could be used or three broader categories might be used: (1) literal (knowledge level from *Bloom's*), (2) interpretive (comprehension, application, and analysis), and (3) critical (synthesis and evaluation) to classify or categorize instructional objectives. In one audit, the auditors found, as shown in Table 1, a configuration of objectives in a system where the board had called for competency in problem solving and skill in critical thinking.

As shown in Table 1, planning to provide critical thinking in the school system falls short of the stated expectations of the board. The configuration of learner objectives stated in the curriculum materials does not address the board's intentions adequately, making the curriculum in this system internally inconsistent. In addition, even if the configuration were balanced and reflected the board's values, the system

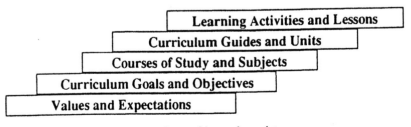

FIGURE 1 Steps of internal consistency.

Table 1. Analysis of levels of thinking in selected courses.

Course Title	Number of Objectives	Literal Level	Interpretive Level	Critical Level
English Literature (nonfiction)	12	17%	75%	8%
Journalism	45	51%	49%	0%
Developmental Reading	16	69%	31%	0%
Theater Arts	24	21%	79%	0%
Social Studies (grade 4)	36	45%	55%	0%
Total/Mean	133	41%	57%	2%

still could be internally inconsistent if the learner activities weren't coherent with the stated objectives.

Configuration Analysis

Still another way to determine internal consistency is to conduct what is called a configuration analysis, or sometimes referred to as a "level II curriculum analysis" (English, 1989). In this analysis, hierarchical linearity is examined among levels of the curriculum. In simplest terms, some type of agreement among the components of the curriculum is sought from one level of the curriculum to the next (goals to objectives to activities, etc.). This examination would reveal consistency from the "macro" level of the system (policy, goals, plans, etc.) to the "micro" level (curriculum guide objectives, activities, etc.). If one level is not predicted by its parent, or higher, level, inconsistency is said to exist.

Conducting a configuration analysis first requires selection of a suitable set of curriculum materials. A curriculum guide used for configuration analysis should be of relatively high quality in terms of its construction and characteristics (see preceding chapter). A score of twelve to fifteen from the level I curriculum guide analysis is thought to be the minimum qualification level of a guide for a level II configuration analysis. Next, the goals or program outcomes must be clearly identified, as well as unit or course of study objectives and learner activities. As many levels as possible need to be defined or located for the analysis. Objectives or activities are then categorized according to their relevance or connection to the next higher level in the curriculum design. Levels are evaluated according to their "fit" with their parent, or antecedent level, and then are sorted by congruence with the higher, or preceding, level. A configuration chart is then constructed, similar to that shown in Table 2. In this example, objectives from three course units have been categorized according to five district goal statements relevant to those courses.

In this table, note that the vertical axis is the "macro" level, graphically depicting the district or system goals (parent or antecedent level). These goals could be drawn from school system curriculum documents, strategic or long-range plans, board policy statements, or similar sources. Then the horizontal axis is the "micro" level, which could be unit objectives, teaching activities, or other curriculum components expected to be drawn from or connected to the system's over-arching goals or expectations. In the example in Table 2, a tabulation of the objectives by unit is conducted and it is possible to see that Course Unit 1 has 24 objectives out of the 38 total objectives for all units, or 63% of the total. On the other hand, we see that Course Unit 3 has only seven objectives connected to district goals, or about 18%. In this case, one unit, Course Unit 1 has 63% of the objectives related to the goals, and it has 64% of the objectives for goal 5. An imbalance is evident. Some course units have more congruence or linkage with district goals than others.

Analyzing the configuration of objectives across goals reveals incongruence of the connections within the curriculum design, or another example of internal inconsistency. Course Units 2 and 3 seem to miss the target established by the system's overall goals. This imbalance of focus or connections indicates that control is insufficient to guarantee consistency in curriculum design or delivery.

Table 2. Level 2 curriculum guide configuration analysis.

District Goal Statements	Course Unit 1 Objectives	Course Unit 2 Objectives	Course Unit 3 Objectives	Total All Units Objectives
Goal 1	5	0	4	9
Goal 2	6	3	2	11
Goal 3	2	0	0	2
Goal 4	4	1	0	5
Goal 5	7	3	1	11
Total	24	7	7	38

Alternative Configuration Analyses

Other types of configuration analysis are possible. With this format, other links from the curriculum chain or quality cycle can be examined. For example, time could be analyzed in terms of system expectations. Designed activities could be analyzed in terms of objectives. Teacher activities could be compared to designed activities. An example of the latter was observed in one system audit where district expectations for students were defined to include "opportunities for communication and interaction with others." However, teaching behaviors observed and documented during an audit indicated that most of the classroom time was being used for "worksheet drills" or solitary seatwork writing answers to textbook questions, leaving little or no time for student communication opportunities.

If hit-or-miss configurations or curriculum internal inconsistencies are evident, the system is failing to demonstrate control of itself, and quality can't be assured. Internal consistency is a necessary ingredient for curriculum quality. Curriculum documents must clearly explicate what teachers are to do related to system goals if curriculum adequacy and quality is to be provided. When the process of curriculum delivery or design is incongruent or disconnected, achievement of desired outcomes is doubtful.

Other Forms of Consistency

Consistency among operational levels is also a key to providing quality control in school systems. Operational levels include schools, individual departments, special programs, and other system support or task units. Overall system integrity is in some measure determined by how all subcomponents of the system work together toward system purposes. For example, schools often develop building improvement plans for developing greater effectiveness in program delivery. By making these efforts congruent with district purposes, consistency can be fostered. With clear connections to the system's purposes or mission, policies, or strategic plans, individual school buildings can contribute to overall system quality, or optimization.

However, one part of a system conceivably could thwart the efforts of other parts of the system and cause suboptimization, where the advancement of one part causes harm to another. If, for example, a school system's procurement office invokes a delivery schedule under an economy plan that limits the frequency of deliveries of equipment and supplies to schools, school programs could be harmed if they required timely delivery of materials. In such a case, the procurement office might be more cost efficient (optimized), but the system mission, or an individual school, could be jeopardized (suboptimized). All components of the system must work in harmony and cooperation for the system's best interests. Support units, separate schools, alternative programs, vocational schools, and other elements of the system must reflect congruence with overarching system goals and purposes. Any configuration of services or programs that is incongruent with system purposes creates a condition that is not only inconsistent, but counterproductive in terms of quality attainment.

CONNECTIVITY AND EQUITY

Healthy cultures and societies are generally thought to be those that use the concepts of fairness, justice, and equity as cornerstones for their organizations (Carrell and Dittrich, 1978). When Thomas Jefferson wrote, "All men are created equal," those words established forever the value and comparable worth of each individual person in American society. This powerful belief of America's founders remains a driving force in advancing the level of attainment and quality of our schools for all children even today. Efforts at school reform continue to grapple with ways and means for improving education for all children. All school clients, regardless of ethnic group, race, religion, national origin, sex, or handicap should have equal opportunity to master the best of what educational institutions have to offer.

Despite years of effort by educators to produce comparable results for all groups of children, inequality in educational outcomes persists (Frasier, 1989). Discrepancies between groups, particularly between low and high socioeconomic levels, have plagued school improvement efforts for decades; however, the value and ethic of providing equal opportunity have not diminished among school policymakers. The words of John Dewey still ring true: "What the best persons in our society hope for their children, society should want for all of its children."

Some unique tools are used for analyzing the nature of educational equity and the quality of education for all groups of children. The tools are a "spin off" of the curriculum management audit and provide a most promising and productive approach to evaluation of schools. Analysis of equity is a major component of the larger curriculum audit and focuses on the factors and circumstances under control of the schools that affect the educational attainment of different groups of students. Education in a democracy is not the servant of power. Rather, it is the "great leveler," providing all individual students with the means to learn and to succeed. So far as the individual local school agencies treat their student clientele according to differential needs, the school agency is providing equity. This section was derived from the underlying beliefs, assessment criteria, and the process of equity analysis described in an article in the *International Journal of Educational Reform* (Poston, 1992).

Assumptions of Equity Analysis

Primarily, equity analysis involves use of an evaluation technique in a largely social system or institution. People, resources, and time are directed in various ways in different school systems. Some systems are better than others at producing results (Edmonds, 1982), and the equity analysis is based on what makes a part of the difference. Given appropriate use of people, resources, and time by any school system, appropriate results should be achieved. Another assumption is that equality, or the quality or condition of being the same as something else, is inconsistent with the principles of equity. Equity results from providing different educational environments, services, and programs to those who have different needs for them.

Procedures of Equity Analysis

Procedures for equity analysis are the same as those of the curriculum audit process. The curriculum audit uses trained and certified professional auditors to review and intensely study a school system's documents, to inspect operations and facilities during an extensive site visit, and to conduct in-depth interviews with school personnel at all levels. The process provides an extensive body of information to be analyzed by the team of auditors.

Once findings have been triangulated, or validated by at least three sources, the team synthesizes the information into a report of findings and recommendations for improvement. The process must incorporate sound principles of program evaluation and research management.

DIMENSIONS OF EQUITY ANALYSIS

Equity analysis focuses on specific characteristics of organizational behavior and characteristics related to its specific criteria. The equity analysis process is directed toward the fifteen specific criteria, issues, and questions listed in Table 3.

Once criteria were selected for inclusion in the process of auditing for consistency and equity, specific definitions for each area were developed and fashioned into a body of data indicators to use in the equity analysis. The criteria are defined and explained, and an example is given for each criterion in the next section.

Administrative and Supervisory Procedures and Practice

Administrative and supervisory procedures and practices are evaluated through uniformity and consistency in documents about and monitoring of instruction, evaluation of teaching, curriculum implementation, and supervisory behavior.

Different situations require different supervisory behavior. Depending upon the needs of the school, its staff and faculty, and its students, supervisory behavior should show flexibility and versatility. Supervisors must diagnose needs of the organization and personnel and apply differential supervisory action congruent with those diagnosed needs.

For example, in an equitable situation, the supervisor may spend more time working with new employees who face an unexpected assignment in working with a new or different ethnic group. The supervisor might provide instruction or direction, and support or encouragement, far differently in this situation than in a situation in which the employee is highly skilled and motivated for working with the ethnic group. Another case in point would be found in administrative situations involving competence in promoting growth and improvement of faculty. If supervisors across schools have substantially different skill levels in guiding or directing instructional improvement or if novice supervisors are assigned to schools with high concentrations of at-risk students, inequity would likely occur.

Class Size Practices

Populations in classes across schools generally should be similar in

Table 3. Criteria for equity analysis.

1. Administrative and supervisory practices
2. Class size practices
3. Course offerings and access
4. Demographic distribution
5. Financial and funding resources
6. Grouping practices and procedures
7. Individual differences considerations

8. Instructional time utilization
9. Materials and facilities
10. Promotion and retention practices
11. Special program and services delivery
12. Staff development and training
13. Student management practices
14. Support services provision

15. Teacher assignment and work load

size in the same grade levels, course offerings, and types of programs following determinatively planned or specifically designed variation if required. Essentially, allocating teachers and programs equally across a highly diversified student population or different schools is ineffective and inequitable. An example of this problem is a policy of equal class sizes across all schools in a large school system. This means that classes will contain equal numbers of students, but unequal numbers of students with intensive needs such as at-risk students. Twenty-five students in a class with a high percentage of at-risk students will have less educational opportunity than a different group of twenty-five students with a low percentage of at-risk students. Class size policies and practices must reflect differential needs of the students within classes, or the standard is not met.

Course Offerings and Access

In this area, the analysis seeks to find evidence of coordination horizontally across the curriculum and across schools in courses, programs, and access by students according to stated goals or plans. Variability outside definitive planned design is inconsistent.

Course offerings may vary across schools by design. However, if the designed difference in offerings precludes certain students or groups of students from accessing any and all courses of any school system, inequity and inequality of opportunity exist. For example, if one school has a course in pre-algebra that is not available or provided to students from all schools in the system, difference exists in the educational program offered to all students in the system.

Course offerings have been found to be disparate across schools in some system audits. In Table 4, selected high school offerings have been tabulated for eight high schools in an eastern-seaboard school system. This system demonstrated an abominable lack of consistency in its high schools' course offerings. Among the eight high schools, 226 courses were offered, but only 42% of the courses were offered in all eight of the high schools. Table 4 shows a small sample of the plotting of course offerings across eight high schools.

With a finding of this type, students have little chance of getting an equivalent menu of educational offerings from one high school to the next. Given no open access to schools across the district, the student is denied equal opportunity in course offerings accordingly. Course offerings must be comparable across schools or be different by design

Table 4. Tabulation of selected high school course offerings.

Course	1	2	3	4	5	6	7	8
Basic Rdg. Skills	1	1	1	1				
AP Lit. & Comp.	1	1	1				1	1
AP Lang./Comp.	1	1	1	1	1			
Creative Writing			1		1	1		
Themes in Lit.				1		1		
Journalism III	1		1			1	1	1
Spch. Sk. Wkshp.			1		1		1	
Writing Styles						1		1
French IV	1		1					
Total	5	3	7	3	3	4	3	3

Course	1	2	3	4	5	6	7	8
Symphonic Band	1	1	1	1		1	1	1
Band Ensemble	1		1	1		1	1	1
Stage Band	1		1	1		1	1	1
String Ensemble			1	1		1		
Orchestra	1	1	1	1	1	1	1	1
Vocal Ensemble	1	1	1	1	1	1	1	1
Art II					1		1	1
AP Studio Art					1	1		
Fine Crafts	1							
Total	6	3	6	6	4	7	6	6

without delimiting opportunity or access by all students to satisfy this criterion in equity analysis.

Demographic Distribution

To meet the requirements of this criterion, populations of all schools in the district should be reasonably analogous in ethnicity, socioeconomic status, accessibility to educational resources, entry to human support services, and other educational opportunities provided by the system.

Desegregation has been common since 1954 in the famous *Brown v. Topeka* case decided by the United States Supreme Court. Despite this case and federal prohibitions against disparate distributions of races and ethnic groups across schools, many communities have failed to establish common characteristics of school populations within local educational agencies. In equity analysis, the concentrations of ethnic and racial groups are analyzed at each individual school unit. The focus of the analysis is to determine how the constituency of the whole is reflected in each of its parts. Generally, more favorable educational results are expected given less sizable concentrations of minority students in individual schools, indicating that a better course of action would be to distribute students evenly across the system in terms of race and ethnicity (Rumberger and Willms, 1992).

Comparisons are made across schools to find if disparity exists in racial or ethnic composition compared with the system norm (Fleming et al., 1978). A good rule of thumb is to compare the school mean with the district mean percentage for racial and ethnic groups. If a given school exceeds the district average by 20%, racial isolation may be present (Iowa Department of Education, 1990). Schools across a school system must approximate the district mean percentage of racial and ethnic groups to meet this standard.

Finance and Funding Resources

In this criterion, comparable and equitable financial resources and other funding sources, such as concessions, fund-raising opportunities, grants, fees, and other economic characteristics, are scrutinized across all schools within the system.

Inequality can result from both funding discrepancies and uniformity. Discrepancy, as uneven or irregular distribution of resources without regard to performance or program requirements, may be inequitable. By the same token, uniform allocations of resources without consideration of performance or program needs may be inequitable. Many school systems use formula systems to distribute resources, often promulgated from input variables such as enrollment, numbers of teachers, or another formulation irrespective of differential needs or requirements. Given different school needs, student populations, and variance in results, resources must be tied to programmatic factors.

Another type of inequity may result due to external funding or resources obtained from outside normal internal school system actions. For example, an energetic parent organization may raise money and equip its neighborhood school with additional special equipment. If this procurement creates a disparity and said disparity creates unequal access to educational opportunity, issues arise about fairness and equity. Parent groups should have the option to provide additional resources to their schools, but if such resources exacerbate inequity, the school system may have to provide compensatory resources to ameliorate inequitable conditions.

School funds and resources must be distributed according to identified and measured program expectations and outcomes, not just on the basis of enrollment numbers. Unless the school system is using a means to distribute resources based on measurable outcomes and requirements across programs, this standard may not be met.

Grouping and Placement Practices

Registration practices and assignment of students to groups for instruction should be based on carefully diagnosed needs for instructional differentiation on specifically and narrowly defined learning objectives for temporary, short-term bases only, and heterogeneity should be the standard method of allocation of students to classes, subjects, and instructional programs without regard to academic ability, achievement test performance, race, nationality, sex, or ethnicity.

Grouping practices are often the most perplexing of the many things evaluated in equity analysis. Often, school systems purport to be providing equal opportunity, but this goal is not reflected in class groupings. Grouping by ability is often used in a way that results in grouping by ethnic or racial characteristics by default. Poor, minority children are often disproportionately represented in the "lower" ability tracks. These assignments are rarely changed, and disparities between higher and lower groups grow in magnitude over time.

Moreover, placement procedures in special programs often result in classifications along racial or economic lines. In one analysis, it was determined that special education placements were disproportionately representative of certain racial groups. The analysis revealed the configuration illustrated in Figure 2.

In Figure 2, several school populations were tabulated in terms of percentage of African-American students in the total school population and in special education. In examining the data, it was noted that a higher percentage of African-American students are in special education in some schools than are in the total school population. This finding appears to indicate a disproportionate percentage of this particular group and may reflect bias or flaws in the special education placement process, especially in the case of schools shown as numbers 3 and 7. If this criterion is to be met, grouping and placement practices should reflect purposes or reasons that are educationally valid or tied to educational objectives.

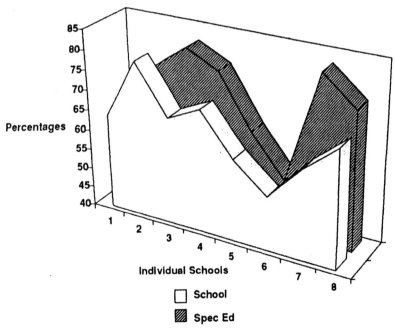

FIGURE 2 African-American percentages in special education compared to percentages in the total school population.

Consideration of Individual Differences

The seventh criterion seeks to find evidence of differentiation in the allocation and use of human and materiel services based upon clearly diagnosed educational needs of a specific clientele in policy or in operations. For example, in one district evaluated, it was learned that educational attainment varied widely across schools. A tabulation of this data is displayed in Figure 3.

This demonstrates that considerable differences exist across schools, at least in terms of mean achievement in reading on the Iowa Test of Basic Skills. Resources of the school system should be targeted accordingly. In this criterion, evaluation is not on the actual allocations of resources themselves; rather, it focuses more on how decisions are made in the allocations. If no adequate assessment system is established in policy and in fact, decisions about allocations cannot assure equity. Interdisciplinary study of student needs is also helpful in providing a sound data base with which to focus and direct the resources of the organization. With a comprehensive, adequate process to identify clearly and define educational needs of individual students and groups, and with implementation accordingly, this criterion would be satisfied.

Instructional Time

This portion of the analysis looks for equitability and evenness in time allocations, uninterrupted blocks of time, use, and monitoring

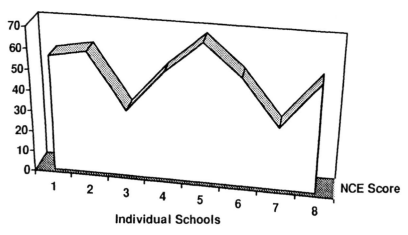

FIGURE 3 Third grade NCE score means across schools.

provided across the district (bell schedules, bus service, recess, administrative interruption, recreation, lunch, and other time using or managing processes).

Perhaps the best way to illustrate this criterion was found in a situation observed in a large school system during a curriculum audit in a southern state. In one elementary school, classes began at 8:15 A.M., and a kindergarten class was being observed at the beginning of the day. The auditor noted that the class was about evenly divided between African-American children and white children. A few moments after roll had been taken, the teacher excused the "breakfast" children to go to the cafeteria. Immediately, all of the African-American and only two of the white children left the room. The teacher then began to teach the remainder of the class, now comprised of all white children, apparently not of poor economic means. The amount of instructional time received by the "non-breakfast" students exceeded that of the "breakfast" students by at least twenty minutes daily. Such disparity is unmistakably inequitable. This actual situation displays how this criterion may not be properly satisfied. Moreover, time allocations are a key prerequisite to control in the delivery of curriculum. Specific expectations for instructional time, when spelled out by the system, provide better uniformity in instructional practice. Without specific guidelines for the use of instructional time, delivery can be uneven, disparate, and inequitable across a system. Time allocations and utilization must reflect fair and reasonable comparability across the system and for all clientele.

Materials and Facilities

Comparable and equitable educational opportunities must be reflected in the distribution of educational tools and materials, including library, audiovisual supplies, computers, and laboratory and classroom supplemental books and workbooks. Facilities should provide equal environmental support, including cleanliness, maintenance, suitability, utility, and general nature.

Schools can have widely different materials, facilities, equipment, and other materiel within a given school system. For example, it is not uncommon for an audit to reveal that older schools (often in high at-risk student neighborhoods) have library book collections that are older and more dilapidated than found in newer schools in upscale neighborhoods. It is occasionally revealed that the older schools and schools located in poor neighborhoods are less well maintained than other schools in the same district. Moreover, some schools are often better equipped than others, especially in terms of idiosyncratic situations, such as highly motivated building-level administrators, preferential treatment, or simple age of the buildings.

To meet this standard, efforts must be evident and documented that equity in materiel (supplies and equipment) and facilities is maintained across schools.

Promotion and Retention Criteria

Pupil promotion and retention practices remain controversial today despite a substantial body of research evidence calling retention into question. Analysis of this criterion looks for evidence of rational criteria and procedures for determining promotion and consistent utilization of fair practices for all children across the district. With appropriate promotion-retention processes, including interdisciplinary team decisions and comprehensive assessment, school systems may exceed the requirements of this criterion.

Equity in this case goes beyond the system following its rules, even if the rules are designed purportedly to achieve justice. This analysis should be construed as a check on the justifiability of specific system actions that are carried out within the educational arena and the arrangements that result from those actions (Secada, 1989). Rational and consistent practices of promotion and retention should be evident across schools. If inordinate amounts of students are retained at any one school compared to other schools, the process is not under quality control.

Policies and regulations must be carefully established for promotion and retention, and such policies must incorporate sound educational and psychological principles. For example, in one system, the auditors observed that over 60% of the retentions were male, and the percentage of black student retentions was nearly twice their percentage in the total population. This inordinate imbalance illustrates inequity. If little or no differences in the incidence of promotion or retention are observed across schools or among ethnic, gender, or racial groups, this criterion may be said to be satisfied.

Special Program Offerings

Demonstration of equity and consistency of program delivery across schools, linkage of curriculum, pull-out activities, extensions of time, or other alternative educational options must be evident following a careful data analysis.

In modern school systems, many "extra" programs are available for students. Some of these auxiliary or special program offerings include summer schools, after-school programs, enrichment tutoring, and alternative schools. It goes without saying that such programs must be equitably provided across the system's schools. Equal distribution of programs is not required, but no deleterious effect should result from offering any special or auxiliary program to one segment of the school population compared to another.

For example, schools may decide to provide after-school tutoring for their students. If this decision were to create an imbalance in educational opportunities for one group but not others in the same system, inequity might result. Or, in one case observed by a curriculum audit team, the district provided an "at-risk" program. In one school, this was an intensive pupil-tutoring program in reading. At another school in the same system, it was a disciplinary room, where miscreants were held (without any educational activities) for the "term of their sentence." It was easy to see how this "extra" program benefitted one group of clients in the system and hampered another.

Decisions about augmenting educational programming should consider not only differences among schools but the effects of any augmentation upon the difference. Any exacerbation of the difference of educational attainment between schools would be undesirable and could comprise nonconformity with this criterion. The reasonable outcome is to close unreasonable gaps in performance and opportunity.

Staff Development

In this case, equity, resources, and diagnosed and individually prescribed training is reviewed for administrators, teachers, and other staff congruent with assessed needs and goals of the district to the extent required.

In a recent audit in a large midwestern city, one middle school with a majority of at-risk students had the largest percentage of first year and nontenure teachers of all the schools in the system. However, no allowances were provided for the additional training and developmental needs for this inexperienced staff, and the training provided was voluntary and based on popular choices (related to nationally popular topics) in content.

Staff capabilities can affect equity within and across schools. Competencies needed for dealing with the educational needs of students may or may not be present within a faculty. If deficiencies are observed in the capabilities of faculty and staff, training and staff development is advisable. In staff development design and delivery, needs must be diagnosed, action prescribed, and results evaluated. It only seems to make sense to focus training where it is needed. "Shotgun," voluntary programs do little to target scarce resources on high-priority areas of system need. Failure to provide adequate training in support of curriculum and instruction requirements causes noncompliance with this criterion and is counterproductive for the school system as a whole.

Student Management Practices

Equity in this criterion's case calls for evidence of comparability in student disciplinary practices and procedures, suspension practices, and other student behavioral control or modification activities. One key factor in examining the extent to which a school system is treating students fairly and equitably is in the area of student management. If an inordinate number of students from one characteristic grouping is subjected to discipline, suspension, or other student management practices across various demographic groups of students are compiled and compared. This type of review is illustrated in Figure 4. In this situation, the percentage of suspensions was tabulated across schools compared to the schools' percentage of the total population.

What Figure 4 illustrates is an imbalance in suspension incidence. East High School (fictitious name) has about 17% of the system population but has only 4% of the suspensions. Central High, on the other hand, has only 15% of the students but 25% of the suspensions. Equity is likely in question in this situation. Given discrepant occurrence or frequency of student management practice, conformity with this criterion may be inadequate.

Support Services

Allocations of support services including administrators, nursing services, counselors, attendance officers, librarians, training programs, logistical support (including office equipment and personnel), and other support services should be equitably and appropriately allocated across the district.

As in other standards, services must be equitably provided across a

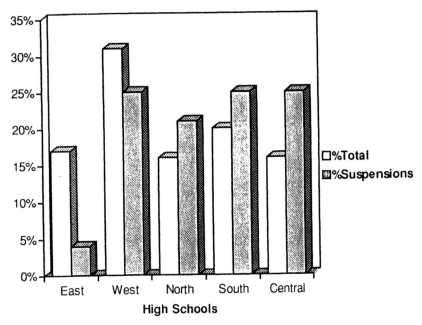

FIGURE 4 Percentage of suspensions compared to percentage of district enrollment by high school.

school system according to the identified needs of the individual schools. It is not uncommon for support services to be allocated and assigned on formula factors, like enrollment count irrespective of school needs. Allocations based on factors other than diagnosed need may not meet the variable demands for individual services. As an example of disparity, one system allowed the allocation of librarian personnel to be up to the individual school principal. In this large system, some schools had libraries open all day long during the week, while others had library services only a few days per week, and then not all day. What this meant is that some students got the benefit of library services more than did others, without regard to diagnosed need or program requirements. Delivery of services should be structured to insure that unequal populations of student clientele receive what they need, not merely the same as other schools or by some haphazard means.

Teacher Assignment and Work Load

This criterion explores the nature of teacher assignments and work load in terms of knowledge, skills, and competence across schools, as well as equitability in terms of work load and direct student contact and in accordance with plans or specific goals.

In this area, staffing allocations should reflect various demographic and program needs. The level of teacher skill should match up with student needs, and staffing must be adequate to properly deliver instruction. The more experienced, skilled teachers normally should be assigned to work with students of greater challenge, such as with at-risk students. Regrettably, audits have generally found that the novice, inexperienced teachers are relegated the work of dealing with difficult and challenging students. In some systems, seniority transfer rights have facilitated the "flight" of senior, experienced teachers to the higher socioeconomic areas, leaving the poor, minority students to junior, less experienced colleagues. Both instances illustrate how inequity or inefficacy can result if teacher assignments are not carefully made and based upon student characteristics and needs. Parents have been known to complain that some schools have become a "dumping ground" for poorer teachers. Administrators have been heard to indicate that "better teachers are with better students, and poorer teachers are with poorer students."

However, incentives and motivation could be provided to retain and support teachers assigned to more difficult teaching situations, and the infusion of outside personnel with special qualifications usually benefits demographically disadvantaged school situations. Unless levels of teacher skills and student needs are considered in assignment of faculty, this criterion might be left unfulfilled.

Besides inequities of staff skill and assignment, inequity can also occur when some positions are not filled, and staffing levels become or are allowed to be inadequate. For instance, in one audit, there were three unfilled positions in special education at the time of the audit team's site visits, and the positions had been vacant nearly four months.

Just as some students could get more instructional time than others, some could also receive different amounts of instruction by faulty staffing allocations. For example, one school with an enrollment of 209 students was observed to have an allocation of .4 of an art teacher, while a school of 359 students in the same district was also allocated .4 of an art teacher. Typically, more art instruction is given to the smaller school's students. If the same amount of art is taught, inequity still exists between work load assignments for the individual teachers.

Occasionally, audits find that work loads across different types of teaching assignments are not comparable. Some teachers have longer pupil contact than others, and often this is due to dissimilar amounts of planning time. Another way for work loads to become unequal is failure to include traveling time between classrooms or schools as part of the work load determination. Levels (elementary, middle, and high schools), special areas (special education, fine arts), and independent assignments (speech pathologists, librarians, counselors) often have disparate work load assignments caused by insufficient definition of work load expectations. If such expectations are clearly defined, consistency and equity are enhanced and subject matter time allocations would be defined accordingly.

EQUITY ANALYSIS SUMMATION

Equity analysis remains under development, and its conceptual framework is highly dependent upon theoretical bases. By identifying and defining various elements of equity, configuring the elements into a structure of criteria, and providing implementation guidelines, the theory and practice of school quality improvement should be enhanced.

Any diagnostic or evaluation tool is only a means to improve the quality of an organization. The equity analysis provides a fresh and useful tool to decide the level of fairness and equity a school system brings to the delivery of educational programs and services. By using equity analysis in school quality improvement efforts, educational leaders and policymakers can establish greater control over quality and greater likelihood of improvement of educational practice and organizational results over time.

Much remains to be determined in the theory and practice of equity analysis. However, the movement of school quality improvement provides an enormous opportunity to use the tool for guidance in improvement activities. More significantly, equity analysis holds substantial promise for improvement of the design and delivery of curriculum and instruction. Quality has always been the product of thorough institutional research and organizational efficacy. Given continued development and refinement, new dimensions can help develop and maintain quality in educational organizations and institutions.

CONNECTIVITY AND STAFF DEVELOPMENT

System thinking in education leads to an understanding of the dynamics of complex organizations, and in education, the systems are people-intensive. People provide the vehicle for design, delivery, and assessment of programs and services, and the needs of people are critical to system success. People, in this case teachers, administrators, and support staff, need training and assistance to carry out system goals and purposes with greater efficiency and effectiveness over time. Staff development programs are essential ingredients for system improvement.

Staff development has often been found in curriculum management audits to be fragmented and dysfunctional. A common type of staff development is focused on currently popular topics, which may or may not be germane to the system's curriculum, and is voluntary, with recipients deciding whether or not to participate. In some cases, staff development has been "one-shot" in nature. In one large system, the entire instructional staff and administration was mandated to participate in an all-day seminar on effective principles of instruction. After the one-day program, the system claimed to be following the principles of effective instruction, but no follow-up activities or actions were taken after the one inservice session. Site visits in that system confirmed that the inservice session did not "take," as teachers seldom were observed using effective principles in their classrooms.

Other districts offer a "shotgun" approach, with a long list of training options available for teaching and support staff, open to teachers to select and attend at their discretion. Often, support staff are not provided much in the way of inservice training. Moreover, rarely have school systems drawn connections between staff development and measures of teacher, student, or system effectiveness. Rather, process focus has been common, with unsubstantiated assumptions that attendance in an inservice program results in a concommitant behavioral change. These anomalies illustrate the need for clearly focused staff development, which is relevant to organizational purposes and mission. Staff development must be carefully defined, designed, and implemented if the system is to maximize its efforts in quality improvement.

Planning for Effective Staff Development

No effort in staff development should begin without a clear understanding of purpose. The nature of the mission to be addressed must be clearly defined, and a statement of purpose must be identified and communicated in the planning efforts. Wide participation in development of purpose and needs assessment builds credibility and system unity of effort. Needs should be identified and documented with particular attention to discrepancies between the current status of the system and its intended future status.

Goals should be established and reduced to writing, with inclusion of measurable criteria for accomplishment. Connections to student and organizational performance should be such that the staff development process is results-based, rather than process-based. Planning should center its attention on the ends to be reached, rather than the means to be employed. Specific staff development activities should be designed, which are supportive of the system goals. Data should be elicited that support the need for specified activities in relationship to goals for consistency in the hierarchical relationship (see internal consistency above). Criteria are needed to ascertain the means and measures to assess goal completion and mission accomplishment. The planning phase should incorporate sufficient definition of expectations so the system can determine whether or not the training fulfilled its intended purpose.

Emphases and priorities for staff development need to be drawn from board and system goals, established pupil expectations (skills, knowledge, and attitudes), needs assessments of programs and services, parameters of written curricula, findings from administrative evaluations of teaching and monitoring of curricula, and teacher-identified needs.

Implementing Effective Staff Development

Once the staff development program has been planned and designed, implementation must be handled to assure consistency and alignment with system purposes. Activities and programs of staff development must be clearly connected to the system mission, policies, and plans. Activities should be directed at those elements of system functioning that impact measured student or organizational performance.

Congruency between staff development and system needs is best handled by vesting responsibility for staff development in a single, high-level administrative position to ensure that such programs are concentrated on key strategic outcomes. Responsibility for program management in staff development is too important to be fragmented. Data on effectiveness need to be gathered following training at various intervals, which confirm the effect of the training on measures of performance. In essence, the "loop is closed" between planning, action, and feedback. Types of data used include criterion-referenced tests in content areas, school climate or culture assessments, time utilization and duration, curriculum delivery problems and processes, cost-benefit analyses, and attitudinal measures on organizational or system factors.

In addition to ongoing evaluation, implementation efforts must include active communication and reporting structures for intraorganizational understanding of expectations and outcomes. Progress should be communicated to appropriate individuals and groups. Troubleshooting and supervisory help should be provided during staff development implementation to overcome unforeseen obstacles and problems. Results of program evaluation should be shared with teachers and staff. Program modifications can then be made based on evaluation results periodically.

Quality staff development programs include the following elements:

- alignment of training with system mission, goals, beliefs, plans, and defined learning standards for students
- reflection of sound instructional practice, including clear statements of purpose and participant objectives, needs diagnosis, differentiation of instruction, diversification of learning activities, training sessions that use productive psychological and social processes coupled with effective learning, and use of principles of motivation and learning when appropriate
- incorporation of participation of affected personnel in design and delivery of the staff development activities, and opportunities for on-the-job application of skills and learnings as much as possible
- use of qualified and skilled staff development trainers and determination of the effectiveness of all developmental activities based on empirical evaluations and documentation of changes in instructional performance and behaviors in the workplace
- assessment of effect and results, particularly in terms of individual behavioral change over time after training

Instructional quality is an elusive goal at best, but without sound and appropriate training and development for the people who are to deliver and support instruction, the goal is unattainable. Consequently, staff development can and must be an integral part of system quality improvement. With constancy of purpose, clear relationships, documentation of needs, effective activities, accessibility to all personnel, transportability across the system, evidence of results, and continual revisions based on data and results, the system is enhanced in terms of quality in its delivery of teaching and learning.

CONNECTIVITY AND INSTRUCTIONAL MONITORING

Curriculum implementation, if left to chance, will quickly become disparate, fragmented, and loosely coupled. Curriculum implementation requires careful coordination, support, and direction from administration if programs and instructional activities are to be working in harmony. Without administrative monitoring of curriculum implementation, the system will not be in control of itself, and inconsistency will result (English, 1988). The administrator's responsibility in monitoring is extensive and involves activities designed to promote individual student progress and success.

Dimensions of Instructional Monitoring

Monitoring activities should focus on the following components:

- compliance and congruence with system policy
- student progress and achievement
- instructional efficiency and effectiveness
- assessment of performance
- revision of design and delivery
- use and allocations of time
- staff development needs and requirements
- communication of program progress and needs
- support and assistance to implementation effort

There are many facets of instructional monitoring—too many to cover adequately in this text. However, quality control would be enhanced with several key components of the monitoring process.

Instructional Monitoring Processes

Monitoring can be a powerful tool to manage and adjust the curriculum by focusing on the central mission of the system. In quality terms, monitoring is congruent with a system's "constancy of purpose." That is, it keeps the planning, development, implementation, and feedback components of instructional delivery working together. Regrettably, audits have often found administrative actions in monitoring lacking. Teachers have often complained that they seldom see their administrator, much less consider them a partner in the instructional implementation process. In one audit, the principal even got lost showing the audit team around his school!

Also, findings have also revealed that instructional objectives are frequently not addressed in curriculum delivery efforts (Steffy and English, 1983). In most audits, few examples of administrative monitoring have been worthy of commendation, leading to finding of fragmented supervision and flawed instructional management. Components of a sound, comprehensive curriculum monitoring process should include the following administrative activities:

- clear definition of the monitoring system's expectations at the system and building level
- frequent and thorough supervision of teaching processes, particularly focused on development of effective delivery procedures
- congruence and inclusion of proper development of lesson planning including curriculum design and time allocations
- determination whether the designed curriculum is being delivered over a period of time
- analysis of use of instructional time, especially on "teacher-added" curriculum and designed instructional objectives
- provision for teacher-administrator conferencing time through use of proxemics and close working relationships
- use of motivation, modeling, instruction (on methodologies and expectations), and support for teaching and support staff
- determination whether curriculum time allocations and learner expectations are realistic
- evaluation of curricular sequencing, resolving ambiguities or curricular conflicts, and interventions for smooth longitudinal articulation and horizontal coordination
- design and delivery of comprehensive staff development and training, including instructional coaching and nurturing of teaching skill development and curriculum improvement
- development of collegial collaboration and team cooperation for realization of shared vision
- constant accumulation, analysis, and judgment of feedback and assessment information for curriculum design, program delivery, and system process improvements

To manage curriculum as a system, monitoring is essential. Adjustments in the system require comprehensive knowledge and intimate understanding of roles, relationships, and activities within the system. Feedback is critical for improvement, and with proper attention to the monitoring role, the system's quality improvement efforts are likely to become more dynamic and highly functional.

STANDARD THREE CONCLUSIONS

Standard Three deals with the connections and relationships within the curriculum and instructional system. Given appropriate relationships and mutually beneficial efforts from all parts of the system, greater efficiency and effectiveness is likely. Tools to achieve quality in system operations are available for educators interested in diagnosing the consistency, equity, and connectivity within their system. Criteria for effectiveness at all levels of the system focus administrative leadership on priority tasks within this standard. With the use of the tools provided in this chapter, improvements in central focus, organizational congruence, instructional delivery, curriculum design, and client achievement and performance are not only encouraged, but fostered. Quality in system functioning is enhanced in no small measure when connectivity and equity are enabled.

REFERENCES

Adams, J. S. (1963) "Toward an Understanding of Inequity," *Journal of Abnormal and Social Psychology*, 67(5):422–436.

Banks, J. A. (1983) "Multiethnic Education and the Quest for Equality," *Phi Delta Kappan*, (Apr. 1):582–585.

Bloom, B. S. (1956) *Taxonomy of Educational Objectives: The Classification of Educational Goals*. NY: Longmans, Green.

Carrell, M. R. and J. E. Dittrich. (1978) "Equity Theory: The Recent Literature, Methodological Considerations, and New Directions," *Academy of Management Review* (April):202–210.

Deming, W. E. (1982) *Out of the Crisis*. Cambridge, Massachusetts: Massachusetts Institute of Technology.

Edmonds, R. R. (1982) "Programs of School Improvement: An Overview," *Educational Leadership* (December):4–11.

English, F. W. (1988) *Curriculum Auditing*. Lancaster, Pennsylvania: Technomic Publishing Co., Inc.

English, F. W. (1989) *Curriculum Auditor's Training Manual.* Arlington, Virginia: National Curriculum Audit Center, American Association of School Administrators.

Fleming, J., G. Gill and D. Swinton. (1978) *The Case for Affirmative Action for Blacks in Higher Education.* Washington, D.C.: Institute for the Study of Educational Policy.

Frasier, M. (1989) "Poor and Minority Students Can Be Gifted, Too!" *Educational Leadership,* 46(6):16–23.

Gay, G. (1990) "Achieving Education Equity Through Curriculum Desegregation," *Phi Delta Kappan,* 72(1):56–62.

Glickman, C. (1991) "Pretending Not to Know What We Know," *Educational Leadership* (May):4–10.

Goodlad, J. and J. Oakes. (1988) "We Must Offer Equal Access to Knowledge," *Educational Leadership,* 88(5):16–22.

Goodman, P. S. and A. Friedman. "An Examination of Adams' Theory of Inequity," *Administrative Science Quarterly.*

Hart, L. A. (1989) "The Horse Is Dead," *Phi Delta Kappan,* 71(3):14.

Iowa Department of Education. (1990) *The Race Review Process.* Des Moines, Iowa: Bureau of School Administration and Accreditation.

Kozol, J. (1991) *Savage Inequalities: Children in America's Schools.* New York: Crown Publishers.

Lanasa, P. J. and J. H. Potter. (1989) "Building a Bridge to Span the Minority-Majority Achievement Gap," Paper presented to the *National Conference on Desegregation,* Durham, North Carolina.

Mitchell, J. K. and W. K. Poston, Jr. (1992) "The Equity Audit in School Reform: Three Case Studies of Educational Disparity and Incongruity," *International Journal of Educational Reform,* 1(3):242–247.

National Center for Education Statistics. (1988) *The Condition of Education.* Washington, D.C.: U.S. Department of Education.

Poston, W. K., Jr. (1992) "The Equity Audit in School Reform: Building a Theory for Institutional Research," *International Journal of Educational Reform,* 1(3):235–241.

Poston, W. K., Jr., F. W. English and C. A. Downey. (1990) *Aspects of Consistency to Audit in a School District* (unpublished document). Arlington, Virginia: National Curriculum Audit Center.

Rumberger, R. W. and J. D. Willms. (1992) "The Impact of Racial and Ethnic Segregation on the Achievement Gap in California High Schools," *Educational Evaluation and Policy Analysis,* 14(4):377–396.

Secada, W. (1989) "Educational Equity versus Equality of Education: An Alternative Conception," In *Equity in Education,* W. G. Secada (Ed.), New York: Falmer Press.

Steffy, B. and F. English. (1983) Differentiating Between Design and Delivery Problems in Achieving Quality Control in School Curriculum Management. *Educational Technology,* 23(2):29–32.

Successful Schooling for the At Risk Student. (1988) (Conference Report and Recommendations, City University of New York, NY). Albany, New York: New York State Education Department.

Taylor, W. L. and D. M. Piche. (1991) *A Report on Shortchanging Children: The Impact of Fiscal Inequity on the Education of Students At Risk.* Washington, D.C.: The Committee on Education and Labor, U.S. House of Representatives.

CHAPTER 8

Standard Four: The Assessment Standard

WILLIAM STRESHLY — *San Diego State University*

THE PURPOSE OF A SCHOOL DISTRICT ASSESSMENT PROGRAM

EXPERTS in program evaluation claim there really is only one purpose for evaluation activity, namely, "to provide feedback in social systems" (Posavac and Carey, 1989). The purpose of a school district's assessment program is to provide feedback about the district's instructional program. Despite the present day's persistent move toward test-based accountability, a well-designed school district assessment program is not composed merely of test results. Rather, it is designed to gather a variety of data that allow school district leaders to evaluate continuously the school district's program. In other words, a district's assessment program is a *feedback loop* that enables the people in the system to judge more accurately how well the district is doing what it was established to do.

This is a tall order under the best of circumstances. The school district's mission embraces most of the global objectives of child rearing. The typical kindergarten through twelfth grade process takes thirteen years. In the world of physical sciences, the time scale needed to evaluate the impact of an intervention in the school setting would be ten years or more. Some writers suggest that the reason educational problems are difficult to solve is because of the long delay between the adoption of poor policies and the feedback indicating a failure of the system (Meadows and Perelman, 1973). Program evaluation, nevertheless, is a powerful tool for improving the effectiveness of any system in the school (Zammuto, 1982). The process of assessing needs, developing goals, designing programs to achieve goals, implementing programs, and evaluating the results comprises the operational core of a rational organization and serves to help these organizations to adapt to changing conditions and to improve operational effectiveness and efficiency.

185

The purpose of this chapter is to discuss the components of well-functioning, comprehensive school district assesssment programs and to analyze the processes and procedures used by districts to manage these systems.

DEVELOPING A DISTRICT ASSESSMENT PROGRAM

Curriculum auditors from the National Curriculum Audit Center, sponsored by the American Association of School Administrators (AASA), base their examination of a district's assessment program on the curriculum evaluation framework developed by English (1987), which is described in Figure 1.

English emphasizes that "Curriculum evaluation must be sensitive to the nature of outcomes as expressed in results and be able to relate results to sets of specific directions which change work in the work place" (p. 293). The functional relationship of the written, taught, and tested curricula is reinforced by the evaluation plan. Evaluation of curriculum must be concerned with the operation of the *total* system. This means examining the connections among the written curriculum, the classroom teaching, and the various assessments of student outcomes. This evaluative framework can form the basis of an effective district assessment program.

Discussing a district's assessment program must include the manner in which the data is analyzed, fed back through the system, and used to make changes in systemic functions. Feedback helps the school district accomplish two purposes. First, it helps to strengthen instruction and to increase the efficacy of programs and services. This purpose,

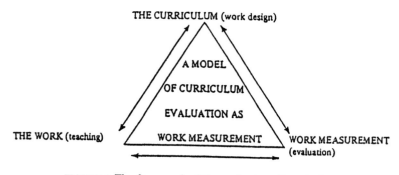

FIGURE 1 The framework of the evaluation of curriculum.

commonly known as formative evaluation, ideally serves to update and improve the program that is being evaluated. The second purpose of feedback is to provide qualitative judgments or program rankings and ratings commonly known as summative evaluations. In recent years, the popular demand for school district accountability and greater responsibility for achieving outcomes has resulted in a push for more summative evaluations. The idea is to eliminate less effective programs and use scarce taxpayer dollars to improve high priority programs. It is no surprise to critics of public education that school district assessment programs are composed largely of formative evaluations. School district services, once established, are very rarely eliminated as a result of summative evaluation. Cook et al. (1985) point out that this is also true of other agencies and organizations whose mission is primarily social service. A functional, comprehensive school district assessment program should include a balance of formative and summative evaluations that provide school leaders a broad array of data for decision making.

Standard Four:

The school system uses the results from system-designed and/or adopted assessment to adjust, improve, or terminate ineffective practices or programs. Common indicators are:

- a formative and summative assessment system linked to a clear rationale in board policy
- knowledge and use of emerging curriculum and program assessment trends
- use of a student and program assessment plan which provides for diverse assessment strategies for multi-purposes at all levels—district, school, and classroom
- a timely and relevant base upon which to analyze important trends in the instructional program
- a way to provide feedback to the teaching and administrative staffs regarding how classroom instruction may be evaluated and subsequently improved
- a vehicle to examine how well specific programs are actually producing desired learner outcomes
- a data base to compare the strengths and weaknesses of various programs and program alternatives, as well as to engage in equity analysis

- a data base to modify or terminate ineffective educational programs
- a method/means to relate to a programmed budget and enable the school system to engage in cost-benefit analysis; and
- organizational data gathered and used to continually improve system functions.

Districts with effective assessment programs have developed institutional systems that accomplish these critical organizational functions. Although the features of these systems differ from district to district, several components are common to all well-functioning programs. These are described next.

COMPONENTS OF AN ASSESSMENT PROGRAM

Components of a successful assessment program fall into three categories: the testing program, surveys and follow-up studies, and audits and reviews. Properly planned and managed, these can combine to provide a balanced, clear, and objective assessment of district performance.

The Testing Program

The first thing that comes to mind when one mentions a district's testing program is the traditional publisher-produced standardized achievement test usually administered to every student in school during a special period of time set aside during the school year. These instruments are awkwardly linked to the curriculum. Consequently, they are not very valuable to teachers and site administrators. English (1988) sums it up this way:

Typically, school officials make very poor use of feedback in the form of standardized test data. There are a variety of reasons for this. For one, such tests are usually adopted independently of any consideration of the curriculum in a district. What that means is that the data provided "floats" around a school system with no specific anchor to classroom instruction.

When that is the case, and the test feedback is distributed to teachers (it is rarely explained), they make very little use of it to change anything in their own work places. The data are considered about children and not about teachers or the curriculum, (pp. 62–63).

School board members and other community interests, however, often apply pressure to school officials for comparative data. They want to know how their students (or their schools and teachers) stack up with other districts in the state and nation. Standardized tests produce such data quickly and efficiently and yield scores that can easily be used by the curriculum management auditor to create trend analyses. Figures 2–5 are examples of common trend analyses using standard test scores.

The weakness of a district testing program built around publisher-produced standardized tests is the tendency for this practice to narrow the taught curriculum. Whether we like it or not, principals and teachers bent on raising scores will acquaint their students with test formats and objectives. Since these typically involve heavy use of multiple choice test technology, training students to perform well on these instruments is actually inimical to the higher order mental processes requiring reflection and creative solutions. Scores rise, but students learn less of what educators want them to learn—higher order cognitive skills.

Feedback in the form of test data is a powerful tool for program improvement when it is designed around the types of student performance described in the written curriculum. Multiple choice questions can be designed as good "indicators" of student performance, but the old adage applies, "You get what you test." For example, the ability to iden-

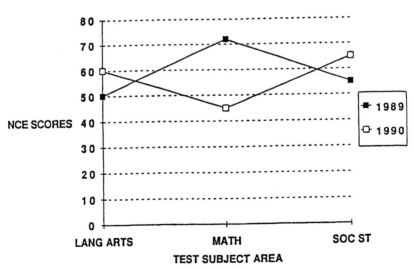

FIGURE 2 Trend analysis using standardized test scores tracing districtwide performance in three subjects over two years.

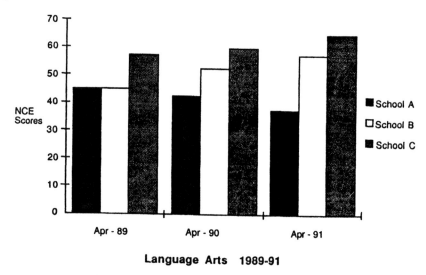

Language Arts 1989-91

FIGURE 3 Trend analysis by school in one subject over three years.

tify correctly pictures of lab equipment can be highly correlated to competence in a science lab. However, when pressure to score well on the standardized tests causes science teachers to spend valuable classroom time drilling students on identifying lab equipment from a series of pictures, the purposes of the district's program have been subverted.

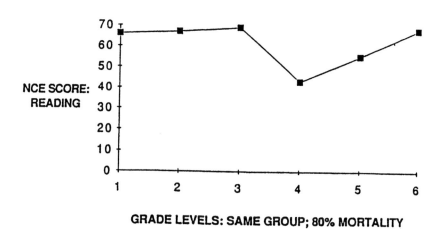

GRADE LEVELS: SAME GROUP; 80% MORTALITY

FIGURE 4 Trend analysis tracing the performance of one group of students over a six-year period.

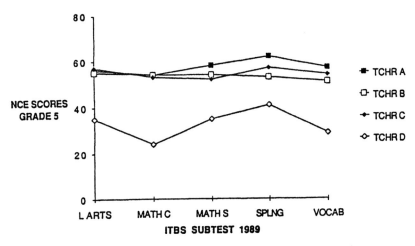

FIGURE 5 Analysis be subtest by teacher at the school level.

Performance-Based Assessment

Performance-based assessment tools should be designed in a manner that allows teachers to accomplish the district's mission by teaching to the test. As Resnick and Resnick (1989) explain:

> Assessments must be designed so that when teachers do the natural thing—that is prepare their students to perform well—they will exercise the kinds of abilities and develop the kinds of skills and knowledge that are the real goals of educational reform. This principal assumes that what is in the assessment is going to be practiced in the classroom in a form close to the assessment form. It directs us to pose for any proposed assessment exercise one central question: "Is this what we want students to be doing with their educational time?" (p. 37)

The simplest type of performance assessment for higher order cognitive skills commonly used in the schools is the essay exam. Performance criteria or rubrics can be applied by trained readers to produce "objective" appraisals of student performance. These scores can be gathered and processed to provide important feedback to teachers and administrators in much the same way standardized test scores are presented. They also provide valuable goals for teachers and establish important performance standards for students. These essays are often graded by two scorers, with a third being brought in to achieve consensus on one or more rubrics when necessary.

A variation to this approach is the use of portfolios. Scorers examine several student products in a portfolio to arrive at a consensus concerning the student's performance. These same processes can be used to judge "live" student performance in much the same manner that the ringside judges score a boxing match or diving judges score a dive using multiple criteria.

Managing a Performance-Based District Assessment Program

Managing a performance-based district assessment program need not be an overwhelming administrative task, providing all of the in-' structional staff are actively involved in assessment scoring and data gathering. The job of the administration is to coordinate the gathering of data in a manner that produces useable feedback to teachers, building administrators, district-level program directors, and policymakers. To provide uniform districtwide data acceptable to the public for accountability purposes, a representative sample of each grade level's work can be assessed on a matrix sampling basis and graded by impartial scorers to produce statistically valid grade level, program, school, and/or district results—both formative and summative. The use of videotape technology can further enhance this process. The data gathered in these processes can be plotted by the curriculum management auditor to produce trend analyses comparable to those in Figures 2–5, which used standard test scores.

USING OTHER STUDENT TEST DATA

A comprehensive testing program also gathers data from outside agencies administering certification or placement tests such as the Scholastic Aptitude Test (SAT), the American College Test, Advanced Placement exams, and the International Baccalaureate exams. These data are not truly reflective of the whole district because the test takers are volunteers. Nevertheless, they provide information about students, which helps with trend analysis. For example, SAT scores can be analyzed in terms of the number of students who take the test, the number scoring above the national average, the number scoring in the top quartile, etc. Over a period of years these data can be linked to other programmatic and demographic events to judge the comparative strengths, weaknesses, and growth of various programs. Figure 6 shows which tests are given by grade level of one district's testing program.

	K	1	2	3	4	5	6	7	8	9	10	11	12
Pre-Kindergarten Observation Checklist	X												
Metropolitan Readiness Tests	X												
Metropolitan Achievement Test Sixth Edition Writing Test				X			X						
Ohio Vocational Interest Survey									X				
Comprehensive Test of Basic Skills (CTBS)				X			X	X	X	X	X		
Life Skills Seminar Test										X			
Competency Based Assessment		X	X	X	X	X	X						
End of Course Examinations								X	X	X	X	X	X
CTBS - Chapter I Schools			X		X	X		X					
Advanced Placement												X	X
Scholarship Aptitude Test											X	X	X
Preliminary Scholastic Aptitude Test										X	X		

FIGURE 6 Matrix of tests administered in the District of Columbia public schools (1991).

The scope of a district's testing program can be analyzed (see Figure 7) by developing a matrix of formal tests administered by discipline area. To determine the percent of scope, the total number of possible areas in which the curriculum could be formally assessed is divided by the number of areas actually assessed. The result is a simple perspective of the scope of districtwide curriculum testing.

Statewide Testing Programs

Statewide student testing programs are usually a prominent part of the district's feedback loop simply because of the widespread publicity received when scores are released each year. Figure 8 is an example of the sort of data typically given to the press.

Like the publisher-produced standardized achievement tests, these state test scores are not usually an accurate reflection of the district's intended curriculum. Moreover, because of the publicity combined with America's traditional faith in the ability of tests to reflect educational progress, these programs, over the past twenty years, have resulted in many of the unsavory side effects of standardized testing in the classrooms of more than thirty states.

Matrix of Formal Tests Administered, Grades K-12 by Discipline Areas as of 1992-93, Wichita Public Schools													
Discipline	Grade												
	K	1	2	3	4	5	6	7	8	9	10	11	12
Art													
Business	•	•	•	•	•	•	•	•	•				
Computer Studies													
Consortium	•	•	•	•	•	•							
English as a Second Language													
English/Language Arts		X	X	X	X	X	X	X	X	X			
Foreign Language		•	•	•	•	•	•	•					
Health								•	•	•	•		
Home Economics	•	•	•	•	•	•							
Industrial Arts	•	•	•	•	•	•							
Mathematics			X	X	X	X	X	X	X	X			
Music													
Physical Education													
Science													
Social Studies													
Technology Education													
Vocational Education	•	•	•	•	•	•	•	•	•				

Key: X = Area is formally tested in some way
        • = Area is not formally addressed in the curriculum at this level.

FIGURE 7 Matrix of tests administered by discipline areas.

In many instances, districts have aligned their curricula to state tested objectives typically stated in terms of multiple choice test technology (School Research and Service, 1991). Despite the plethora of research and scholarly advice warning of its shortcomings, the nation appears determined to take the statewide testing idea one more step and establish a national educational testing program. The success of this endeavor will, of course, depend upon who develops it, how it is developed, and how it is used in the local district. Information concerning the progress of schools is important at all levels of policy-making, but for obvious reasons, the greatest potential for impact on instructional improvement is at the local level. To be effective, nationwide or statewide test data must be embraced by the local district as an integral part of its assessment program.

Why Some Testing Programs Fail

In many districts, sophisticated student testing constitutes the foundation of successful systemwide assessment programs which are ac-

This report is based on 3,900 seniors.

Quality Indicator Performance Levels	1989-90 Percent	Target Met[1]	1-Year Growth[2] from 1988-89	Growth[2] from Base[3] 1987-88	1989-90 Relative Rank[4]
CAP Achievement					
Reading - commendable & above	27		-1	1	65
Reading - adequate & above	71	•	1	3	76
Mathematics - commendable & above	36	•	0	5	84
Mathematics - adequate & above	76	•	0	4	79
Direct Writing - commendable & above	24	•	1	1	78
Direct Writing - adequate & above	57	•	1	1	80
Curriculum					
Geometry completion	53.7		-1.7	-0.6	47
Four or more years of English	79.5		2.3	4.2	61
a-f course enrollments	38.4		1.3	-1.4	26
Dropout Complement (100 minus % dropping out)					
Three-year derived rate[5]	94.9	•	6.3	10.1	81
College Bound					
a-f course completions	23.7		1.3	3.4	40
Four-year college attendance	13.2		1.3	-1.0	38
SAT verbal - at least 450	15.9		-0.2[b]	-0.4[c]	67
SAT mathematics - at least 500	16.8		-0.1[b]	-0.3[c]	62
Advanced placement - 3 or better	11.2		-0.2[b]	-0.2[c]	67
Average Performance Value	51.3	•	1.8	3.3	78

Summary	1990 Average Performance Value	Target Met[1]	Percent Change from 1988-89	Percent Change from Base	Relative Rank
District values	51.3	•	3.6	6.9	78
State values	48.9		1.9	3.4	N/A

Percent change is the increase in the pool of students who met performance levels.

FIGURE 8 California Department of Education. District Performance Report Summary, 1989–90.

cepted and supported by the instructional staff, as well as the administrators and policymakers. In other districts, student testing programs have failed and are looked upon with suspicion by classroom teachers. The reason for this phenomenon is associated with an often misunderstood and misused concept of accountability understood as "blame." Accountability in a school setting too frequently focuses on standardized test scores. Consequently, teachers view standardized testing with anxiety and resentment, because the results threaten to judge their efforts incorrectly. In truth, some school administrators do look at testing as another means of teacher supervision or surveillance, but this tends to minimize the value of the feedback to teachers. As the advocates of total quality management point out (Gabor, 1991), surveillance is not effective in the long run. Rather, employees must take responsibility for quality. The attitudes and perceptions of teachers about the part they play in decisions concerning district curriculum and testing, as well as their perceptions of relations between themselves and the administration, have profound implications for the success of state and national educational reform (Glatthorn, 1987).

The emerging literature on organizational effectiveness suggests that student assessment programs be based at the local level with the full involvement of teachers (Duke, 1987). A study of the statewide student assessment program in Texas concluded with these powerful recommendations (Lutz and Middrala, 1987):

(1) Eliminate the practice of publicly reporting the ranking of school districts by test scores.

(2) Involve teachers in considering ways to improve the tests for all students.

(3) Use the test scores primarily as a means to improve teaching/learning.

Developing a District Curriculum Testing Model

Clearly, the success of district testing programs, whether or not they are aligned with statewide or nationwide tests, depends upon enthusiastic acceptance and eager commitment by teachers and parents. The best time to forge these links is during the curriculum development and review process. In other words, savvy districts put assessment at the core of their teacher-driven curriculum development process.

Four guiding principles have emerged from districts successfully using this approach:

Principle 1: Reinvention of the Wheel

Another way of saying this is that the districts start at the beginning and don't make assumptions. They begin by involving all teachers at every grade level to decide what should and should not be taught at each level. They establish a system of larger subject area councils for studying articulation and alignment. Once drafts of revised curriculum are created, they are fed back to teachers for grade level review and discussion. The goal is to give every teacher in the school system a stake in the finished product and its success.

Reinventing the wheel is also effective when developing the testing processes and instruments—for all the same reasons. If teachers don't have faith in the tests, they won't consider them valid measures of student performance, and if that happens, the program will lose its impact and won't serve as the catalyst for reform. To create this sense of ownership in the tests, many successful districts have created cadres of talented teachers to help develop the tests. The selected teachers— who are recognized staff leaders representing every school—then are trained in test development.

It is also essential that test construction training be of the highest quality possible. For most school systems, it makes sense to hire expert consultants to provide the inservice training, oversee the test construction process, and validate the test instruments. Often, these experts also provide invaluable assistance in the development of computerized data reporting systems. Since the testing program is only one part of a larger curriculum management system and since the reporting function plays a crucial role in connecting test data to other organizational functions, it is important that districts develop this reporting system at the same time the testing program is constructed.

Principle 2: Prohibition of the Use of Program Evaluation Data for Individual Teacher Evaluation

Experience has shown that when student competency tests or program assessment tests are viewed as a teacher evaluation tool, they lose the all-important staff acceptance and support. The program is likely to fall victim to sabotage by frightened teachers who will teach to the test—or worse, who will limit the number of skills they teach to a targeted few, resulting in restricted learning. If this happens, the value of the testing program is significantly lessened or even nullified. Because of the many variables involved in testing (student's varying backgrounds and abilities, for example), the test data are extremely questionable as measures of teacher competency. Districts with successful testing programs realize that it doesn't make sense to junk a superior, effective, fully operational quality control system just to produce another small piece of questionable evidence in a dismissal case.

Neither does it make sense to evaluate principals using these criteria. To do so could tempt principals, as well as teachers, to subvert the system. For these same reasons, systemwide progess is emphasized. Comparisons are made by grade levels or demographic groups, not by school or classroom.

Principle 3. Involvement of a Cross Section of Parents and Community Members in the Curriculum Review Process

Parents and other community members play an essential part in developing and supporting a successful district testing program. Several strategies employed by districts to enhance a comprehensive community review process include the following:

- personal invitations to representatives of many segments of the community to meet with the teachers involved in the design of the curriculum and the construction of the tests
- careful records of all comments from community members, taking special care to list and define their concerns, fears, aspirations, and hopes
- time devoted to educate the community representatives about the purposes of the curriculum revision and quality control testing program and how it will work
- instructions to the subject area curriculum committees to listen to community views carefully and revise the curricula as warranted
- procedures to inform participants about the results of their contributions

Principle 4: Full Management Support

The final ingredient is support and leadership from the school system's principals. The reason for this is simple. In order for a testing program to be effective, principals must use the data as integral elements in their instructional supervision. Again, this does *not* mean using the results to evaluate teachers. Principals use the test data for school planning, and the school's faculty is encouraged to establish yearly goals that relate to the test data. The central office coordinates with principals to integrate emerging staff development needs into the district's inservice training program. In short, the district's testing program is a foundation for the district's assessment program, which, in turn, is at the center of the total instructional support system.

New Test Criteria

As Herman (1992) points out in her introduction to a synthesis of research, "Educational assessment is in the process of invention" (p. 74). The traditional testing practices are being seriously challenged, and new assessment techniques are being developed. The good news is that these more authentic measures of student capabilities tend to support classroom strategies. In California, for example, studies indicated that the eighth grade writing assessment program encouraged teachers to require more writing from students and to give them a wider variety of writing experiences (Herman, 1992).

The new age of testing has prompted Linn et al. (1991) to suggest new criteria for validation of testing instruments and strategies. In addition to the traditional tests of reliability and content validity, these criteria include the following:

(1) *Consequences:* The validity of assessment results can be significantly impacted by the way the results are used, including the consequences of their use.

(2) *Fairness:* Cultural background and the opportunity to learn can penalize minority and economically disadvantaged students.

(3) *Transfer and Generalized Ability:* Authentic performance-based assessment naturally raises questions about the reliability of the scorers.

(4) *Cognitive Complexity:* The new testing technologies focus on higher order thinking skills.

(5) *Content Quality:* Assessment activities can be devised that are stimulating to students being tested and that promote student interest growth.

(6) *Content Coverage:* An assessment program should closely match the written and taught curriculum. Like content quality, the con-

tent coverage criterion is a judge of the entire assessment program.

(7) *Meaningfulness:* The test activities must have meaning and should motivate the student to perform well.

(8) *Cost/Efficiency:* Tests must be affordable. One great appeal of the multiple choice test was low cost. The new tests must compete.

Surveys and Follow-up Studies

A comprehensive school district assessment program typically employs several other general types of measures to augment student assessment data. Some of these techniques employ self-reported impressions. Others involve instruments that purport to measure attitudes and values. In concert with student assessment data, these instruments can provide information that will give district staff and leadership a more distinct picture of how well the district's mission is being accomplished.

The most popular technique for evaluating programs in education is the written survey. Since surveys are usually not expensive to construct or administer, they are a cost-effective means of collecting feedback. Guidelines for writing survey questions can be found in any good textbook on research methodology.

Student Surveys

Surveys of students involved in various school programs can provide valuable feedback. Ratings made by students may be very reliable if they focus on relatively objective perceptions. Usually, the conditions for administration of the survey can be controlled, and the return should be high. Some school districts routinely survey all of the graduating senior class during the latter part of the year. The survey, typically, is revised annually by principals and program heads and focuses on the most immediate concerns of the staff. Figure 9 is an example of a student survey.

In addition to student perceptions of program, the survey can also ask for information about student background, aspirations, needs, and other demographic data that can be correlated with other surveys and follow-up studies.

Total Surveyed: 1376   Total Completing Form A: 752
Not all responses will total 100%, since some questions were left blank or filled in incorrectly.

1. What grade are you in?

9th	10th	11th	12th
28%	29%	20%	21%

2. Sex

male	female
45%	54%

CLASSROOM INSTRUCTION

3. This semester, how much homework are you usually given each day?

less than 1 hour	1-2 hours	2-3 hours	more than 3 hours
17%.	33%	22%	9%

4. This semester, how much homework do you actually do each day?

less than 1 hours	1-2 hours	2-3 hours	more than 3 hours
35%	33%	15%	5%

5. This semester, the amount of work you have to do at school is

too much	too little	about right
24%	6%	68%

6. This semester, your school work is usually:

too hard	hard, but possible	fairly easy	too easy
7%	65%	26%	1%

Rate each course you are taking this semester

7. Art

excellent	good	fair	poor
31%	32%	25%	12%

8. Bilingual/ESL

excellent	good	fair	poor
32%	39%	21%	8%

9. Business

excellent	good	fair	poor
32%	41%	17%	11%

10. Computer

excellent	good	fair	poor
20%	38%	23%	19%

11. Drama

excellent	good	fair	poor
29%	39%	17%	15%

12. English

excellent	good	fair	poor
21%	45%	26%	9%

13. Foreign Language

excellent	good	fair	poor
29%	49%	16%	6%

14. History/Soc Science

excellent	good	fair	poor
32%	42%	16%	9%

FIGURE 9 Student survey total surveyed: 1376. Total completing Form A: 752. Not all responses will total 100%, since some questions were left blank or filled in incorrectly.

15. Home Economics	excellent	good	fair	poor
	28%	36%	21%	15%

16. Industrial Arts	excellent	good	fair	poor
	37%	32%	22%	9%

17. Mathematics	excellent	good	fair	poor
	26%	40%	23%	11%

18. Music	excellent	good	fair	poor
	60%	21%	13%	6%

19. Physical Ed.	excellent	good	fair	poor
	37%	37%	19%	7%

20. Science	excellent	good	fair	poor
	28%	45%	22%	6%

21. Special Ed.	excellent	good	fair	poor
	25%	34%	17%	23%

22. This semester, how many of your classes are usually well–behaved?

0–1	2	3	4	5 or more
6%	8%	19%	29%	34%

23. Do you think that the instructional materials used in your classes (textbooks, films, etc.) are

completely adequate	adequate	inadequate	no opinion
9%	51%	15%	22%

24. This semester, how many of your courses are interesting to you?

0–1	2	3	4	5 or more
12%	23%	28%	20%	15%

25. Do the number of required courses (those you must take) prevent you from taking courses in your major area of interest?

yes	no	no opinion
44%	33%	23%

26. This semester, do you think that you and your fellow students are treated with respect, even when being disciplined?

yes	no	no opinion
39%	31%	26%

27. This semester, how many of your teachers explained their grading system?

1	2	3	4	5 or more
9%	11%	18%	18%	42%

28. This semester, how many of your teachers usually return your papers corrected within two days?

0–1	2	3	4	5 or more
35%	25%	21%	10%	7%

29. This semester, when you put all of your classes together, how many essays or compositions are you are usually assigned each week?

none	1	2	3 or more
13%	34%	29%	20%

FIGURE 9 (continued) Student survey total surveyed: 1376. Total completing Form A: 752. Not all responses will total 100%, since some questions were left blank or filled in incorrectly.

30. When essays or compositions are returned, what do teachers usually write on your papers?

- 30%   usually, just the grade
- 20%   usually, just the grade plus grammar and spelling corrections
- 64%   usually, the grade, grammar and spelling corrections, plus comments about the content of your paper

31. Can you read well enough to do well in all your courses?

yes	no
87%	9%

Answer question 32 ONLY if you answered NO to question 31; otherwise leave it blank.

32. Rate how well the school is teaching you to read:

excellent	good	fair	poor
30%	35%	23%	12%

33. Can you write well enough to do well in all your courses?

yes	no
80%	11%

Answer question 34 ONLY if you answered NO to question 33; otherwise leave it blank.

34. Rate how well the school is teaching you to write:

excellent	good	fair	poor
31%	29%	29%	11%

35. Can you speak and listen well enough to do well in all your courses?

yes	no
80%	10%

Answer question 36 ONLY if you answered NO to question 35; otherwise leave it blank.

36. Rate how well the school is teaching you to speak and listen better:

excellent	good	fair	poor
21%	42%	21%	16%

37. Can you do arithmetic well enough to do well in all your courses?

yes	no
73%	15%

Answer question 38 ONLY if you answered NO to question 37; otherwise leave it blank.

38. Rate how well the school is teaching you arithmetic.

excellent	good	fair	poor
15%	33%	31%	21%

39. In how many classes do you feel challenged to do your best?

0–1	2	3	4	5 or more
15%	19%	25%	16%	14%

40. Give your school an overall rating:

excellent	good	fair	poor
15%	43%	19%	6%

FIGURE 9 (continued) Student survey total surveyed: 1376. Total completing Form A: 752. Not all responses will total 100%, since some questions were left blank or filled in incorrectly.

Graduate Follow-Up Studies

More expensive and less reliable is the information obtained through graduate follow-up studies. In addition to lower rates of return, surveys asking former students to give overall impressions of school experiences are not highly reliable (Posavac and Carey, 1989). On the other hand, if steps are taken to control the return, responses may be quite reliable and valuable when they focus on historical behavior and current data such as training completed, jobs held, wages earned, current problems, and future plans.

Parent/Community Survey

Parent and community surveys properly conducted can produce indispensable feedback to district staff. Like the graduate follow-up study, steps must be taken to account for a low rate of returned surveys. Experts in conducting surveys maintain that the responses of those who do not respond would be significantly different from those who returned surveys (Posavac and Carey, 1989). However, the results can be adjusted by follow-up interviews with a sample of nonrespondents. Again, it is wise to focus the questions on objective observations as much as possible. It is also important for the district to establish a system to feed back to the parents and community the results of the survey and the district's response to those results. That response should also be emphasized as a preface to the next parent/community survey. Figure 10 is an example of parent/community survey questions.

Teacher Motivation and School Climate Surveys

Teacher satisfaction surveys and various types of school climate measures are valuable for a number of reasons. Probably most important, they provide symbolic measures of the district's values. Creating a good place to work should be a major objective of any school district leadership. Staff satisfaction and school climate surveys help communicate to the staff the values and intentions of the district leadership. In return, the data produced help administrators and teachers create a workplace where teachers can succeed in accomplishing the mission of the district.

The culture of the school is the tone and the atmosphere that gives each school its unique character. The culture is made up of the shared values, ideas and beliefs of the school community, and is demonstrated through the activities that are conducted throughout the school.

1. The school is a safe, good place to learn, and a pleasant place in which to be.
   a. strongly agree   b. agree   c. disagree   d. strongly disagree   e. don't know
   Comments:

2. The discipline policy is known, fair, and consistently applied.
   a. strongly agree   b. agree   c. disagree   d. strongly disagree   e. don't know
   Comments:

3. The school staff deals effectively with cultural diversity and helps each student to feel welcomed and valued.
   a. strongly agree   b. agree   c. disagree   d. strongly disagree   e. don't know
   Comments:

4. The school staff involves the parents and community members in exploring solutions to problems and concerns facing students in today's world including peer pressure and substance abuse.
   a. strongly agree   b. agrpe   c. disagree   d. strongly disagree   e. don't know
   Comments:

Student Paths

During high school, each student takes a selected path through the courses offered. This path should take the student through a core of learning expected of all high school graduates, and should go beyond this core through courses and learning that enable the students to meet pre-selected goals and prepare for success in higher education and for the work place. With this in mind, please respond to the following:

5. Your student is encouraged to plan and follow a four-year path of courses that help to realize his or her highest potential and prepare for future pursuits.
   a. strongly agree   b. agree   c. disagree   d. strongly disagree   e. don't know
   Comments:

6. In addition to the core curriculum of English/Language arts, history/social science, science, mathematics, fine arts and foreign language, your student is guided to take courses that will prepare for entrance into college and -or employment in a chosen career.
   a. strongly agree   b. agree   c. disagree   d. strongly disagree   e. don't know
   Comments:

7. Your student is satisfied with the path of courses selected.
   a. strongly agree   b. agree   c. disagree   d. strongly disagree   e. don't know
   Comments:

8. Students and parents receive accurate, clear and timely advice from the school staff regarding choosing the right selections of courses.
   a. strongly agree   b. agree   c. disagree   d. strongly disagree   e. don't know
   Comments:

FIGURE 10 Parent/Community Questionnaire.

9. Your student can make adjustments in the courses taken according to his or her needs.
   a. strongly agree   b. agree   c. disagree   d. strongly disagree   e. don't know
   Comments:

10. Parents and school staff work together to help students select courses aimed toward their highest, most realistic goals.
    a. strongly agree   b. agree   c. disagree   d. strongly disagree   e. don't know
    Comments:

11. The goals for your student's education are shared and communicated to you effectively.
    a. strongly agree   b. agree   c. disagree   d. strongly disagree   e. don't know
    Comments:

12. The school provides an opportunity for your student to extend learning through participation in co-curricular activities (special interest groups, clubs, athletics) on a regular basis.
    a. strongly agree   b. agree   c. disagree   d. strongly disagree   e. don't know
    Comments:

13. The assignments your student receives are appropriate.
    a. strongly agree   b. agree   c. disagree   d. strongly disagree   e. don't know
    Comments:

Improvement Processes And Organization

The improvement process is made up of all the activities that involve the school community in a continuous improvement of the quality of the instructional program.

14. You have been offered ample opportunity to become involved in school improvement activities, including parent-teacher conferences and advisory meetings.
    a. strongly agree   b. agree   c. disagree   d. strongly disagree   e. don't know
    Comments:

15. The improvements in the quality of the instructional programs are preparing your student to lead a successful and productive life after high school.
    a. strongly agree   b. agree   c. disagree   d. strongly disagree   e. don't know
    Comments:

16. There is open communication between the school, staff, parents, and the community.
    a. strongly agree   b. agree   c. disagree   d. strongly disagree   e. don't know
    Comments:

Additional Comments:

FIGURE 10 (continued) Parent/Community Questionnaire.

DETERMINING MOTIVATION POTENTIAL OF THE SCHOOL: A CASE STUDY

Frase and Heck (1992) developed an approach to school district restructuring built around a model and survey designed to determine the motivation potential of a school. Restructuring these days has apple-pie appeal. It promises a great deal. But equally promising innovations such as new math and the open classroom came and went, leaving little or no substantive change. Few restructuring projects are accompanied by an evaluation component characterized by more than superficial analysis of current circumstances (Frase and Heck, 1992). The following paragraphs summarize a research-based approach to restructuring built around a feedback loop. Like the curriculum revision model described above, it began with widespread involvement of the staff creating a sense of ownership of the final plan.

The Steering Committee

In keeping with the belief that change must begin with those it will most affect, the steering committee was composed of a teacher and principal from each school, representatives from central office, instructional specialists, and a consultant.

Development of the Survey

The committee's fist task was the development of a staff survey to include topics shown by research to be key factors in the health of schools and other organizations. Just as good curriculum development is built with sound assessment in mind, the district's restructuring project was built upon a sound assessment program. After a thorough review of the literature, the committee decided to use a staff survey based on a modified version of Hackman and Oldham's Job Characteristics Model (Figure 11).

The Restructuring Process

The committee was adamant that this project not become a one-year, one-time effort that comes and goes without resulting in substantive change. The members also realized that the diagnostic and implementation phases must be repetitive to ensure this change. Therefore, the committee agreed to take the following action:

- Diagnose the schools.
- Analyze the data.
- Develop restructuring (intervention) strategies.
- Implement the restructuring strategies.
- Analyze the feedback.
- Revise the restructuring strategies.

Each step of the restructuring process is discussed below.

Conducting the First Diagnosis

In the early Fall of 1989, the committee members were trained in the administration of the survey instrument. The questionnaire, known as

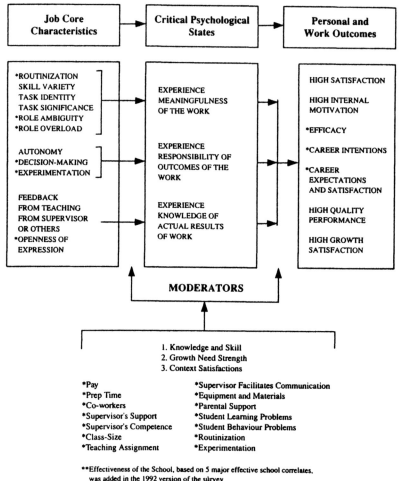

Job Core Characteristics	Critical Psychological States	Personal and Work Outcomes

Job Core Characteristics

*ROUTINIZATION
SKILL VARIETY
TASK IDENTITY
TASK SIGNIFICANCE
*ROLE AMBIGUITY
*ROLE OVERLOAD

AUTONOMY
*DECISION-MAKING
*EXPERIMENTATION

FEEDBACK
FROM TEACHING
FROM SUPERVISOR
OR OTHERS
*OPENNESS OF
EXPRESSION

Critical Psychological States

EXPERIENCE
MEANINGFULNESS
OF THE WORK

EXPERIENCE
RESPONSIBILITY OF
OUTCOMES OF THE
WORK

EXPERIENCE
KNOWLEDGE OF
ACTUAL RESULTS
OF WORK

Personal and Work Outcomes

HIGH SATISFACTION

HIGH INTERNAL
MOTIVATION

*EFFICACY

*CAREER INTENTIONS

*CAREER
EXPECTATIONS
AND SATISFACTION

HIGH QUALITY
PERFORMANCE

HIGH GROWTH
SATISFACTION

MODERATORS

1. Knowledge and Skill
2. Growth Need Strength
3. Context Satisfactions

*Pay
*Prep Time
*Co-workers
*Supervisor's Support
*Supervisor's Competence
*Class-Size
*Teaching Assignment

*Supervisor Facilitates Communication
*Equipment and Materials
*Parental Support
*Student Learning Problems
*Student Behaviour Problems
*Routinization
*Experimentation

**Effectiveness of the School, based on 5 major effective school correlates,
was added in the 1992 version of the survey
*Additions to the original Hackman and Oldham model

FIGURE 11 Modified Job Characteristics Model.

the Job Diagnostic Survey (JDS), was administered to all teachers and administrators in November. The resulting data were organized for each school and for the district. School scores were compared to norms. The district average and tests of significance were conducted to determine significant differences between schools and the district mean. Scores for each school were kept confidential and given to the school's committee representative.

Analyzing the First Diagnostic Data

The diagnostic data package for each school consisted of the school's score on each item shown in the Job Characteristics Model. Comparisons with the district average and averages for other school divisions were also compiled. Individual school teams used this information to determine their problem areas.

Developing Strategies for Restructuring

School teams utilized planning sheets to develop restructuring/intervention strategies for each problem area. The form required specification of objectives to be attained, persons responsible, activities, completion dates, and resources needed for each step in the intervention strategy.

Implementing the Strategies

Strategies were implemented in November of each year and conducted through the remainder of the year when the JDS was administered again to provide feedback on the strategies.

Analyzing the Feedback

A comparison of the results of the first and last administration demonstrated the effects of the intervention strategies.

Repeating and Revising the Cycle

The entire cycle described above has been repeated four times. This long-term approach offers the school district an opportunity to monitor and evaluate the process, try various intervention strategies, and modify or discard them based on their success. The latest study indicates the process improvement of the work environments and teacher satisfaction in the schools using this process (Matheson, Frase, Heck, 1994). It ensures the continued success of the intervention strategies. In short, it demonstrates the power of a carefully developed assessment program.

AUDITS, REVIEWS, AND OTHER DATA ASSESSMENT SYSTEMS

A comprehensive assessment system should formally include the results of internal and external audits and reviews of school district programs and operations. These include the traditional inspections experienced by all districts, such as federal and state compliance audits, accreditation studies and reports, state and intermediate agency quality reviews, and the annual audit of the district's finances, as well as internal program evaluations. Like the various surveys and follow-up studies described above, these audits and reviews contain valuable data to further clarify the district's effectiveness, efficiency, and viability. Figure 12 is an example of one district's program evaluation reports.

Program Evaluation Reports Prepared, 1989-1992 Wichita Public Schools	
Title of Report	**Date of Report**
All Day Kindergarten Evaluation Update	June 1989
Behavior Disorders with Dignity: Formative Evaluation	June 1989
Chapter 1 Evaluation Report	1988-1989
Parent Participation Program Evaluation Update	July 1989
Writing-to-Read Evaluation Update	June 1989
Bilingual/English-as-a-Second-Language Study	December 1990
Foreign Language Formative Evaluation	May 1990

FIGURE 12 Program evaluation reports.

In addition, districts occasionally contract with accounting firms, management consultants, or intermediate educational agencies to perform management studies. These reviews can be directed by the administration to probe areas of school district operations not readily scrutinized by student assessment programs, surveys, or the normal audits and reviews. These include reviews of operations such as personnel, payroll, purchasing, maintenance and operations, risk management, facilities development, and so on.

Finally, the customary student summary reports on dropouts, migration, promotion, retention, and attendance should all be included and analyzed as part of the district's total assessment program.

AUDIT CRITERIA FOR JUDGING THE QUALITY OF AN ASSESSMENT PROGRAM

The quality of a district's feedback loop is determined by how its data are used by the staff to improve instructional operations. When a curriculum management auditor from the AASA's National Center for Curriculum Auditing examines a school district's comprehensive assessment program, six criteria are used to judge its quality. These are as follows (English, 1988):

(1) The assessment program is keyed to a set of goals and objectives adopted by the board of trustees.

(2) Assessment program data are used extensively at the building level to engage in program review and modification.

(3) Assessment program results demonstrate consistent improvement over a longitudinal time period.

(4) Assessment data are used to terminate ineffective educational programs.

(5) The comprehensive assessment program produces data that are used as a base to establish needed programs.

(6) Assessment program results are publicly reported to the board of trustees and the community on a regular basis.

School district assessment programs that demonstrate these exemplary characteristics are usually the result of staff, parents, and community working together. School districts are organizations composed of human beings and the success of any component of a comprehensive assessment program depends upon enthusiastic acceptance and eager commitment by the staff and parents. Involving them in the design, implementation, review, and ongoing revision of the system is essential to its success. A school district's assessment program is as essential to its operations as our own eyes and ears are to us. In the final analysis, it provides input into the system necessary for the system's survival. The time and effort spent developing effective, fully operational feedback loops is eminently worthwhile. Deployed properly, they become the driving force for positive changes in a school system.

REFERENCES

Cook, T., L. Leviton, and W. Shadish. (1985) "Program Evaluation," In *Handbook of Social Psychology, 3rd ed.*,G. Lindzey and E. Aronson (ed.), New York: Random House.

Duke, D. (1987) *School Leadership and Instructional Improvement.* New York: Random House.

English, F. (1987) *Curriculum Management for Schools, Colleges, Business.* Springfield, Illinois: Charles C. Thomas, Publisher.

English, F. (1988) *Curriculum Auditing.* Lancaster, Pennsylvania: Technomic Publishing Co., Inc.

Frase, L. and G. Heck. (1992) "Restructuring in the Fort McMurray Catholic Schools: A Research-based Approach," *The Canadian School Executive,* 11(8):3.

Gabor, A. (1991) "Deming's Quality Manifesto," *Best of Business Quarterly,* 12(4):6–10.

Glatthorn, A. (1987) *Curriculum Leadership.* Glenville, Illinois: Scott, Foresman.

Herman, J. (1987) "What Research Tells Us about Good Assessment," *Educational Leadership,* 49(8):74.

Linn, R., E. Baker and S. Dunbar. (1991) "Complex Performance-based Assessment: Expectations and Validation Criteria," *Educational Researcher,* 20(5):15–21.

Lutz, F. and J. Middrala. (1987) *State Testing in Texas: The Teacher Response.* Commerce, Texas: East Texas State University.

Matheson, R. L. Frase and G. Heck. (1994) "Restructuring with Praxis," *The Canadian School Exercise,* 13(8):3–12.

Meadows, D. and L. Perelman. (1989) "Limits to Growth," In *Program Evaluation,* E. Posavak and R. Carey (eds.), Englewood Cliffs, New Jersey: Prentice Hall.

Posavac, E. and R. Carey. (1989) *Program Evaluation.* Englewood Cliffs, New Jersey: Prentice Hall.

Resnick, L. and D. Resnick. (1989) "Assessing the Thinking Curriculum: New Tools for Educational Reform," In *Future Assessments: Changing Views of Aptitude, Achievement, and Instruction,* B. Gifford and M. O'Connor (eds.), Boston: Kluwer Academic Publishers.

School Research and Service. (1991) *Proposal For a New Direction in Assessment.* Mission Viejo, California: School Research and Service.

Zammuto, R. (1982) *Assessing Organizational Effectiveness.* Albany, New York: SUNY Press.

CHAPTER 9

Standard Five: The Productivity Standard

SUE GREENE—*Assistant Superintendent, University Place School District, Tacoma, Washington*

INTRODUCTION

ACHIEVING results is the main focus of Standard Five of the curriculum management audit. This analysis highlights the relationship of results and costs and specific efforts to improve over time. But it also relates to the educational context of classrooms, materials provided, and the "hidden curriculum" of the school environment in general.

Productivity connotes a range of meanings for the practitioners of quality control, whether the context be a manufacturing or service industry. For educators, the use of the term *productivity* also typically evokes apprehension because of the traditional insistence that effective education cannot be measured. "It involves so many subjective, intangible factors," say those whose resistance is stirred.

However, one curriculum management audit premise is that results can be assessed and that there should be a relationship among goals and objectives, priorities, and costs. The results and costs are studied to determine whether improvement has occurred over time within the same financial parameters.

William K. Poston, Jr., a lead auditor and the trainer who developed the current auditor training for curriculum-driven budgeting, points out the assumptions of this type of budgeting in a way that underlines the application of *productivity* to the educational organization in a curriculum management audit.

(1) Outcomes of curriculum programming can be defined.

(2) Levels of achievement may be measured.

(3) Knowledge of results can be translated into program needs.

(4) Needs and program priorities change over time.

(5) Program needs can be expressed as budget requests.

(6) Budget requests generally exceed available financial resources.

213

(7) Assessment data may be used to establish priorities (Poston, 1990).

Assessment data used in the audit typically refers to test data. The audit approach to productivity, however, does not ignore current authentic assessment strategies in its treatment of assessment data. Rather, the organization itself is expected to determine its goals, objectives, priorities, and assessment criteria. Those decisions then drive the analysis of results and costs and their relationship over time to the organizational goals and plans.

The criteria for Standard Five also recognize that neither the school board, superintendent, principals, nor teachers completely control all of the critical variables to improve pupil performance. But the system is expected to take identifiable, rational steps toward improvement regardless of funding levels.

Auditors look at a cycle of results, costs, and improvement in the Standard Five analysis. They observe linkages among goals, direction, feedback data, interventions, allocations of human and financial resources, decision making, and results over several years. Fenwick English (1988) noted appropriately in his curriculum management auditing textbook, "It is important that [Standard Five] is the last standard, too. It makes little sense to talk about costs or reducing costs until one knows if the required results are being obtained (effectiveness)."

STANDARD FIVE CRITERIA

Standard Five, called the *productivity* standard, is met when a school district demonstrates:

- planned and actual congruence among curriculum objectives, results, and financial costs
- specific means that have been selected or modified and implemented to attain better results in the schools over a specific time period
- a planned series of interventions that have raised pupil performance levels over time and maintained those levels within the same cost parameters as in the past
- a financial network that is able to track costs to results, provide sufficient fiduciary control, and is used as a viable data base in making policy and operational decisions

- school facilities that are well-kept, sufficient, safe, and orderly, that comply with all requirements, and facilitate delivery of the instructional program

Planned and Actual Congruence between Curriculum and Costs

To look for planned and actual congruence between the curriculum and costs, auditors focus on the budget document and its planning process. They seek evidence that major policy and priority decisions have been addressed and that curriculum goals and objectives are in place prior to the development of the budget. This curriculum-driven budgeting process insists that these decisions then be reflected in a programmatic budget format for ultimate demonstration of the linkage of goals, costs, priorities, and evaluation/results.

In addition to a budget format that reflects the connection among goals, priorities, and dollars, the process must ensure that a particular sequence of decisions occurs and that representative participants and stakeholders in the system are involved in those decisions. Finding the balance between effective involvement and system accountability and cohesiveness is not always easy. The more tight and systemwide the district's assessment measures, for example, the greater is the need for centralized budget decisions. But that centralized system must still ensure meaningful participation by the front-line educators at the building level.

Three ingredients of participation are expected:

(1) Dialogue focused on needs, goals, and priorities

(2) Propositions that link interventions to program criteria and identified problems

(3) Resource plans that guide and support implementation of improvement strategies

These involvement factors let the curriculum (goals and priorities) drive the budget. Otherwise, the financial plan and student services are driven by predetermined funding allocations directed from a data vacuum.

Specific Means to Attain Better Results

Schools intent on improving student achievement and attaining other goals customarily take ongoing and varied steps to improve. Sometimes these steps are simply curriculum review and revision or textbook changes; others are more complex, data-based efforts.

Changing standards for hiring and placement of personnel, personnel evaluation programs and procedures, and promotion or advancement of personnel are also indicators of productivity improvement efforts. Auditors usually see these specific means referred to in board minutes, often associated with follow-up to testing data presentation or organizational reports or audits.

A systematic approach to selection of improvement strategies shows up in budget proposal narrative, especially if the school district has a more programmatic type of budget format. In that instance, auditors see the identification of changes in a program with indicators of the evaluation standards to be applied to implementation of the change.

A Planned Series of Interventions to Raise Pupil Performance

When the efforts to attain better results respond to specific performance feedback, a district may demonstrate a planned intervention strategy. For example, intervention might be indicated by a restructuring of the instructional staff to address content areas shown by test results to need particular focus or by an adoption of different instructional materials to improve alignment of the curriculum.

Another example of planned intervention comes from a district seeking improved alignment of its curriculum with the state curriculum and state assessment instruments. The staff developed a four-step strategy. First, they found an external consultant to assess the existing alignment and report to them. The following semester they selected a company to assist in creating the needed alignment changes by use of an extensive data base of objectives and test items. The first area selected was math because the student performance on the state test had historically been less satisfactory in that area. Then teacher teams of four were created to work about twenty hours with the district curriculum coordinator on the project and serve as assistants in inservice training on the new curriculum objectives. A specific step for monitoring progress and adjusting procedures was built in before the next budget year so that the math project could become a model for the subsequent work on science and language arts.

Commonly, a specific intervention program might be developed to address a specific student population need. A school system in North Carolina developed an alternative 7th and 8th grade program when they discovered that teen pregnancies were increasing steadily in the 9th grade year.

Staffing of intervention strategies is only one way auditors see the linkage of priorities to results. Provision for staff development and training in areas of critical need is another.

A Financial Network to Track Costs to Results, Provide Fiduciary Control, and Create a Data Base for Policy and Operational Decisions

Any organization intent on being productive and achieving goals must have a system that is capable of creating linkage between expenditures and results attained from the services and/or commodities purchased. As they review procedures and forms related to the financial and budgetary system of a school district, curriculum management auditors look for inclusion of information about the intended results. They seek information on data on which the goals have been based, details of the planned use of resources being allocated, and clear performance indicators of the results sought. It should be evident how the system will be able to assess its progress during the budget period and how it can base future decisions on the data used during both preparation and implementation of the budget.

A general review of the financial audits, procedural documents, and policies should reveal that the system has its financial management under control. They scan these areas of policy and operations with an eye for appropriate control systems, responses to audit findings, and congruence of practice with policies adopted by the board.

If the financial planning system is thorough and complete, it will provide the kinds of information that contribute to relevant and informed decision making. Policies will emerge in areas of appropriate needs rather than in reaction to problems. Operational decisions will have such information as cost-benefit analysis, research or experience data bases that fed into recommendations, and data on results over time and through several budget cycles.

The effectiveness of the budget and financial network system within a school district is a significant contributor to the district's ability to achieve both educational and operational productivity.

School Facilities that Enhance and Facilitate Delivery of the Program

School facilities provide the physical environment for delivery of the educational program. The basic requirements of space, safety and physical comfort must be met so that attention can be directed toward the primary jobs of teaching and learning. For those functions to be carried out most effectively, the kinds of rooms, physical equipment, and support services provided are important. When the facilities and support services are inadequate, it is not uncommon to see direct relationship between these problems and program effectiveness. Additionally, there are mandates which if not met may lead to financial penalties against a district and drain resources from the coffers, thus impacting the funds available for the educational program. Schools in which frequent temperature control problems exist impact teacher and student comfort and attention to teaching and learning quite directly. Buildings that are not used to capacity can impact resources by requiring additional administrative, clerical, and custodial staffing. When teachers must teach 30 to 35 students in classrooms originally designed for 24 to 26 students, the types of teaching strategies used will of necessity be limited due to the lack of options for furniture arrangements for particular instructional activities grouping.

This particular criterion does not require that a school be recently constructed to be supportive of the educational program. Rather, what auditors see often is an older school that is made effective by the creative thinking that underlies staffing, student and program placement, scheduling patterns, and similar tactics to create acceptable or even advantageous learning situations out of formerly disadvantageous or problematic settings. When the problems with facilities become so bad that it is no longer cost effective to avoid new construction, a comprehensive information base should be available that lays out the comparative costs in time and dollars of continued use versus new construction. The district owes accurate and full information to the public about its facility investments, even when the picture is a bit ugly. The effect on educational quality cannot be avoided in these analyses and reports. A district that avoids delivering bad news about facilities to the public may be one that is exacting an unfair price from the students directly. Auditors look at the full context of facilities from the operational efficiency to the program support available through appropriate, safe, and well-maintained schools.

DATA SOURCES FOR STANDARD FIVE ANALYSIS

Standard Five uses documents, interviews, and site visits as data sources in assessing the school district's productivity in accordance with the curriculum management audit standard.

Documents

The major documents for Standard Five review are the budget, budget development forms, related process documents, and annual external financial audits and management letters. Other sources useful to developing a comprehensive productivity assessment are accreditation and other external reports, strategic or long-range plans, and updating documents, assessment data, and policies. A useful step taken by auditors is the review of board meeting or work session minutes related to feedback data reports, program evaluations, or budget decision discussions.

The annual budget document is a primary data source in Standard Five assessment. An audit assumption says that a structured and logical relationship must exist between the curriculum and the budget. Reviewing all of the budget-related documents allows an auditor to trace the evolution of the annual financial plan and assess its connection with the curriculum and with districtwide, as well as school, needs and priorities. Auditors study evidence of the use of adopted goals, feedback data, and research sources in annual financial planning. Often, evidence is found in the memoranda and request/revision/ranking forms used in the budget development process. These often reflect a range of requests differentiated by levels of service and relationship of the funding levels to the program or system goals or priorities.

External financial audit reports are also valuable. Fiscal problems noted in the audits may reflect impediments to curriculum and instruction productivity if poor management of resources prevents appropriate priority allocations. Examples noted in some curriculum management audits are chronic over-expenditures of particular budget areas that impact resources available for curriculum priorities, noncompliance with legal or regulatory requirements that impact student achievement opportunities, and cost inefficiencies. Management letters accompanying the financial audit reports, likewise, may provide notes on system control or operational problems that impact productivity efforts.

Considering productivity requires a look at any data reporting *output* of the various district *inputs*. These may be such documents as test score summaries, student marks (grades) analyses, achievement progress reports, or the familiar "report cards" prepared by districts or other agencies. Auditors seek information about what the system's response to the feedback data was, how the response was translated into specific actions, and how the resources were redirected to support those actions. They then look for reports of results from those actions and reallocations. If improvement has been documented and it occurred within the same general parameters as previous operations, the productivity standard has been exemplified.

Interviews

Interview sources for Standard Five analysis usually include board members, the superintendent and business manager, other administrators, teachers, and, occasionally, representatives of the community. Interviews reveal the extent to which decision makers consciously use systematic, program-driven decision making to guide the district toward improved results and achievement. Questions asked by auditors in gathering Standard Five data vary among the interview sources, but the questions have three common threads:

(1) Linkage between curriculum goals and priorities and the budget
(2) Participation roles in the budget process
(3) The rationale and data bases for budget decisions

In the interviews, auditors readily determine the degree to which the school district has widespread ownership in the budget as a resource plan for implementing the educational program. If the decisions are closely held and minimally explained, the concept of the budget as a plan is lost entirely. Rather, the budget becomes a restrictive expenditure guide requiring the specific permission from a single, all-powerful source for resources to be applied to the program.

Site Visits

Productivity is assessed primarily through documents and interviews, but site visits offer several opportunities for data collection. Auditors observe visual evidence of attitudes and messages related to achievement and success, those consistent or inconsistent with espoused missions and goals. If districtwide long-range or strategic planning has occurred in the district, auditors usually see mission statements and goals posted throughout schools.

The audit team assesses the capability of the physical plant of a school system, including its equipment and auxiliary services, to support the educational enterprise as described in policy, plans, and the budget. The environmental factors are recognized in Standard Five as enhancements or impediments to productivity because they influence the ability of people within the system—professionals and "clients"—to realize progress toward goals and desired outcomes.

It is in Standard Five that auditors focus on "the hidden curriculum." The hidden curriculum refers to the messages that are unstated but are part of what a student learns during his or her presence in that school. For example, if all poster pictures of students portray white boys and girls, the student of a racial minority sees reinforcement of his/her differentness and may feel even more out of place. The student who sees a banner announcing that "You are special!" but who uses a restroom with no stall doors for privacy will have a hard time believing the banner message.

Another example is the presence or absence of messages reinforcing a district's goal to improve student self-esteem. A school district with emphasis on multicultural education in the curriculum will typically have numerous visual demonstrations of that focus in the school buildings.

TYPICAL FINDINGS IN STANDARD FIVE ANALYSIS

Auditors find few school districts that meet all of the Standard Five criteria for productivity. They often find districts lacking in the budget criteria particularly, but succeeding in meeting facilities or other expectations. The criteria used to assess a district's budget document and the development process are reflected in Figure 1.

The most critical factor is the linkage of the district's programs (curriculum) and priorities to the budget. Achieving this linkage is inherently easier with a more programmatic budget format. The curriculum or program decisions should precede the budget decisions so that the budget becomes "how to get there" rather than "whether to go," as a curriculum management audit intern clarified the issue to himself.

Components of a curriculum-driven budget and the rating of the budget and process			
Criteria	Adequate	Partially Adequate	Inadequate
1. Tangible, demonstrable connections are evident between assessments of operational curriculum effectiveness and allocations of resource.			
2. Rank-ordering of program components is provided to permit flexibility in budget expansion, reduction, or stabilization based on changing or priorities.			
3. Cost benefits of components in curriculum programming are delineated in budget decision making.			
4. Each budget request or submittal is described so as to permit evaluation of consequences of funding in terms of performance or results.			
5. Budget requests compete with each other for funding based upon evaluation of criticality of need and relationship to achievement of curriculum effectiveness.			
6. Priorities in budget process set by participation of key educational staff in the decision-making process. Teacher and principal suggestions and ideas for budget priorities are incorporated into the decision-making process.			

FIGURE 1.

While districts vary in how they label programs, the other procedures are relatively similar if the criteria are being met. For example, in a district meeting the Standard Five budget criteria, a systematic procedure would be in place to allow the proposals at various funding levels to compete openly in a ranking process that involves several stakeholder participants. The participation stages may vary from district to district for specific staff or stakeholders, but the outcome of shared decision making and linking of the budget to the programs will be evident and similar.

The following finding excerpted from an audit performed in 1992 is a typical budget-related finding.

Finding 5.1: The Budget Process and Document Impair the District's Productivity Progress

To address the adequacy and effectiveness of both the budget documents and procedures, the auditors reviewed policies, budget documents, reports, and memoranda presented.

The auditors found that the budgeting process does not force linkage with the organization's goals and objectives or with articulated annual priorities determined by various assessment and feedback results. Documents used in budget requests identify changes and ask for rationales behind those recommendations. However, auditors found nothing in the procedure or forms to require consideration of goals and priorities. These deficiencies inhibit the ability of the school system to ensure that annual spending plans move educational operations increasingly toward desired results.

Auditors were told by most board members that they felt they knew what various programs cost and could decide appropriately where to approve funding. The auditors found that this confidence results more from the thoroughness of the budget briefings in the annual budget workshops than from information provided in the traditional line-item budget document. They found that without preparers' interpreting the line item budget, a public reader cannot ascertain any linkage among goals, objectives, and priorities and expenditures. The documents do not set forth goals and tie resources, timelines, measurement standards to those goals/priorities.

No public or executive summary of the budget was presented to auditors, and no other document provided the necessary links among annual goals and priority statements and the proposed expenditures.

Auditors found that the budget development process involves primarily the central office administrators. Discrepancies among schools were evident in interviews as to who participates in the budget development process and how that participation is implemented. Central office staff indicated that the budget begins in the schools with the principals and their staffs.

However, many teachers indicated that they had never been given an opportunity to help develop requests at the building level; some principals indicated they submit the requests themselves. Further, no evidence surfaced in interviews that site-level staff are involved beyond the request stage unless the principal is invited to discuss an item with either the finance officer or another central administrator. It was reported to the auditors that the central administration team discusses and recommends decisions and that the superintendent and finance officer decide on the administration's budget for presentation to the Board.

Auditors found that little public participation occurs until the school system's budget request goes to the county commissioners, at which time advocates of various interests surface. Reportedly these voices are heard only at that stage, even though the commissioners do not legally exercise line-item decisions on the budget. Rather, they approve the level of county funding.

Findings related to facilities range from those districts in which the facilities are in severe disrepair to those in which the facilities clearly support the educational program and exceed usual standards of quality. Most typically, auditors find a mix of circumstances. For example, the following finding resulted in a district with a mix of very old schools and several recently constructed school facilities.

Finding 5.5: School Facilities and Equipment Are Generally Adequate to Serve the Educational Program

The auditors visited school facilities and reviewed facility plans and expenditures. The purpose of this part of the audit work is to address the climate and environment as indicators of the school system's ability to deliver the educational program effectively and to demonstrate productivity over time.

The auditors found that the facilities in the ["Example"] School System were generally very well maintained both on a daily custodial basis and in their ongoing preventive and operational maintenance. The schools have been upgraded and remodeled periodically to serve the educational programs better. Frugal use of outer buildings at some sites enabled the school district to meet expansion needs of the 1980's and other modification needs. Efficient use of school district maintenance staff and contractors has allowed these efforts to move forward even with limited funds.

However, the auditors found some disparities among schools in the amount and quality of space available for instructional use. These disparities are most noted between older and newer facilities. The differences are noted in classroom size, lighting, and space availability for resource instruction, physical education, music/arts programs, and computer labs. Among elementary schools, disparities were noted in playground areas. Parent groups' fundraising revenues have enhanced a few playgrounds while others await funding to improve or upgrade the equipment.

The auditors found that air conditioning is now present in all schools in response to a long standing concern recorded in numerous planning documents over the last decade.

Interventions and specific means chosen for improvement are not always identified in an audit. Many times the auditors find these to result from new funding and therefore not consistent with the Standard

Five requirement that improvements be undertaken within the same general parameters to be considered for *productivity*. The following 1992 finding is representative of audit results in many districts.

Finding 5.3: No Intervention Efforts to Improve Student Achievement Have Occurred Recently

Productivity is improved in a school system when it takes steps to intervene in response to identified needs. Usually the feedback to the district comes from student performance on tests, discipline and dropout data, follow-up studies on students served by the school district, or anecdotal messages to the school district from the community. Such responses do not necessarily require an increase in funding. More common is the reallocation of resources to address the identified need.

The auditors reviewed a variety of documents dating back to 1975, including a document dealing with the attitudes and opinions of the staff of the district regarding curriculum goals and the quality and performance of the educational program. They studied test data and looked for subsequent actions by the district in response to that data. No evidence was presented of any curricular or instructional interventions having been implemented in response to feedback. Neither did the audit team see information to suggest that changes had been undertaken to improve performance or program results based on recommendations from district committees, task forces, or staff. Because the budget is not programmatic, auditors saw no information reflected there to suggest intervention efforts having been planned and funded.

When asked about intervention efforts or programmatic changes adopted to improve student achievement, staff and board members offered no clear examples of such actions.

TYPICAL RECOMMENDATIONS FOR STANDARD FIVE FINDINGS

The recommendations for Standard Five commonly focus on the budget format and process, developing a systematic approach to consider interventions and specific improvement strategies and addressing facilities/equipment needs. Other recommendations have pointed to facilities' use practices, human resource management improvements in general, and support services. Occasionally, an audit team recommends action related to personnel evaluation if the improvement efforts are countered by ineffective or inefficient evaluation and supervision practices.

The following recommendation was given to a district in which the budget did not reflect curriculum priorities or programs and where there was minimal participation in the budget development process.

Recommendation 5: Adopt Program-Focused Budgeting and Budget Development Procedures

The auditors recommend that over the next three years the school district implement a programmatic budgeting format and process. Programmatic budgeting can offer an efficient way for the board and the superintendent to allocate resources with a cost-benefit system. This change should accompany strategic planning and other efforts to link goals, instructional activity, testing, and student outcomes with resources. It will also allow for clarity of communication about the district's goals and resource commitments.

The current budgeting system (see Finding 5.1) builds on previous budget and program allocations, with limited involvement and limited cost-benefit analysis. Participation in budget development should be expanded to increase feedback data, ideas for alternatives, and "ownership" of the budget process and outcomes. Because so many staffing and related decisions are currently locked into employee negotiated contracts, the district and its employee groups will need to redesign contract contents to maximize the options to prioritize both financial and human resource expenditures.

THE USE OF THE CAMERA IN STANDARD FIVE DATA

Facility visits offer auditors an opportunity to record some of the audit data by photograph. While other criteria of other standards invite photographic documentation for purposes of showing consistent school program features, visual instructional data, and classroom techniques in practice, Standard Five emphasis on facilities and the environmental support of the curriculum is greatly enhanced by photographs. It is appropriate to describe a hallway in which students must regularly dodge tubs catching water from leaking ceilings; showing that problem visually gives a stronger message. Portraying a photograph of two different gyms used by junior high school students demonstrates without words the inequity of physical education program space in those two schools. Likewise, commentary is hardly needed with a photograph of first graders sitting in a classroom with their coats on because of frequent heating malfunctions.

Photos 1–4 illustrate the types of camera documentation used by auditors during site visits. The first two photographs point out missing floor tiles, which create a potential safety problem, and trash barrels

PHOTO 1

PHOTO 2

PHOTO 3

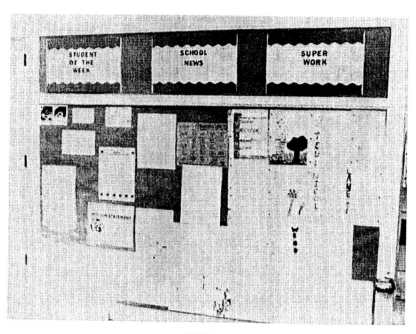

PHOTO 4

228

catching water from leaking ceilings, which had been in disrepair for some time. The auditors' captions relate the picture to the condition, the way in which the condition demonstrated a problem in creating a safe environment for learning, and any other factors that had surfaced in that audit that could be illustrated with those pictures. Photo 3 of a computer lab being used at less than fifty percent capacity was used to demonstrate a lack of planning for maximum use of instructional technology in which the district had invested. Photo 4 is the type of picture used to demonstrate messages about the school climate. The signs and displays on the bulletin board relate to student recognition with a student of the week posting and displays of student work. The school news section posts items of interest to students. The focus of visual displays are be discussed by the auditors in the text.

STANDARD FIVE SUMMARY

Productivity, in the context of Standard Five of the curriculum management audit, refers to the relationship between the costs (all resource "inputs") and the attainment of any determined level of "outputs," or results. Productivity occurs when the same or increased/improved results are achieved with the same or fewer costs over time. Standard Five analysis for the curriculum management audit unveils the organization's productivity in a comprehensive way.

REFERENCES

English, F. W. (1988) *Curriculum Auditing.* Lancaster, Pennsylvania: Technomic Publishing Co., Inc., pp. 132–133.
Poston, W. K., Jr. (1990) AASA Curriculum Audit Training. American Association of School Administrators. Standard Five training transparencies.

CHAPTER 10

Preparing the Board, the District, and the Community for the Curriculum Audit

CAROLYN J. DOWNEY—*San Diego State University*
VIRGINIA C. VERTIZ—*American Association of School Administrators' National Curriculum Audit Center*
LARRY E. FRASE—*San Diego State University*

INTRODUCTION

THIS chapter outlines recommended steps a superintendent might take to prepare the district for a Curriculum Management Audit. It is divided into four sections: before the audit, after deciding to have an audit, during the audit, and after the audit. It is not necessary to engage in all these steps; neither are they presented in lock-step order. However, the better prepared the school community, both inside and outside of the school system, the more open they will be to receiving the audit report.

LEARNING ABOUT THE AUDIT

Before conducting a Curriculum Management Audit, the superintendent of schools should learn as much as possible about what the process entails. Information about the service should also be disseminated to the community while the superintendent and board are thinking about whether or not to have an àudit.

Learn about the audit:

- Attend sessions on the audit at national conventions and conferences. The American Association of School Administrators (AASA) offers sessions on the Curriculum Management Audit each year at its annual convention. One session features superintendents of school districts who have had curriculum management audits conducted. The 1993 convention also included a session that featured the relationship between the curriculum management audit and quality principles.

231

- Attend Fen English's one-day preconference workshop at AASA's annual convention. Each year, Fen English conducts a one-day overview of the Curriculum Management Audit at the convention.
- Read *Curriculum Auditing* and *The Curriculum Management Audit: Improving School Quality. Curriculum Auditing* (English, 1988) is the first definitive text on curriculum auditing. This early text from Technomic Publishing Company presents essential background information, the audit model, standards for the audit process and the audit team, and real case studies. Direction is given for how to conduct site interviews, how to write the audit report, and how to use photographs to illustrate salient points. The book you are currently reading, *The Curriculum Management Audit: Improving School Quality* represents the most current thinking and practice on the curriculum management audit.
- Obtain a free information packet from AASA's National Curriculum Audit Center (NCAC). The address is 1801 North Moore Street, Arlington, Virginia 22209. The phone number is 703-875-0752.
- Talk to the director at AASA/NCAC for more information.
- Talk to other superintendents who have had audits done. AASA maintains an updated list of districts that have had audits conducted. Other superintendents are the best source of information about client satisfaction with the audit process and product. Anecdotal data are also available elsewhere in this book from those superintendents who had audits between 1981 and 1993.

BEFORE THE AUDIT

There are many ways in which the community can be prepared for the audit. A list of suggested activities follows:

- Discuss the audit with board members.
- Discuss the audit with administrative staff.
- Hold open meetings for staff and faculty to disseminate information and answer questions. *Indicate that the purpose of the audit is not to evaluate individuals or individual schools but to provide systemwide diagnostic information for improvement.*

- Include community groups in deliberations about whether or not to have a curriculum management audit done.
- Obtain at least one sample audit report from AASA/NCAC and circulate it among board members and administrative staff. Let others know it is available for perusal.
- Have the AASA/NCAC director or designee speak to your board or community group about the process.
- Prepare a press release. Focus on the courage of the superintendent and board to undergo such a rigorous review. A sample follows.

SAMPLE PRESS RELEASE

The _____ Public Schools announced today that they will contract with the American Association of School Administrators for a Curriculum Management Audit. The audit will be conducted on (Date) by a team of certified auditors.

The auditors will analyze district documents, visit all school sites [if over sixty, they will visit a representative sample of school sites] and interview key personnel, as well as anyone on the staff or in the community who wishes to be interviewed. Five standards guide the audit process and its assessment of a district's total curriculum system. They concern the school system's ability to:

- control resources, programs, and personnel
- establish clear and valid objectives for students
- demonstrate internal consistency and rational equity in program development and implementation
- use the results from district-designed or -adopted assessments to adjust, improve, or terminate ineffective practices or programs
- improve productivity

The end product will report problems and make recommendations to take the client district forward to the next level of excellence in student achievement and instructional success. The district will promptly pursue those audit recommendations consistent with current district direction and not requiring additional resources. Others will require long-range strategies and allocation of resources to implement successfully.

(continued)

The superintendent of schools _____ states, "[that reflects the reason for conducting the audit, acknowledging that some good things are happening in the district, and adding a statement about the desire to move the school district on a new path toward true educational reform]. The rigorous external review of the curriculum's total management system was seen as a means of doing just that."

A spokesperson from AASA said, "Only committed and courageous school districts subject themselves to the extensive scrutiny of a curriculum management audit. The _____ School District is distinguishing itself by joining those districts that are not afraid to take this bold step."

AFTER YOU HAVE DECIDED TO HAVE AN AUDIT

Once you have decided to conduct the audit, large scale communications are needed. These are some suggested activities:

- Encourage everyone to conduct business as usual when the team visits.
- Select a district liaison to work with the lead auditor in making preparations for the audit. Initial duties include gathering of materials (list included in the latter part of this chapter) and designating a private and secure work/meeting room for audit team and audit materials.
- Prepare the building principals for site visits. A sample memo follows.

SAMPLE MEMO TO PRINCIPALS
FROM SUPERINTENDENT

DATE: Audit Time, 1995
TO: Principals
FROM: Superintendent
SUBJECT: AASA Curriculum Management Audit

This memo is to advise you of the upcoming visit of the AASA curriculum management audit team. The team will be conducting

---

(continued)

formal interviews with all principals at a central location. In addition, two auditors will make a short visit to your school. These auditors may or may not be the same team who conduct the formal interview. Schedules for both interviews are attached.

One of the primary purposes of the site visit is to identify any facility problems you may have. One member of the team that visits your school will photograph both facility problems and activities that will help illustrate points that will be made in the audit.

Because of the short time available, please start the tour of the building and classrooms as soon as the auditors arrive. They will need to see as much of the total facility as possible. Please do not plan to offer them food or ask them to visit your office.

Visits to classrooms are very short; *auditors will not be evaluating teachers*. In most cases, the auditors would like you to enter the classroom first so that there is as little disruption as possible. The auditors want to see the normal routine of the school, so business should be conducted as usual.

Please remind all staff that they may make appointments to meet with the audit team if they choose. This should be entirely voluntary. To make an appointment, please ask them to call (name) at (phone number).

Thank you for your assistance.

- Develop a schedule for the site visit; a sample follows. Please note that the following guidelines are for a three-day audit; a shorter or longer visit by the audit team will require adjustments.

SCHEDULE GUIDELINES

A. General Overview (The following is a proposed schedule for a three-day audit. A longer audit will require extrapolating from this schedule).

Evening Dinner meeting or regular meeting with board and or
Before: central office administrators to explain audit (or breakfast meeting on Day 1). Note: Some superintendents invite media and union president, etc.

(continued)

Day 1: Interviews with: superintendent, assistant superintendents, business manager, directors/coordinators, principals, teachers' organization, executive board, parent organization groups (Teams A and B—opposite site-visit team) (All Teams)

Site Visits: Begin site visits of schools

Day 2: Interviews with: assistant principals, media (if desired), business/industry group, complete district staff interviews, department chairs, individual board members (schedule board president with Team A), walk-in opportunities for teachers, other employees, parents (Teams A and B)

Site Visits: Visit schools (Teams A and B)

Note: Evening meeting with superintendent. Meetings with the superintendent at the end of each day are recommended.

Day 3: Interviews with: any remaining individuals

Meeting: Exit conference with superintendent

Meeting: Meet with school board at the end of Day 2 or the beginning of Day 3 or noon to hear report on preliminary findings (if desired by the superintendent).

Note: Day 3 is over at 2:00 P.M.

Note: Breaks and drive time from site to site should be built into the schedule. Maps of school system and a list of names of drivers for Teams A and B to site visits should be prepared for and given to auditors.

B. Interview Guidelines (The following are general guidelines for five allocations for individuals or groups to be interviewed).

Person/Group	Time Allotment
1. Superintendent*	1-1/2 hours
2. Assistant superintendent/business manager*	30 minutes each

*These interviews should be scheduled prior to interviewing principals.

3. Directors/coordinators*	30 minutes each
4. Principals (individual)	30 minutes each
5. Assistant principals (group by school level group)	45 minutes
6. Teacher organizations' executive board (group)	1 hour
7. Individual board members (should be scheduled on Day 2 and 3)	45 minutes
8. Teachers, employees, other groups (send letter from superintendent one week prior to audit informing teachers that they may set up twenty-minute appointments to talk with audit team), individual interviews (set up late afternoon)	30 minutes
9. Department chairpersons (as group or as individuals)	1 hour
10. Parent advisory group	1 hour
11. Newspaper representatives (as group)	30 minutes
12. Business/industry group	45 minutes

- Schedule time for everyone listed to be seen. Include all groups represented by stakeholders.
- Prepare a press release (see sample).
- Schedule drop-in time for community members, parents, teachers, press, and anyone who wishes to speak with the audit team. Ensure that notice has gone to all employees and community members.
- Communicate with individual schools about what they should expect at the time of the audit team's visit (see sample letter).
- Gather the documents listed at the end of this article. The lead auditor will indicate when and where to send some of these documents.

DURING THE AUDIT

These activities that may take place during the audit which will enhance the gathering of data by the audits and preparation of staff.

Logistics and Facilities

During the audit the site-liaison's responsibility is to ensure the following:

- The schedule is followed.
- The audit team's requests for materials are fulfilled.
- Materials requested are logged.
- There is convenient access to a copy machine.
- Drivers are identified for site-visits.
- Refreshments (coffee/soda/fruit) are available to auditors.
- The designated audit team meeting room is available to the auditors and is secure.
- Arrangements are made for individual conferences with auditors.

AFTER THE SITE VISIT

After the on site work, it is crucial that the superintendent, based on the exit interview, begins to prepare the district to receive the report. Some suggestions are:

- Discuss with key individuals how the system plans to react to receipt of the report
- Discuss with relevant staff anticipated findings and recommendations and how to prepare the organization for change
- Use internal and external communication vehicles to thank people for their participation, outline expected timelines, and encourage receptivity to the report. Continue to gather your own data to support tentative findings so you can productively receive the report and provide personal examples.
- Receive the draft audit and review it with designees, if any, noting corrections of fact
- Begin to frame the superintendent's response to the audit

UPON RECEIPT OF THE FINAL REPORT

When the district receives the final report, there are some immediate strategies to be undertaken.

- Prepare the superintendent's response to the audit
- Set up communications strategies (see next section) for open communication to everyone concerned, insuring that the board is the first to hear
- Arrange a formal presentation to the board at an open meeting
- Meet one-on-one with board members and appropriate staff members regarding their perceptions of how the organization can use the audit data
- Send a press release containing findings and recommendations and the system's response

AFTER THE AUDIT

- Identify the group that will be responsible for implementing the recommendations
- Create a means of monitoring progress on implementation
- Report periodically to the board and public current status of audit recommendation implementation

ONGOING PUBLIC RELATIONS AND COMMUNICATIONS STRATEGIES

Based on what the superintendents who have commissioned curriculum management audits report in Chapter 10 and the research findings reported in Chapter 11, public relations is one of the most important considerations a district has in regard to a curriculum management audit. Communication to the community and staff has been highlighted throughout this chapter. However, communication must be a well-planned, ongoing process. The following are ideas we have found useful for communicating with the many publics in a school district before, during, and after a curriculum management audit:

- Prepare press release at point of board consideration for conducting an audit, including purpose of audit and why the board would consider such—to help us continually improve.
- Have press at a presentation by a lead auditor to the board regarding the purpose of an audit, standards, and the audit process.
- Hold a press conference for newspapers and television media to

discuss the possibility of an audit—with a group of stakeholders present for interviewing—business person, teacher's union president, board president, parent leader, superintendent.

- Release notice of board action on approving the undertaking of an audit—using all types of communication devices both internal and external.
- Prepare and disseminate brochure on purposes of the curriculum management audit, standards, and process prior to site visit.
- Put out an "all call" for anyone who wishes to make an appointment with the auditors while they are on site—television coverage is great for this, along with normal distribution vehicles.
- Set up for press to be interviewed by auditors as part of the data-gathering activities so that these individuals can experience the process.
- Hold a press conference during the site visit to explain the presence of the audit team and what their activities entail.
- Participate on a local news show about the purposes and process of the audit during the site visit.
- Have the press interview the lead auditor, while on site, regarding the audit process.
- Participate in a television news show to release some of the probable findings and recommendations you might be expecting (take from final draft sent to the superintendent) so it looks like staff are beginning to proceed even before the report comes.
- Make public the full report of the audit plus a synthesized version prepared by the school system for dissemination on the same day the report is made public.
- Hold several open forums to make the full report public along with the superintendent's recommendations.
- Disseminate report prepared to respond to the audit.
- Develop periodic updates highlighting changes in the system in relation to audit recommendations.
- Disseminate annual report on the changes in the system based on the curriculum management audit [list adapted from Downey (1992)].

SUMMARY

As with any organizational activity, planning for an audit, adhering to the plan, and following up is crucial to the success of a curriculum management audit. This chapter has provided the basic information for such planning.

List of Documents to Be Gathered Prior to Site Visit

(1)** All relevant board policies on curriculum, instruction, testing, budget development, pupil evaluation, grading, and courses

(2)   Any past external reviews/consultant reports regarding program or curriculum, including accreditation reports (for the past five years

(3)** All curriculum guides (send two to three samples—keep others at auditor work site)

(4)   All test data within the last five years and all public reports of that data

(5)   Two copies of the last two years' final budget documents

(6)   Any and all internal memoranda from administrative officers to principals and from principals to staff regarding curriculum, testing, evaluation, or program

(7)** Course descriptions for the secondary schools

(8)** Job descriptions of all major administrative officers and table of organization chart with names

(9)   Any surveys done of staff or community on program or curriculum

(10) Any follow-up studies of students completed in the last five years

(11)** A copy of the procedures to adopt textbooks

(12)** A copy of the current teachers' union/association contract

(13) A copy of any and all staff handbooks

(14) Any and all long-range plans for the district or school(s)

(15) Minutes of major district curriculum groups regarding program or curriculum issues

(16)** Copies of the independent CPA's audits within the last three years (please include the management letters as well)

(17)** A copy of any analysis of school facilities

**These items are to be sent to the lead auditor. All items, including those with asterisks, are to be sent to the work site.

(18)** Any document that presents a history of the school system from its inception to current times

(19)** Background data on system (e.g., history, size, number of schools, location in state, honors, business/school/community relationships)

(20) Statement for lead auditor on why you have undertaken the audit and what you hope to expect from the audit

(21)** Any and all documents regarding enrollment trends/analysis

(22) Any and all documents created by the staff or district that guide teaching/instruction/curriculum or program in any way

(23) Evaluation instruments and procedures for all instructional type staff (teachers, principals, assistant superintendents, superintendent, etc.)

(24) Salary schedules

(25)** Grade distribution reports for each school (by class)

(26)** Demographic data on students—ethnic, enrollments in schools by grade level, class size data

(27) Master schedules of actual enrollments by high school and junior high school

(28) Evaluation instruments and procedures for all groups impacting instruction, board, superintendent, district office administrators, principals, and teachers

(29) 15% Random sample of tenured teacher and 15% random sample of nontenured teachers' evaluation reports and professional improvement plans for the most recent complete two school years (Delete names from evaluations if desired. Organize distribution of ratings display for each group. Prepare summary of all board actions regarding dismissal of teachers and administrators.)

(30) Time allocations by discipline, by grade, if such

(31) Start and end times of schools, bell schedules, and bus schedules

(32) Homework policies and guidelines—district, school

(33) Workload schedule of art, physical education, and music teachers at the elementary level, library, counselors, nurses, and other support staff

(34) Administrator's contract

(35) Demographics of teachers by schools

(36)   Accreditation documents

(37)   Policies on retention, grouping, class placement, textbook selection, and access to courses

(38)   Staff development plan and evidence of program offerings, evaluation, and attendance

(39)** Demographic data, socioeconomic status, and ethnicity of each school

(40)   Special program opportunities, list of all programs, major objectives, and any effectiveness data

(41)   Discipline policy in the district/school and data on in-school suspension or off-campus suspension by school

(42)   Special grants for special schools, etc., and how they are determined

(43)   Guidelines for fund-raising activities

(44)   Examples of program innovation

(45)   Library book guidelines, A-V equipment, computers, and actual counts in schools

(46)   Copies of all board meeting agendas for the past eighteen months

REFERENCES

Downey, C. J. (1992) "Working with, Not Against, the Media in a Curriculum Audit," *Education*, 113(2):193–194.

English, F. W. (1988) *Curriculum Auditing*, Lancaster, Pennsylvania: Technomic Publishing Co., Inc.

PART III

THE CURRICULUM MANAGEMENT
AUDIT: RESEARCH EVIDENCE AND
SUPERINTENDENTS TESTIMONIALS

CHAPTER 11

Benefits of the Audit:
The Superintendents Speak

VIRGINIA C. VERTIZ—*American Association of School Administrators' National Curriculum Audit Center*

INTRODUCTION

SUPERINTENDENTS of school districts that have undergone Curriculum Audits by the American Association of School Administrators' (AASA) National Curriculum Audit Center (NCAC) are the best source of information regarding the process. Opinions from their unique perspectives are worthwhile sources of information for superintendents of school districts contemplating an audit, as well as AASA/NCAC, which is continuing to grow and develop.

This chapter comprises statements from superintendents whose districts were audited from January 1981 to February 1993. Of the seventy-one districts that have been audited as of this writing, twenty-three superintendents present testimony about twenty-six school districts. This group includes all superintendents who (1) returned completed 1992 surveys to the NCAC; (2) have written about the audit independently or for the NCAC; (3) who have had audits since the NCAC director has been in place; (4) have participated in panels at the last two annual AASA conventions; and (5) who responded to the request to be interviewed for this chapter. The two most recent districts audited—Wichita, Kansas and Fountain Hills, Arizona—have not yet received draft reports, so they were not asked to respond.

The majority of districts not included are those that were audited many years ago, those where there has been so much turnover in administration since the time of the audit that the institutional memory of the audit is lost, and those that were audited through the Kentucky State Department of Education. However, two of the latter, who returned surveys, were invited to respond. Superintendents were asked to give background information about their districts, the reasons for having an audit, what resulted from the process, and any advice they might have for other superintendents contemplating an audit. Except

247

where there has been more than one audit, appraisals are presented chronologically. For that reason, there will be a difference in perspective, in that those from the districts most recently audited will not yet have recommendations in place.

Most of the information is from telephone interviews conducted in late May and early June 1993, while some is from presentations made by superintendents at national conventions and/or from published articles. The author is indebted to those who have contributed.

The reader may be interested in specific school districts or superintendents or, rather, in a particular time period during the life of the curriculum management audit. For those interested, recurrent themes are summarized below.

One of the most prevalent themes throughout the interviews was the relationship between the curriculum management audit and strategic planning. Where the planning function had occurred beforehand, superintendents felt that the audit gave focus to planning efforts. There was some feeling that the audit should precede the planning function, creating a built-in action plan for change.

Recommendations were found to be concrete, on target, and presented in a way that they could be implemented by districts. Implementation of the recommendations helped districts restructure; renovate curriculum; align the written, taught, and tested curricula; and focus the district. Superintendents talked about change in staff development, policy, and other specifics, including board relations, the testing program, and textbook adoption.

Finally, many superintendents talked about the importance of having an outside, objective validation of many things they already knew were going on in the district. Having an objective report also afforded the opportunity to make changes that would otherwise take years. And while some superintendents have said that it is important to have a curriculum management audit in the early phases of the superintendency, others have said that, as long as the public and board are properly prepared, any time can be the right time.

THE SUPERINTENDENTS

Leonard Burns, Bellflower Unified School District, Bellflower, California

The Bellflower Unified School District was audited in January 1981. The school district had about 10,000 students, and enrollment was declining. The district was about 30% minority, which was a mixture of Hispanic, Black, and Asian students. Bellflower serves mostly blue collar families and is considered a low wealth school district, with one of the lowest per-pupil expenditures in California. This district originally had a lot of Dutch students, who moved into private schools and were replaced by minority students. Before the audit, student scores on the California Achievement Test were in the 30 percentile in the state.

Our district was in utter chaos after Proposition 13. The curriculum was set aside; no one was talking about education and expectations for learning. I used the audit to focus the district on its mission, curriculum and instruction, and student learning, which it did.

After the audit, we went over the 50th percentile on the California Achievement Test. The self-esteem of teachers went up; we created a model school district relative to what we were doing. We made other significant improvement: more students going to college or enrolling in college-type courses. Before the audit, we had only one algebra course with 30 students. Afterward, with the audit as catalyst we added ten algebra courses.

Leonard Burns, Parkway School District, Chesterfield, Missouri

The Parkway School District was audited in October 1985. At that time, the district had 23,000 students, 4,000 of whom were black and bussed in from the city of St. Louis under voluntary desegregation. Parkway served an upper middle class population, 98% of whom were white, not including those who were bussed in. The remaining 2% were made up of a few Hispanics and Asians. With the additional 4,000 black students from the city, the population became 18% black.

Parkway was a fine school district, but it had no systemic curriculum development process. For that reason, I requested a curriculum audit.

The audit targeted and focused us; we developed a long-range, multi-year plan for curriculum development and a new set of policies. We included all instructional programs in curriculum development. We had a lot of curriculum coordinators to do the work. The audit really helped us focus. We created alignment with testing and evaluation and our staff development program. The audit really helped us deal with the changing demographics I described.

The curriculum management audit is a tool you can use as a catalyst for change and reform and for improving student learning. Superintendents ought to consider using the curriculum management audit as a major restructuring/reform effort. I've been using it for years. I'm a strong supporter. I had external audits conducted in two school districts where I was superintendent, and I'm using it in a third district to build a pre-K–16 program in cooperation with the University of Southern Colorado.

Gary Livingston, Topeka Unified School District 501,* Topeka, Kansas

The Topeka Unified School District 501 was audited in 1981. The school district had 15,000 students, 30% minority and 45% on free and reduced price lunches. Major employers are the state government, Good Year, DuPont, the national office of Payless Shoe Stores, and two major hospitals. Student achievement was above the national average and slightly above the state average on the ACTs. Per-pupil expenditure for education was about average for the state. The school district is in a semi-urban, reasonably conservative district that is becoming more urbanized.

We decided to have an audit because we felt that we were not in control of the curriculum. I was accustomed to looking at individual student needs, having come from a special education background. I heard about the curriculum management audit and Fen English's approach to gaining control of the curriculum, since Peat, Marwick, Mitchell was doing our fiscal audits at the time. We wanted to do better, to be more accountable, to have more control. There wasn't a documented curriculum that anyone could identify, and there was a willingness to allow the textbooks and tests to be the curriculum. We were controlled by textbook companies and test makers. In other words, we had curriculum by default. We were frustrated; it was clear that something had to be done.

The audit gave us some real solid, practical recommendations — things we could implement and a sense we could get in control. The recommendations were so candid and concrete that we had some hope. We totally renovated the curriculum. We knew what teachers were teaching; we could give new teachers a curriculum document, and we could share our expectations. We began making better decisions about textbook adoptions and much better decisions about staff development expenditures. These were confirmed by the post audit.

We decided to have the post-audit because we felt comfortable that

---

*Topeka is the only district as of this writing to undergo a post audit.

we had responded to the audit's recommendations, but we wanted an objective snapshot of how we'd done in the last eight years. We wanted verification. We asked Fen to come back; no one had asked him to do that before. He verified some things and challenged us in some areas. To some extent, the audit had become more sophisticated. He took a closer look at the school district and identified the next level for the district to take. The recommendations were more outcome-based.

To a superintendent considering having a curriculum management audit, I would say that even if you think you've got control of your school district, it's an inside perspective. It is good to bring someone in to be objective. Even with the post-audit, we thought we knew what was going on; internal validity and external accountability are big issues. I think school boards are expecting superintendents to demonstrate that the curricular program has integrity. The audit helps establish confidence in the relationship between the board and superintendent. Explore the curriculum management audit and see if it fits. Ask yourself: Do you know what you should be teaching? Do you know what the teachers are teaching? Do you know what the kids are learning? If the answer is no, consider looking at the curriculum management audit.

John M. Whan, Montabella Community Schools, Edmore, Michigan

The Montabella Community School District was audited in June 1985. Montabella is a rural school district serving approximately 1,500 students. Located in mid-Michigan, the community is farm country, growing mostly potatoes. There is one major industrial plant, which is an important employer. Other members of the community work in Greenville and Lansing, each an hour away. The schools are less than 1% minority.

We decided to have an audit because we felt we needed to take a long look at what we were doing and where we were going. Before making long-range plans, we had to assess where we were. We had no middle management to do the work and for that reason felt we needed external help.

The curriculum management audit brought staff, administrators, and community together and helped bring focus to issues and needs. The audit was very successful in laying the groundwork to develop our first five-year plan to improve the curriculum and the learning experiences of students. It made district staff become more cognizant of the need for a balanced curriculum. The audit developed a mechanism for curriculum development. The next time we hired a principal, we hired one with curriculum background who served a dual role as an elementary principal and curriculum coordinator. He has been a real asset. Now we have a curriculum council, made up of cluster coordinators, who are teachers paid an extra stipend and given release time. The cluster coordinators worked with curriculum groups to develop K–12 curriculum, which has greatly improved alignment. After the audit, a team of eight or nine attended a curriculum workshop conducted by Fen English at AASA. The audit has helped staff have more input into the decision-making process. I saw some people really grow professionally as a result of this participation. They learned a lot and gained appreciation for what administration is like. We have increased our budget for professional development, as well as curriculum development.

Robert Henley, Independence School District 30, Independence, Missouri

Independence, Missouri is in the Kansas City metropolitan area. At the time of the audit, in April 1988, we had about 11,000 students. We were a low wealth district, spending about 15% under the Missouri average per student, which placed us well below the national average. We had some uppermiddle and middle class families and a lot of working class families; 40% of our students were eligible for Medicaid.

For these reasons, we needed to make every dollar count. Although it is called a "curriculum management audit," the way it's done, you get a very comprehensive look at the district in general—not only the way the instructional programs are aligned and effectively operating, but what can be done in the future to make the system the best it can be with available money. As superintendents fighting all those alligators, it's real easy to get sloppy in the area of curriculum where the voices of change are not always real strong.

The way we got into the curriculum management audit was this. Our school board had heard Fen English speak and wanted to pursue a curriculum management audit. At that time, I was still in the early "John Wayne" stage of my superintendency, so I said, "Pilgrims, if we want to look at our curriculum, by God, we're going to do it ourselves." But the idea kept coming up, so I decided to find out more about the curriculum management audit. I sent away for a few copies of previous audits, and I asked some staff members to attend a meeting where Fen English was presenting. I wanted to be certain in my own mind that we were getting a practitioner, not just a theoretician. The staff was impressed.

In looking at the sample reports, we knew we were going to get a tough-medicine report; we knew some things that needed to be changed. We weren't completely happy with the way we had organized the instructional program, and we felt that the audit, sensibly arranged and thought out, would help us plan for the future. We were prepared; we knew it wouldn't be candy-coated, but would go right to the heart of the matter. We thought it would be the best use of our time and money.

What we got was a report that enabled us to make steady and substantial improvements in what we were doing. All the recommendations were helpful. Strategic planning was one suggestion. We found through examination of our curriculum guides that our written, taught, and tested curricula were worlds apart. Fen was able to find only one person in our secondary program who knew anything about curriculum organization. We worked with the press. They praised us for taking a nontraditional means of looking at school change. They wrote that other wishy washy knee jerk superintendents hadn't the guts, but our superintendent and board would take the strong medicine. At the time of audit, I'd been superintendent for thirteen years.

Changes have been constructive; things that resulted have certainly improved our system. With a curriculum management audit, you get the good, the bad, and the ugly. The media and dissident board members tend to celebrate the ugly. You might as well know that. Tough medicine was a positive; people had been used to sugar-coated, softly stated suggestions. You don't have to be a rocket scientist to realize that what needs to be done is presented in a straightforward manner. The report was defensible in terms of its recommendations; we found little to disagree with. Many of the recommendations have been implemented.

The curriculum management audit was a vehicle for substantial improvement in our district. We received strong, but good, medicine. Anyone considering an audit should read previous reports and go to meetings where the reports and process are explained. Orient your board and community that you're calling for a hard, no-holds-barred report.

Larry Coble, Durham County, North Carolina

At the time of the audit, in May 1988, Durham County had approximately 17,000 students. The student body was 67% white, 32%

African-American, and 1% other. Durham County was an affluent suburban school district with some urban characteristics. Student achievement was high, and the levels of family income and parents' education were high among whites and minorities. A high preponderance of parents in this area are employed in the Research Triangle Park area. The economy is supported by Liggett Myers Tobacco, Duke University Medical Center, Duke University, North Carolina Central, and the University of North Carolina at Chapel Hill.

The purpose of the audit was to make a really good school system even better in an effort to begin to see ways to develop a national reputation. Even though Durham was a top quality school district prior to the audit, strategic planning efforts in curriculum and instruction had been inadequate. Most of the district's energies were devoted to maintaining existing programs and implementing state mandates. We were searching for the kind of information and direction that could thrust us into another level of improved student achievement.

The curriculum management audit process assembled a group of outside experts who could be as objective as possible for the purpose of doing an honest evaluation of the instructional program. The main result was that it laid the groundwork for a strategic plan. The audit and the planning process go hand in hand, with the audit providing the kind of information the superintendent needs to develop a strategic plan.

Larry Coble, Winston Salem/Forsyth County School District, Winston Salem, North Carolina

Winston Salem/Forsyth County was audited in February 1990. At that time, the school district had 38,000 students. It had been merged in 1963. The district was 62% white, 37% African-American, and 1% other. Winston Salem/Forsyth County can best be described as a district that truly represents urban, suburban, and rural characteristics. It has a major inner city population with a number of schools located in the inner city, as well as suburban and rural areas. A handful of major companies support the economy: R. J. Reynolds Tobacco Company, Sara Lee Corporation, Wachovia Bank, Integon Insurance, and a number of new-growth industries moving into the area. Winston Salem/Forsyth is rapidly taking on the characteristics of an inner city, and we have not been geared up to deal with the issues of inner city problems on a large scale.

When I came to the district, the board wanted a change agent, and as a new superintendent, I was looking for high leverage activities for the purpose of implementing change. The curriculum management audit was one of the tools available. We audited just the high school program because we were getting good reviews for the elementary program, and the middle school program was in the process of being restructured.

Before the audit, we were offering so many courses at the high school level that it would have taken thirty-one years to take all the courses. We had a divisive tracking system at the high school level, with five levels of tracking. I wanted to learn as much as I could as quickly as I could about the eleven high schools; I wanted the audit team to become my eyes and ears.

The audit team certainly was my eyes and ears. We have implemented every one of the audit's recommendations. The most profound and controversial recommendation, to eliminate ability tracking, was approved by the board and has had a profound, positive effect on students. The first year after the audit, we reduced the number of electives in the high school program by sixty-seven courses. Since that time, we have eliminated about another fifteen. The curriculum management audit has helped us more than anything else we've done here to restructure schools during my more than four years.

The audit is invaluable in identifying and interpreting need for major education reform. I would recommend that all superintendents who accept an initial assignment to a school system have an audit conducted by an external team. For a superintendent who wants to get a handle on where his or her school district is in terms of curriculum and delivery of the instructional program, the curriculum management audit is a must. In particular, the audit is essential for superintendents who want to leverage productive change in trying to move away from the status quo. The people inside were taking bets that we would never reduce the number of tracks; bureaucracies are famous for never dismantling anything; the audit enabled us to do that and more. The curriculum management audit is absolutely essential to true school reform or restructuring.

The audit made a significant positive impact on our school system. We received more support of the audit and the audit recommendations from the board, staff, public, and media than I expected. Having outside consultants increased the support of the audit and the probability of making needed changes. I derived great benefit from the audits in both Durham County and Winston Salem/Forsyth.

Paul Hagerty, Springfield School District R 12, Springfield, Missouri

The Springfield School District R 12 was audited in November 1988. At the time, the district had 23,000 students, 95% of whom were white. There were significant pockets of poverty, with all schools having students on free and reduced price lunch. Half the schools qualified for Chapter 1 funds. The school district serves what is thought of as middle America. There are a broad range of industries, including the center for health insurance for Southwest Missouri and the international headquarters for the Assembly of God Church and Baptist Bible College. This conservative community felt that the education system was sufficient. There was satisfaction with the status quo and what was accomplished with the small amount of money spent on education.

The curriculum specialists had heard Fen English speak, and they said it would be valuable to go through a curriculum management audit. To me, it seemed similar to a North Central accreditation visit. It struck me that here was a well established, highly objective process to do the same thing on a systemwide basis, rather than the accreditation process, which was school-by-school.

The audit was a major force in moving the district along the path toward looking at student learning outcomes, the idea that you should have course objectives, look at what students learn, and that the written, taught, and tested curricula should be aligned. The idea of having final examinations at the end of the semester was foreign to the school district before I got there. I thought it was important. Fen said there should be commonality of objectives as well as end of course assessment. Algebra I, for instance, should be the same across the district. The audit helped create internal consistency for courses and a sense that, yes, it is time that assessment of student learning be done on a regular objective basis at the end of the learning experience.

If you are considering a curriculum management audit, be ready for a totally honest, frank appraisal of your system. The warts will be uncovered. For people who believe in open, honest communication and sharing information, good or bad, the sharing of this information will be the basis upon which growth and improvement will occur.

Although the curriculum management audit and strategic planning process were conducted as separate activities in Springfield, it is a happy coincidence that one led into and reinforced the other. In both cases, the focus was on an outcome-based approach to education. The audit gave the district a means to address the district's need of holding itself more accountable, and acted almost like a built-in action plan. The curriculum management audit and strategic planning process were mutually beneficial activities for the district. The curriculum management audit is a very powerful analysis of the total school operation from a curriculum perspective, in contrast to the typical accrediting reports that tend to be bland and self-serving. The curriculum management audit zeroes in on the fundamental issues and presents both strengths and recommendations in a way that commands a response.

Terry Grier, Darlington County School District, Darlington, South Carolina

The Darlington County School District was audited in December 1988, when the student population of about 13,000 was approximately 50% black and 50% white. The school district had ignored a 1970 court order to desegregate. As a result, there were separate and unequal schools. For instance, there was an elementary school that was 90% white one mile away from one that was 90% black. The inequities were similar to what Jonathan Kozol talked about in his book, *Savage Inequalities*. It would break your heart; it would make you cry. He could have written it in Darlington. I was the eighth superintendent in ten years. The previous superintendent killed himself halfway through his first term. Only half the general adult population had high school diplomas. There was a twelve-member board, very political, with a 6–6 split. They constantly fought. Two or three members were micromanaging; most of principals had come up through the ranks in the school district. There was a true southern "good old boy" mentality. The majority of the board was very much interested in reform and change. They wanted "new blood." We hired talented people as part of our reform initiative.

I was there for only a short period of time when I realized the inequities that existed for black students, and I realized that no new superintendent was going to bring about that kind of change by him- or herself. I looked at audit reports from other districts, and I went through audit training with two members of the staff. They had been in the district for some time and were trusted by the board. I later sent another two people to training. A Fortune 500 company paid for two-thirds of the audit. They felt that change wasn't going to come at all without an outside opinion of what needed to be done.

The audit gave us clear direction. It reinforced what we knew needed to be done. It also uncovered some things we hadn't anticipated and really rattled a lot of cages. One board member said he felt like he was running around the courthouse naked; it exposed the district to that degree. Another board member said had he known it would be that blatant and clear, he would never have agreed to have it done. A third board member said, "I don't know what you're so upset about; there's really nothing here we didn't know; this all came from our people and our district." There was a lot of denial, and people were pointing fingers of blame. Some said I had brought in friends to empower me to do the things I wanted to do.

We used the audit as a springboard into a five-year strategic plan, a modified version of the Cook model. Recommendations tied into goals the board had established to improve the district. It is just uncanny how well the recommendations fit the objectives of strategic planning. All we had to do was develop strategies to achieve them. I've heard a lot of people say over the last five years that this concept of the curriculum management audit and strategic planning are at odds with each other. That's a silly statement; they complement each other. If I were going to do both, I'd definitely do the audit first, and then use the recommendations to develop a strategic plan to address the recommendations. Of course you're not limited to those recommendations; there may be other things you and the community want. But an audit is pretty thorough.

The audit helped us make changes in a three-year period that would have taken us ten to fifteen years otherwise. Some of the changes were painful for people who had been working here and were particularly bothersome to school board members who were satisfied with the status quo. I strongly recommend a curriculum management audit, but you need to assess your current situation. I would advise working with your business advisory council or chamber of commerce. If you have been working to improve your school district, you need to ground your community and board in terms of what the audit will look like and what the audit process will involve, and not belittle everything they've done in past. If the school district is in bad shape or you haven't been engaged in school reform efforts, even better communication is needed.

The curriculum management audit process is not an end. Critics of the report will want to deep six it. You need to do an annual progress report on how well you've done to implement recommendations. Do a district wide report card for the community. But when you receive your report, you're going to find that it gets right to the point. Don't expect kudos for doing what is expected. As Fen English says, people should not applaud when the train comes in on time.

Daryle D. Russell, Saudi Arabian International School, Riyadh, Saudi Arabia

The Saudi Arabian International School at Riyadh was audited in November 1989. At the time, the school had 1,921 students from fifty-nine countries, 46% of whom were from the United States. Achievement on standardized tests placed our students at least 1.5 grade levels above the United States' national public school norms, and 95% of our students are expected to complete college.

At the time we decided to have an audit, we were midway in our accreditation cycle and looking for an entry into strategic planning. The auditors were friends of mine and suggested a curriculum management audit. We had the financial resources and board support, so it seemed like the logical thing to do.

The audit exceeded our expectations. Fen had told us at the onset that they were not here to "tell us that our trains run on time—we expect that." Although most of our recommendations were "boiler plate," they served to move us quickly in the right direction, including a commitment to complete a strategic plan.

The service provided by the National Curriculum Audit Center exceeded our expectations. We were provided a good, tough document with acceptable recommendations. Those recommendations were helpful in getting us to focus on strategic planning as a means to bring about desired changes. I have presented several workshops to overseas superintendents about the curriculum management audit.

I am absolutely dumbfounded why more schools are not involved in a curriculum management audit. Ironically, we think nothing of spending considerable money for an annual financial audit. Why not, by board policy, subscribe to a curriculum management audit once every five years? Boards and parents would easily buy into this procedure. I suspect that the resistance is top-side among the administrators. There is a built-in fear of the audit results. There is also the need for substantial follow-up activity. I know it is a hard sell, especially to my overseas colleagues.

We recently became the first school to hold paradigmatic accreditation from the Middle States Association of Colleges and Schools. We credit the curriculum management audit with having moved us to this level of sophistication.

Dr. Edward L. Kelly, Prince William County, Virginia

The Prince William County Schools were audited in October and November 1990. The school division had 42,000 students at the time of the audit, with a growing number of minority students, then about 22%. Prince William County is a bedroom community, with most of the parents working in or around the Washington, D.C. area with the federal government or the military. Some parts of the county have a high student mobility rate. The county is diverse, with the eastern end being much more dense and urban and the western end semi-rural. Prince William is a county in transition, both in numbers and the level of sophistication of its schools and county government.

We requested the audit because of perceived weaknesses in our written curriculum and countywide testing program. Before we went off half-cocked, we wanted some basis for making decisions, not just doing what our instincts told us.

The audit provided us with valuable information regarding instructional deficiencies in Prince William County Schools and included recommendations needed to strengthen our program. The audit gave us an analysis of areas where we had to do some work. Although the audit does not indicate strengths, you can deduce from the comments where your strengths are.

I would encourage any superintendent to have an audit. But be realistic. I was told that having an audit is like having to run naked down main street. I don't know that it's all that bad, but it does expose a lot of weaknesses. Go into it knowing that and prepare your board and staff and community; tell them you need to know areas that need improvement, so when they're exposed you don't feel like jumping off a cliff. Those people need to know the purpose of the audit.

Chuck Morris,** Alamance County Schools, Graham, North Carolina

The Alamance County Schools were audited in December 1990. Alamance is a school system of approximately 10,100 students with

**Chuck Morris was acting superintendent when Alamance County Schools were audited. During the time of the audit team's visit, he moved to Mount Airy City Schools, so he did not discuss the results of the Alamance County audit.

four high schools, four middle schools, and twelve elementary schools. It is a county system, and there is also a city system in the county. At the time of the audit, the school district was 78% white and 22% black. The racial distribution was uneven, however, as some schools had no minority students, while others had around 34%. The economy is supported by light industry, including textile and service industries. Although Alamance County is the tenth wealthiest school district in the state, it ranked 132nd out of 134 districts in spending for education. Student achievement was around the state average on the California Achievement Test, but varied among schools. SAT scores were considerably below the state average.

We decided on a curriculum management audit because we wanted an objective look at what was going on in the school system in terms of curriculum in order to initiate change. We felt that using an outside source would generate recommendations that people could buy into. We really had never had anybody look at what we were actually doing. It is real hard to do that from the inside, as you cannot always be objective. The audit was the first step to bring about change and to make people aware that change was needed.

Chuck Morris, Mount Airy City Schools, Mount Airy, North Carolina

The Mount Airy City Schools were audited April 1991. The school district has one high school, one junior high school, and two elementary schools, with a student population of 1950. The Mount Airy City Schools have a mixed population, with 87% white and 13% minority students. About half the students have well-educated parents, while the other half come from homes where the parents have not completed high school. All of the housing projects in Surry County are located in Mount Airy City, as is the county's most prestigious neighborhood. The populace is supported primarily by the textile industry. Mount Airy City is one of the top twenty school systems in the state in terms of performance on standardized tests. Their SAT scores exceed both national and state averages. The district ranks twenty-fifth in terms of per pupil expenditure for education and is supported by a supplemental tax, while the county system ranks eighty-ninth.

I was a new superintendent coming into a school district that had a reputation for excellence and a school board that wanted changes, even though the scores were up. They felt that the curriculum needed improvement, with an emphasis on twenty-first century direction; they wanted to see use of more technology, more reform, getting away from the traditional high school day, and bringing about a difference in teaching methodologies. I wanted a curriculum management audit to give me a foundation, instead of the changes being just a new superintendent's program. Although the board saw the need for change, the staff viewed the system as not needing change.

Once the audit came in, it allowed us to use recommendations to implement writing our own curricula, looking at curriculum policy, and going to zero-based budgeting. The audit opened the eyes of the board to some things that needed to be looked at. The recommendations gave us a launching pad for a four-year plan for where we wanted to go. We got exactly what we expected. We hadn't done a lot in curriculum, evaluation, or anything to make us accountable in terms of programs. We put programs in and didn't evaluate whether they were working or not. We needed to see how successful these programs were. The audit provided food for thought for those in the system, particularly the administrators. It initiated thinking that might not have happened any other way. The audit gives superintendents and boards credibility in bringing about change. It needs to be reemphasized that, in relation to national standards, schools may not stack up that well. Whereas your district may look all right compared to your state, you might not be doing that well from a national perspective. You can't rest on your laurels.

The curriculum management audit is an eye opener in the sense that, even though there may be things you see, it acts as a confirmation. The superintendency is a pretty lonely job; you don't have anyone to turn to. The audit allows you to have some confirmation from someone else's point of view about what you're feeling and observing. It also gives you some basis to begin something. Some of the recommendations are not complicated, but they are visible and are things you can do immediately to show that something's going on. It is important to a new superintendent for people to see that things are happening. For that period of time you're not by yourself; you have a book that says these are things we need to work on and do.

Larry G. Rowedder, Cumberland County, North Carolina

The Cumberland County Schools were audited in January 1991. The school system had 45,000 students at the time of the audit, 46% of whom were minority. The district had sixty-nine school buildings, 30,000 plus teachers, and a budget of $180 million a year. The major livelihood came from Fort Bragg and Pope Air Force Base, which employ 40,000–45,000 soldiers. Twenty-five percent of students' parents work in the military. Other major employers are Kelly Springfield Tire, DuPont, Westinghouse, and Black and Decker.

One of the poorest counties in North Carolina, Cumberland County is considered a low wealth district, with about 50% of students on free and reduced price lunches. For 1989, student achievement was about at the 50th percentile since 1989, but it has risen steadily to the 65th percentile since that time.

One of our goals was to take a major look at our curriculum and do some innovative programming. We believed the first step was to assess where we were and to conduct a curriculum management audit. We had a strategic planning team interview several groups to determine who should conduct the audit. AASA clearly offered the most comprehensive program and one of the things we wanted to do was get a really honest and accurate assessment. We believed that AASA's process could best deliver that.

When we decided to have the audit, we didn't realize the exact format and the brutal frankness that would be contained therein. We probably got more than we expected. We wanted an objective assessment and we got a brutally frank objective assessment; we got more than we thought we'd get. That was good. If we are going to make meaningful change in our schools, we must become dissatisfied with the status quo. It's dissatisfaction that moves you toward changing things. The audit creates dissatisfaction, i.e., a reason for change.

For obvious reasons, my advice would be to do an audit upon going into a school system; it's a good place to begin. One of the problems in any organization is that the organization has a need to assess blame, which is a waste of energy, as far as I'm concerned. If the superintendent and the board are new, the need does not exist. If people are all in place, they may want to determine whose fault it is that things aren't better. The curriculum management audit can be taken as a starting point. When I look at visioning, I see three major steps. First, determine objectively where you are. Second, be able to visualize where you might be some day. Third, communicate the vision to those involved. The curriculum management audit serves the first function very well; it provides a rich store of resources to help you assess where you are.

John DiBuono, Community Consolidated School District No. 93, Carol Stream, Illinois

The Community Consolidated School District No. 93 was audited in February 1991. It is a consolidated school district in New Page County, one of the wealthier counties in the state, encompassing four different communities. It is a growing K–8 district, about 3,500 students at the time of the audit. The population is middle class, with upper blue collar and lower white collar workers. There are not many professionals in the community. Students were doing very well, scoring above the national average on national achievement tests.

We had a curriculum management audit because we were very much interested in improving the curriculum. We wanted to improve our position in curriculum and instruction.

The audit gave us a lot of insight into what we were doing right and what we could improve. We got thirteen recommendations, have set up a number of study committees, and have assigned a faculty member as a curriculum management audit assessment person. The results were very good for the entire educational community. They brought teachers, administrators, and parents together and became the focal point for administrative goals. The board became very involved; it opened up a lot of doors for them to be involved in the curriculum. The audit channeled the energies of the board.

I think that an audit is a great opportunity for districts to take an inside picture of what is actually going on and to give the school district a great sense of how to bring the school district together, especially the board and staff, to understand what needs to be done to have a good curriculum.

Taras Herbowy, Utica City Schools, Utica, New York

The Utica City Schools were audited in March 1991. Utica City is a medium-sized city school district in upstate New York, with an urban population not unlike what you'd find in larger urban areas. Seventy percent of the students were on free and reduced price lunch. There was a high mobility rate between schools, with an in-migration of limited English proficient students from higher concentrated urban areas in New York, especially New York City. This inmigration is directly related to the prison system, as families of incarcerated adults move into Utica to be close to loved ones who are transferred from prison systems elsewhere. Utica's tax base has been declining, and the city suffering from municipal over-burden. The families who receive social services are concentrated in Utica because of the lack of low income housing in suburban areas. Property owners are typically not parents of the students served by the district. Thus, there is no direct relationship between the quality of programs and the support of programs. Industry is declining.

As a new superintendent, I had the audit conducted because of the ominous rule over district funds and functions. The board had been intrusive, and because they did not represent the majority of the students served, there was incongruity between the focus of programs and the efforts of the educational program. There was an absence of policy based on student information. For a new superintendent, it was very important to do the audit.

The audit team very quickly, in a logical presentation, made recommendations that verified what was common knowledge in the school district. It was presented with objectivity and credibility. As a result of the audit, we have improved understanding and work on the testing program and have a new staff development program under way through Syracuse University, essentially focused on understanding and describing student needs and focusing instruction on those needs.

In the area of policy, we have almost completed a new policy manual, which, for the first time, will be compatible with regulations and law. We brought in a consultant from the state who has worked very closely with us on policy. For the first time, we are automating the business department, including all spending, purchasing, and personnel functions. We are working with the state department on that. We added an acting assistant superintendent for business. We are establishing a testing committee, which has developed formative evaluations at the secondary level by department, where we previously had only summative evaluations. We are also conducting mid-year evaluations of all students at the secondary level. Even in the last board election, the audit was referred to a lot.

As a result of criticism in the audit report about the way in which our magnet schools were conceived, a lot more planning is going into magnet schools, very deliberately involving parents and the community. Because of this, the planning is much better in magnet schools than in other school sites. The curriculum management audit is referred to in all applications for funding and programs. It has bolstered the issue for competitive grants. There is a sense of renewed commitment because of the curriculum management audit.

If we are going to address the issue of accountability and we're going to make a difference in our schools, and we know that there are problems, I think it is very critical that one take advantage of a credible source in being able to enumerate and find what you know actually exists and provide you with some logical recommendations for implementation. New superintendents especially have to go to the curriculum management audit. Immediately afterward, you have to implement the recommendations. You have to get your board to establish a curriculum management audit task force of district officials and community members and parents, and a standing committee to report on progress and success of implementation, using the audit report as a guide.

Franklin Smith, District of Columbia Public Schools, Washington, D.C.†

The District of Columbia Public Schools were audited in October 1991. Sixty square miles of land, the boundaries of the school district are coterminous with those of Washington, D.C., "the capital of the free world." At the time of the audit, the schools served 80,618 students in 175 schools, with an operating budget of $519,344,000.

When I was appointed superintendent in April of that year, the NAEP scores had just been released and Washington, D.C. was next to the bottom. The only reason that D.C. was not last was that the Virgin Islands had the flu the week before. The media were calling and asking what I was going to do about it. Test scores were down, morale was low, board members were interfering, the mayor was cutting the budget, and the buildings were falling down. I responded, "I'm going to have a curriculum management audit." Little did I know what I was asking for at that time. The board concurred with me, so we went ahead with the audit.

When the audit was released, the headlines read: D.C. school district mismanaged from top to bottom. Since that time, some members of the community have been using what was meant to be a tool as a weapon. I have been using my time and energy for talk shows and going back to Congress and council members. I will have to release progress reports to the media to get the resources I need. Even with all we're going through, I still believe that the best thing for me and my leadership is

---

†These comments were made at the AASA annual convention in San Diego, California, in February 1992 just after the audit was released.

to have gone through this audit and have all this on the table now. I was told all these things before I came to Washington. We had other reports—the Cope, Rivlin, and Peat, Marwick reports—which all correlated with what AASA said. I wanted a report from a firm that knows education. They said the same things.

Be prepared to deal with the media in terms of responding to negative issues. As Virginia Vertiz said, they are not in the marketing business. The board and superintendent must feel secure with each other. Be prepared to deal with the credibility issue of the audit. The principles of the audit are the same, regardless of the size of the school district. Make sure people who come to your district are credible. The AASA training assures that. Also, review the draft report in detail.

I believe that the audit will afford me the opportunity to make Washington, D.C. the urban model I've talked about. I look forward to working with it to improve the district.

Russell Working,‡ Clinton City Schools, Clinton, North Carolina

The Clinton City Schools were audited in November 1991. Clinton is a small rural school district with a student population 45% white, 45% black, and the balance Indian and Hispanic. The poverty level is quite high. A low level achievement pattern is traditional, especially among minorities. There is a population schism, in that the white population is typically involved in leadership roles in the community and in business and industry; blacks are not involved in higher paying positions. The type of instruction in the classroom has been largely whole group instruction, with a primary focus on instruction at the middle and lower middle achievement level, which has resulted in brighter students not doing as well as they might and very low achieving students not doing as well either. The focus has been at the average level, with very heavy emphasis on drill and practice. For the large part, most of the teachers have been carrying on the kind of instruction that generally had the support of the community, as it was the type of instruction that they had received. There has been a need to alter the instructional mode, focus on instruction, and adjust the curriculum so there could be greater flexibility in teaching and more focus on higher level thinking skills.

We had a curriculum management audit to validate the need for

‡Russell Working left the Clinton City Schools before the audit was released.

change and to bring focus to the kinds of changes needed, targeting more students more effectively, with a variety of teaching skills and curricula that hold students' interest and keep them involved. Without the audit, neither the board nor the parents who had been involved with decision making would give credence to the need for drastic change.

Ray Brayboy, Bladen Schools, Elizabethtown, North Carolina

The Bladen County Schools were audited in January 1992. At that time, the district had approximately 5,600 students, 51% minority, primarily black, and 49% white. The school district is primarily rural, with at least 30% of the students living in poverty. There is not a very strong economic base. It is primarily geared to agricultural activities, with limited industrial development. Although there is a higher than average tax rate, there are limited dollars for education.

The major reason we had a curriculum management audit was because we needed a focus for curriculum. We needed to develop congruence between the written, taught, and tested curricula. We also wanted to use the audit recommendations for strategic planning. We had problems generating positive student outcomes, as measured by test scores, attendance rates, and other indicators. We needed to do something to turn it around. We didn't have a lot of objective information about the district; it lacked focus for instruction or curriculum.

The audit gave us the momentum to effect changes. The audit validated the areas of weakness and need. We plan to implement all recommendations of the audit. The audit report, along with our developing strategic plan, will provide the blueprint to guide our school system toward further improvement. We are fusing the two to provide one clear direction.

The results of the audit were very straightforward, meaningful, and objective. The auditors did a very thorough job, based on the school system's data. It was completely objective. I feel very good about the quality of information generated through the process.

If you have any guts, have a curriculum management audit. If you're really interested in promoting excellence within your district, the curriculum management audit is a valuable tool in assisting you with this process. Don't worry about the cost; it will be dollars well spent and will increase productivity.

William P. Ward, Newington Public Schools, Newington, Connecticut

The Newington Public Schools were audited in February 1992. Newington is a suburban community that is best described as an inner ring suburb. It is between two cities, Hartford and Newport. Employees work in Hartford in the insurance business, for the state government, and in light manufacturing. The community is middle and upper middle class.

There are about 3,800 students in this K–12 system. The student body is 9% minority, and the remainder of the student body is white. There has been no dramatic change in ethnographic data over the past twenty-seven years. Students score well above the state average on Connecticut Mastery Tests and above the national, New England, and Connecticut average on SAT tests. Eighty percent of the students go to college. Several of Newington's schools received recognition from the national blue ribbon panel. Newington ranks in the top 10% for per pupil expenditures and pays among the highest teacher salaries in the state.

Because my assistant superintendent for instruction thought it was a good idea, we decided to have a curriculum management audit. At the time, we'd been developing curriculum and we decided to stop and have an audit and see what we were really doing. It was part of our strategic plan. It was time to stop, catch our breath, and determine where we had been and where we were going. I had heard about the audit a long time ago, and I had read all the material and heard Fen English speak.

The audit was a very good report, very helpful, very straightforward. We have been able to use it. We have developed a new plan for developing curriculum. We have changed the format and focus of curriculum development. It was nice to have someone from the outside tell us the good things. They also told us the things that were missing without making us feel threatened, so we didn't feel like we had to defend the status quo. We did discover the holes in what we were doing. It was the staff's idea to take a look at ourselves; there were no negative attitudes that they didn't want looked at. The audit wasn't something the superintendent was forcing on the district.

When the lead auditor met with the staff and told them about the process, it wasn't done in a threatening way. She said, "We're here to help you; we would appreciate your assistance." The audit team spent time and took care in meeting with staff and parents. It was a very thorough process that focused on curriculum.

If you ask me about conducting an audit, I'd say do it. It's simple; just get it done. You have to have a commitment from the community, staff, and school board. The superintendent has to believe in the process. Learn about the audit; hear Fen English speak. The ultimate person that benefits is the student in the classroom.

Walter Tobin, Orangeburg School District 5, Orangeburg, South Carolina

Orangeburg School District 5 was audited in May 1992. The school district is located in the southeast part of the state. The county student population is 45,000, which is served by eight school districts. Ours is the largest, with 6,700 students. Our student body is 79% black, 20% white, and 1% other. Sixty-six percent of our students are on free and reduced price lunches.

Ours is a tremendously diverse community, with two historically black colleges and one community college. We have a wide range of economic levels, with a large black middle class, a lot of poverty, and some very wealthy people, as well. We have a relatively low dropout rate, largely attributable to the fact that we keep track of those students who leave our system. Some of those who leave go to adult education, some to the department of youth services, and some to other school systems. Although we have a large percentage of graduating students enrolling in college, we felt we needed to serve the others better.

We wanted to take a look at what we were doing for students and how our use of resources affected them. We have among the highest per pupil expenditures and teacher salaries in the region, so we wanted to know how it was affecting children and if we were getting the kind of results we should expect for the investment. We had some notions about it, but we wanted an outside source to give us an objective report. Those who told me about the audit said we'd get what we wanted in that respect. We also went through strategic planning and wanted to see if the two efforts had some congruence, and they did, even though they were independent efforts. The curriculum management audit gave us a basis of where we were, the strategic plan will give us direction, and quality management will drive all of those.

The audit was right on target. There were some things we believed were taking place in the organization, areas where we hadn't been effective and practices that were not good for children, even in the area of personnel issues. The audit helped us redirect resources, making sure people were where they could be most productive. The audit gave the board a good source of information to make some decisions on, which will be reflected in policy.

If you decide to have a curriculum management audit, make sure you understand the information you might get may not be in a format to which you have been accustomed. Usually, commendations and recommendations are matched, and language is couched in such a way that real problems are not detected. You have to understand that there are some harsh revelations. These do not necessarily reflect on the organization. We are not used to looking at our programs in so much depth. We tend to resolve problems by adding programs and people, without ever eliminating them. The audit allows management to make decisions based on program recommendations. The smaller the organization, the easier it is to pinpoint personnel problems.

Randy Stortz, Bay Village City School District, Bay Village, Ohio

The Bay Village City School District was audited in October 1992. Bay Village is a suburban Cleveland school district, middle and upper middle class, and 97% residential, with little business or industry. One-third of the community is taken up by a park, located right in the center of Bay Village. Seventy-five percent of the people in the community no longer have children in school. There has been a rather dramatic change in demographics, as this is a reverse of the statistic ten to fifteen years ago, when about 75% of the residents had children in school.

The student body of 2,450 is basically white, with very few minority students. The school district has four K–12 schools and its own day-care center. Our kids are great; they have all kinds of experiences that many young people do not have: trips, books, access to media. They achieve in spite of us, not necessarily because of our programs. It is easy to lull ourselves into the attitude, "If it ain't broke, you don't have to fix it."

Bay Village became a plan-driven district in 1988; the mission statement in the plan set goals a lot higher than what we had before. We stretched as far as we could, but we missed alignment issues. The audit provided a legitimate impetus for change. I like the term *audit*. We spend so much money for a financial audit; no one had ever questioned spending the tens of thousands of dollars mandated for the fiscal program. Why aren't we doing the same thing for a curriculum management audit? I think it's a powerful argument.

When I came to the district in 1986 as the assistant superintendent for curriculum and personnel, I realized we didn't have a focused curriculum. We had no alignment that Fen speaks about. We had made a number of advancements since 1986, but better alignment was needed. The existing paradigm about how people thought about curriculum and instruction wouldn't stretch further; we were far short of alignment needed to produce high quality. We needed the audit for impetus to move forward and stretch ourselves.

The results weren't surprising. In order to move the organization forward, we have to involve our community; the audit left inside will not produce the change, but, shared with the community, will produce a healthy tension. We have held a meeting of the administration and board; there will be meetings in each of the buildings; there will also be meetings to share with key communicators in the community. Those will include the citizen advisory council and PTA presidents. We have already had one of AASA's other lead auditors do a session on curriculum-driven budgets.

Do a curriculum management audit; it makes a whole lot of sense, especially for a new superintendent. The audit fits perfectly with strategic planning. I would recommend doing a curriculum management audit in your first year of the superintendency and doing a strategic plan in year two. It is better to have the audit first, then the strategic plan. That would be ideal. Because our strategic plan focused on alignment and curriculum and instruction, it worked all right the other way around. Other important components include consensus-building and conflict management.

Eric J. Smith, Newport News Public Schools, Newport News, Virginia

The Newport News Public Schools were audited in November and December 1992. At the time of the audit, the school system had about 31,000 students, approximately half of whom were black and half white. One-third of the students were on free and reduced price lunch. Newport News Public Schools is in an urban area, which is part of a larger metropolitan area that comprises one-third of the total school population in Virginia. The economy is dependent on military expenditures, with major military bases, NASA, and Newport News Shipbuilding as major employers.

We decided to have a curriculum management audit because of strong interest in school reform and equity in academic achievement. The audit was exactly what we hoped it would be. It is very comprehensive. It touched on the critical issues that need to be addressed in our school system if we are going to become truly competitive on an international scale. Although it provided recommendations for reform, those recommendations were not a cookbook variety, but were structured in such a way that they gave community members, including employers and school system employees, ample opportunity to be actively involved in the implementation of change. Had those recommendations been extremely prescriptive, they would have been useless. Those opposed to the prescription would have killed the utility of the report. If there were single correct answers to problems in education, we wouldn't have any problems. Education is a living process; it has to breathe. The curriculum management audit allowed the community to wrestle with the issues that surfaced without putting us in a straitjacket.

Those superintendents who are dissatisfied with the status quo and current results, the level of academic achievement of students, or other related issues should consider having a curriculum management audit. The superintendent has to feel fairly secure about managing the change process. This includes security with the board and readiness to take on very difficult issues. It doesn't have to be for a superintendent early in his career. The homework is different, but it can be done successfully. It's an open admission to the public that you're not satisfied with where you are; you have to go at it again. Make sure you fully understand the audit process and what the product is you will be receiving; make sure your board understands; make sure you're prepared to deal with the most critical issues, those we usually try to keep in the closet; be prepared to have to face those; be certain you have either access to staff or others in the country to look at things in a fresh way. All educators are struggling with tough issues. It puts you on a roller coaster ride.

R. Robert Jones,§ Deer Valley School District, Phoenix, Arizona

The Deer Valley School District was audited in January 1993. The district had 18,000 students K–12, 90% white and 7% Hispanic. The

§At the time of the audit, Bob Jones was co-superintendent of the district, responsible for Curriculum, Instruction, and Assessment.

school district encompasses 380 square miles and has nineteen schools. It is basically a middle class district, with some upper middle class families who live off the country club fairway and other poor families, living in tents, sleeping bags, and in their cars, off the freeway. Of the thirteen elementary schools, six were Chapter 1 schools; we have Chapter 1 in one of three middle schools and one of the two high schools. We had one school in our district that was rated as one of the top five elementary schools in the state that was least at risk and one of the top twenty-five that was most at risk. The people work in industry: American Express, Honeywell, and small businesses. Achievement scores were above the state for Iowa tests and were in the upper half for the city of Phoenix.

We had the audit because we felt we needed as firm a direction as we could possibly get to make our district truly curriculum-driven. There was a lot of talk about it, but we were very strongly business-driven, not curriculum-driven. We were a small district that got large fast. Ten years ago, we were a small elementary school district. Now Deer Valley is a rapidly growing district that has high schools as well. Curriculum hadn't been well developed for the high schools. The curriculum just appeared with no common philosophy. We wanted to have the audit for two reasons. The first was to help give the department a direction so we were moving with a plan that would help create a district that was top in the area in curriculum and curriculum development. The second was to help wake up people to the fact that it is easy to say we're curriculum-driven but we really aren't. The best thing to do was to have an audit. If I was wrong, okay; if I was right, it would help others realize we weren't even close to being curriculum-driven.

We got exactly what I expected. Out of our whole audit, the only surprise was that the vocational training center in the district was not getting the attention that it needed. Everything else in the report confirmed what I also felt was there; it was great to see that being verified by other professionals. Everyone in my department (Curriculum and Instruction) felt exactly the same way.

It's risky doing a curriculum management audit because people want to blame others. But you have to get over that to make the kind of changes needed. Lay it on the table that here's what you need to do, here's what needs to happen—that you have to design a plan based on this direction. The audit could pull the district out of the fire very quickly. Any superintendent going into a district who wants to get a handle on what's going on based on what schools should be about, the first thing they ought to be doing is a curriculum management audit and have that information for the direction for strategic planning. I'm really glad we did it and had the chance to go through the process. I'm a real advocate. I'm now in a new district. It is smaller, but it needs an audit badly. People have to wake up to that fact. The district has had the highest test scores, and people have become complacent. It is becoming an inner city district, and people are starting to point fingers. A lot of work is needed to upgrade the curriculum and teaching methods for the different kinds of students we are seeing. The district is no longer the bedroom community it was previously. June Cleaver doesn't live here any more, or at least there are a lot fewer June Cleavers than lived here before. It is still a very upper middle to middle class district, with high standards. The board is made up of lawyers and doctors. It is important to have someone go through curriculum management audit training who understands the process. It is a valuable component, even if you never do the audit—a real plus.

Ron Saunders, Huntsville City Schools, Huntsville, Alabama

The Huntsville City Schools were audited in February 1993. The district has 25,000 students, 60% white, 35% African-American, and 5% other. The school system has some of the most affluent, as well as the poorest, families in the state. With an average household income of $39,000, it is the wealthiest in terms of per capita household income. The district has 3,044 employees; of those, 1,600 are certified teachers and administrators. The top employer is Red Stone Arsenol, which is headquarters for MICOM (Missile Command), as well as NASA Space Station. We have several large companies that support MICOM and NASA through space industry contracts. We also have Nichols Research, which came up with Star Wars.

Our school district is ahead of other school districts in Alabama in terms of achievement test scores, but we are showing signs of becoming a metropolitan, inner city school system. Test scores are dropping, particularly among students of low socioeconomic status. Our counterparts are now the big cities.

I felt that having a curriculum management audit was a challenge and that for this system to remain at the forefront of the state, we had to reexamine ourselves to see if we were heading down the right path. The school system was changing and we needed to be prepared for it. I really liked the idea of someone from the outside coming in and looking at the curriculum in detail and seeing if we were heading in the right direction.

I got more than I expected; more detail than I ever expected. There were some eye openers. I realized some of the things were there, but I didn't realize to what extent. I believe I have the makings of a roadmap for this system that I can strategically plan on for the next five years to move us forward to provide proper instruction for all our students.

If you are considering a curriculum management audit, think carefully about it and make sure you really want to do this because it is a great undertaking. Make sure you have the board's full approval and a good relationship with the news media. Work very hard on how you present this to the board and the public because it can be taken out of context and if you're not careful they will take it as negative instead of as a challenge. Even with all the work involved, I would do it again.

CHAPTER 12

A Follow-Up Study of Three School Districts

HARRY J. KEMEN — *Oakhill School District, Cincinnati*
KAREN S. GALLAGHER — *University of Cincinnati*

INTRODUCTION

A question frequently asked about any systematic review of school programs is, "So what difference did it make?" The assumptions underlying the curriculum management audit presuppose the utility of intense examination of curricular practices and documents from a school system against standards of control, direction, consistency, and productivity. The curriculum management audit process produces findings that specifically outline gaps between practice and standards, offering recommendations that suggest ways to narrow these gaps. As an outcome, the expenditure of money, time, and administrative effort to conduct a curriculum management audit should result in a more efficient and effective school system.

The "so what?" question is implicit in this study of three school districts who underwent the curriculum management audit. We sought to find out what influence the audit report had on management practices and how the audit report was used once the audit team completed its task. Specifically, we asked the following questions:

(1) To what extent were the recommendations in the curriculum management audit report implemented by the district's management?

(2) What unanticipated, audit-related effects (positive and negative) occurred in the district after the audit?

(3) Were the benefits of the audit perceived to have improved the management of the district?

(4) Was the audit broad enough in its scope and analysis to enable the district's board of education and administrative team to develop or extend a process of systemwide strategic management?

(5) What aspects of the curriculum audit were similar across districts?

METHODOLOGY

The case study method was used to identify the realities of the districts concerning the impact of the curriculum management audit. Just as the curriculum management audit itself is shaped by those who authorize it and the time frame and value system in which it is conducted, these detailed examinations of three settings try to capture the situational characteristics unique to each district. A case study investigation is concerned with everything that is significant in the evolution of the case. This method intensively analyzes the interaction between factors that produce change. While case study methodology lacks the facility to generate broad, generalized conclusions, a case study does serve as an appropriate way to present the meaning of the curriculum management audit process as perceived by those who went through it.

AASA Audit Population

Sixty-five curriculum audits had been commissioned nationally at the time of this study. Approximately one-half of these occurred prior to the American Association of School Administrators' (AASA) sponsorship of the audit process. Table 1 indicates the geographic spread of the

Table 1. AASA-sponsored audits conducted by 1992 (by geographic region).

Region	State	Number of Audits
West	Arizona	1
	California	1
Midwest	Illinois	1
	Indiana	1
	Missouri	3
Northeast	Connecticut	1
	New Jersey	1
	New York	1
	Pennsylvania	1
South	Arkansas	1
	Kentucky	16
	North Carolina	3
	South Carolina	1
	Virginia	1
Total		33

Table 2. Demography of school districts who
commissioned an AASA audit.

Range of Enrollment Size	Number of Districts with Audits	
1–2,500	8	
2,501–10,000	16	
10,001–100,000	5	
over 100,000	4	
Financial Carryover	Pre-Audit	Post-Audit
Less than $500,000	10	13
$500,001–$5,000,000	17	14
Over $5,000,000	6	6
Method of Audit Commission	Number of Districts	
Voluntary	26	
Mandated	7	

thirty-three districts that requested a curriculum management audit under AASA's sanction.

A preliminary review of these districts shows how broad the range of participation has been. Audits have occurred in: (1) all settings (inner city, rural, suburban, and urban), (2) districts with a variety of financial resources available, (3) districts with enrollments that varied from fewer than 500 to over 100,000 students, and (4) districts whose superintendent's tenure varied from newly hired to long-term service. Audits have been financed through the use of district funds, as well as underwritten by state and private sources. Table 2 displays the districts sorted by district size, pre- and post-audit financial carryover, and the method of audit selection.

Selection Criteria for Sample

Only those districts that had commissioned the audit through the AASA between the years of 1988 and 1990 were considered for inclusion in this study. This two-year period was selected to allow sufficient time for audit recommendations to be addressed by the district. Additional criteria for selection into this study were whether the curriculum management audit was voluntarily commissioned or mandated by some regulatory body and whether the financial position of the district at the time of the audit was stable. The categories of financial position were

Table 3. *Contrast of AASA-sponsored audits showing voluntary versus mandatory selection and level of carryover.*

Level of Carryover	Method of Selection	
	Voluntary	Mandated
High	6	0
Middle	14	0
Low	6	7
Total	33	7

based upon the district's *carryover* at the time of the audit, that is, the dollar amount available at the end of the fiscal year. The categories were low or less than $500,000; middle or $500,001 to $5,000,000; and high or over $5,000,000. Table 3 shows the resulting matrix of districts in the population pool.

The three districts selected for study represented a variety of the selection criteria. Table 4 shows how the three districts compared across the selection criteria: selection process, student enrollment size, date of audit, and post-audit carryover.

Data Collection and Analysis

Evaluation data were collected by the same triangulation process used in an audit: surveys, document analyses, and interviews. Individuals who had been involved in the audit, including members of the boards of education, administrative team members, certified staff, employee union representatives, and parents, and community members, received a survey designed specifically for their district. Using the recommendations from the final audit report, a survey was custom designed for each district. Each recommendation of the audit team was

Table 4. *Characteristics of sample.*

Characteristics	District A	District B	District C
Student Enrollment	3,000+	9,000+	3,000+
Pre-Audit Carryover	$500,000	$4,000,000	$6,500,000
Selection Method	Mandated	Voluntary	Voluntary
Date of Audit	1990	1989	1988

Table 5. Return rate for implementation-impact survey.

Respondent Group	Number of Completed Survey		
	District A	District B	District C
Board Members	1	3	1
Administrative Team	6	9	8
Certified Staff	3	4	2
Employee Union Members	0	1	1
Parents and Community	1	2	2
Total	11(18)	19(22)	14(20)
Return Rate	51%	86%	70%

listed with key descriptors from the audit included. Each survey recipient was asked two questions pertaining to the recommendation: (1) To what degree was this recommendation implemented? and (2) What impact did the implemented recommendation have on the district? Table 5 indicates the return rate for each district.

After survey data were analyzed, a site visit was made to each district. Interviews with individuals were scheduled at this time. The purposes of these interviews were to clarify implementation and impact issues and to expand upon previously collected responses. In addition, related district documents such as goal or mission statements, organizational charts, budget documents, board meeting minutes, and administrative reports were examined.

RESULTS OF IMPLEMENTATION-IMPACT SURVEY

The purpose of the implementation-impact survey was to determine the status of each audit recommendation, the impact of each recommendation's implementation, and any unanticipated effects linked to the audit. Respondents were asked to identify the status of each recommendation and to rate the impact of the recommendation's implementation on the district. Finally, the survey requested the respondents to list any positive or negative effects resulting from the audit.

Table 6 displays the combined content of the audit recommendations by audit standard for all three districts. Four recommendations were common to all three audit reports:

(1) Audit Standard I

Table 6. Audit recommendations by standard for each district.

Standard I: Control of Resources, Programs, and Personnel

Recommendation Content	District		
	A	B	C
Develop a Long-Range Strategic Plan	yes	yes	yes
Develop a Comprehensive Policy for Curriculum Design, Delivery, and Evaluation	yes	yes	yes
Revise the Table of Organization	yes	yes	no
Expand the District's Curriculum Division	no	yes	no
The Board Must Abide by Laws and Policies	yes	no	no
The Board Should Spend Proportionally More Time on Education	yes	no	no

Standard II: Establish Clear and Direct Objectives

Recommendation Content	District		
	A	B	C
Develop a Comprehensive Plan That Directs Curriculum Management	yes	yes	yes
Uncouple Testbook Adoption Process from Curriculum Development	no	yes	no

Standard III: Documentation

Recommendation Content	District		
	A	B	C
Develop a Comprehensive Staff Development Program	yes	yes	no
Refine the Teacher Evaluation Model	no	yes	no
Develop Multi-Cultural Curricular Activities	no	yes	no
Implement a Comprehensive Approach to Curriculum Review and Development	yes	no	no
Eliminate Extensive Tracking	yes	no	no
Continue the Innovative Program at the High School	no	no	yes

Standard IV: Use of Assessment Tools

Recommendation Content	District		
	A	B	C
Adopt Guidelines for District Testing and Data Utilization	yes	no	yes
Develop Plans for a Needs Assessment	yes	no	no

Table 6. (continued).

Standard V: Improve Productivity			
	District		
Recommendation Content	A	B	C
Implement a Curriculum-Driven Budget	yes	yes	yes

- Establish a comprehensive policy framework for curriculum development and management.
- Develop and implement a long-range management plan.

(2) Audit Standard II
- Engage in significant revisions of the system's curricular documents.

(3) Audit Standard V
- Revise district budgeting procedures to be directed more by curricular priorities.

Our study found that recommendations calling for revision of curricular documents and the improvement of curriculum development and management were implemented by all districts. Only one district implemented a long-range strategic plan. None of the three districts implemented a curriculum-driven budget.

Three recommendations were common to two audit reports:

(1) Audit Standard I
- Clarify and revise the table of organization for the district.

(2) Audit Standard III
- Develop a comprehensive staff development plan and program.

(3) Audit Standard IV
- Develop guidelines for district testing and utilization of test data.

Seven of the twenty-eight recommendations were unique. These seven recommendations were very specific to the individual district programs. For example, a recommendation for District C involved the continuation and expansion of an innovative program at the district's high school.

Categorization of Audit Recommendations

After we identified the content of the audit recommendations, we categorized them using Kaufman and Herman's (1991) three management levels. The *mega- or strategic, management* level refers to audit recommendations intended to cause interaction between the district and its external constituencies. *Macro- or tactical, management* level refers to audit recommendations intended to impact within and across the district. And the *micro- or operational, management* level refers to audit recommendations tailored to specific functions, programs, or schools within the district. Using Kaufman and Herman's classifications, we found the following breakdown as displayed in Table 7.

The majority of the recommendations included in the audit reports were aimed at the macro- and micro-management levels. This observation is consistent with the purpose of the curriculum management audit as an independent, objective examination of data pertaining to the educational practices of a school district. One recommendation, common to each district but implemented by only one, was the mega-management level recommendation to develop a strategic planning process for the system.

ANALYSIS OF RESEARCH QUESTIONS

Four of the questions guiding this study were answered from two perspectives. First, each district is described independently. Then we compared District A, where the audit was mandated, with Districts B and C, where the audits were voluntarily chosen. We also contrasted the three districts by their carryover classification.

Table 7. Breakdown of audit recommendations by Kaufman and Herman's (1991) levels of management.

Level of Management	Number of Audit Recommendations			
	A	B	C	Total
Mega or Strategic	1	1	1	3
Macro or Tactical	6	6	4	16
Micro or Operational	5	3	1	9
Total	12	10	6	28

Table 8. Breakdown of audit recommendations, implementation, and levels of management for Distrist A.

Recommendation Level	Total Number Received	Total Number Implemented
Mega or Strategic	1	0
Macro or Tactical	6	1
Micro or Operational	5	2
Total	12	3

In this section, we will briefly describe what we found in each district and answer the four research questions posed above. The quotations included represent responses made during individual interviews or on the implementation–impact survey.

District A

Question 1. To What Extent Are the Recommendations in the Curriculum Management Audit Report Implemented by the District's Management?

District A implemented three of twelve recommendations of the audit report. Table 8 shows the implementation compared by management level. Two years after the audit, only 25% of the recommendations had been implemented, and the likelihood of any additional changes tied directly to the audit were slim.

Question 2. What Unanticipated, Audit-Related Effects (Positive and Negative) Have Occurred in the District Since the Audit?

In a general sense, the audit process was seen as a "focus to look at [district] problems" using "credible, professional people." While the majority of the respondents stated that they were "not surprised with the results" and felt that the "audit process was in principle valid," the fact that the audit had been imposed by the state department of education overwhelmed all other reactions to it. Two of the seven district administrators interviewed believed that the audit was "used in an unethical manner to paint a bleak picture of how things are." Four administrators stated that the audit "hurt morale" and "teachers felt the audit was directed at them."

All administrators interviewed expressed the belief that the imposition of the audit upon the district inhibited any effort to aggressively address the recommendations of the audit. However, more significantly, the Kentucky Education Reform Act (KERA) was implemented shortly after the completion of the audit. KERA required massive changes in the educational practices of the district. The district administrators stated that the district channeled its resources into accommodating the changes required by KERA rather than addressing the audit's recommendations. Thus, implementation strategies for the recommendations of the audit report were never seriously addressed. The three recommendations implemented coincided with KERA required changes.

Question 3. Are the Benefits of the Audit Perceived to Improve the Management of the District?

The impact of the curriculum management audit on the management practices in District A was minimized by several factors. First, the instability at the superintendent level, which existed prior to the audit, continued after the audit's completion. This lack of instructional leadership perpetuated a segmentation of the district. The majority of district and building administrators reported feeling isolated and lacking a unified direction or purpose. Five of the seven administrators interviewed stated that this segmentation encouraged individuals to continue to protect themselves and their programs rather than working cooperatively as a system to implement the audit recommendations. Second, the issue of educational reform within the state undercut the strength of the audit as an instrument of change. Four of those interviewed stated that the audit was abandoned due to the coming legislation and the accompanying changes that would be required. Finally, the audit became a minor battleground between the state department of education and the district. Once the department mandated the audit, the district, as a whole, saw the audit as an unfair, critical effort to make them look bad. As an organization, they were unable to transcend this negative perspective and accept the audit as a means to improve the district.

Administrators in District A implemented only one of six audit recommendations at the macro-management level. This tactical recommendation called for a "consistent, comprehensive approach to curriculum review, revision, and development" (Curriculum Management Audit Report, District A). It was implemented in two curricular areas in the middle school, with plans to expand implementation to other curricular areas in the future. Thus, we found that the improvement of management practices of this district resulting from the audit was minimal.

Question 4. Is the Audit Broad Enough in its Scope and Analysis to Enable the District's Board of Education and Administrative Team to Develop or Extend a Process of Systemwide Strategic Management?

The curriculum management audit's ability to foster the development of a strategic management posture was restricted by the circumstances surrounding the selection of the audit and the educational climate within the state following the audit. These conditions seemed to ameliorate the audit's recommendations, thus restricting any strategic management development.

Interestingly, the interviews with members of the management team did indicate that the audit process was seen as a conceptually sound "means to promote action toward a system-oriented management approach" and "generally, it could be a powerful tool toward strategically managing the district." All respondents stated that the curriculum management audit process could, in other circumstances, enhance the strategic management of a district.

District B

Question 1. To What Extent are the Recommendations in the Curriculum Audit Report Implemented by the District's Management?

District B implemented nine of ten recommendations. Table 9 shows the implementation by management level. This implementation record of 90% took three years to accomplish.

Question 2. What Unanticipated, Audit-Related Effects (Positive and Negative) Have Occurred in the District Since the Audit?

The audit was perceived by those interviewed as a "unique, in-depth process, from the point of view of the curriculum." In general, most

Table 9. Breakdown of audit recommendations, implementation, and levels of management for District B.

Recommendation Level	Total Number Received	Total Number Implemented
Mega or Strategic	1	1
Macro or Tactical	6	5
Micro or Operational	3	3
Total	10	9

stated that the audit was able to focus the district, "bringing the curriculum to the forefront." The majority of those interviewed expressed some surprise regarding the thoroughness of the audit process. Four respondents stated that the audit changed their perspective concerning how the district, as a whole, functioned and, particularly, how they fit into the system. One often repeated quotation from the audit report described the district as a "system of schools and not a school system." Seventy-five percent of the respondents said the district "became aware of the communications and interactions that need to exist in a school system" as a result of the audit.

The audit was identified by all as a vehicle of change, empowering the actions of the district's leadership. Statements such as "The audit pointed out what we had already seen, but gave us the power—that extra push to move on it" and "It didn't find anything new, but gave direction and made action possible" were common.

Question 3. Are the Benefits of the Audit Perceived to Improve the Management of the District?

The data collected by the impact survey, the examination of documents such as the administrative Table of Organization, board minutes, and administrative reports, and the interview process indicate improvement of the management practices of the district as a direct outcome of the audit process. There was unanimous agreement among those interviewed that the audit propelled the district toward restructuring the management process, moving from a "system of schools" to "a school system." District B demonstrated the greatest implementation rate

(90%), implementing every recommendation except one at the tactical-management level.

Question 4. Is the Audit Broad Enough in its Scope and Analysis to Enable the District's Board of Education and Administrative Team to Develop or Extend a Process of Systemwide Strategic Management?

The audit was seen by those interviewed as a "unique, in-depth process" that provided the "framework and direction" for the "restructuring of the district and the development of a strategic planning process." All data collected confirmed the audit's impact in fostering the development of a strategic management process in the district. The audit was credited by all those interviewed as identifying the need for a systemwide management approach, providing direction for the development of a strategic management process, and empowering the organization to implement the necessary changes.

District C

Question 1. To What Extent Are the Recommendations in the Curriculum Audit Report Implemented by the District's Management?

District C implemented four of six recommendations. Table 10 shows the implementation by management level. Commissioned in

Table 10. Breakdown of audit recommendations, implementation, and levels of management for District C.

Recommendation Level	Total Number Received	Total Number Implemented
Mega or Strategic	1	0
Macro or Tactical	4	3
Micro or Operational	1	1
Total	6	4

1988, the curriculum audit recommendations implemented by administrators in District C were completed within three years.

Question 2. What Unanticipated, Audit-Related Effects (Positive and Negative) Have Occurred in the District Since the Audit?

One of the recommendations not implemented by District C management suggested the development of a long-range strategic plan. This was because of the superintendent's belief that any system planning exceeding one year was not effective. He believed that the issues confronting his district changed so rapidly that no long-range plan could anticipate such changes effectively. Central office administrators stated that, prior to the audit, the superintendent's perspective blocked any efforts at long-range planning by other members of the administrative team. However, after the audit, they found the audit recommendation, while not adopted, provided "credence to long-range planning within the district" and "promoted such [long-range] planning in particular areas such as technology."

Half of the individuals interviewed said the audit was an "absolutely necessary procedure" to provide a "stimulus for the district that can't be provided by ourselves." The audit was viewed as an impetus, "particularly for veteran administrators," for district self-analysis, dialogue, and change. The audit process and report forced the system to "articulate very explicitly our purposes." The audit was clearly viewed by all individuals as focusing the district on self-evaluation and improvement.

Both the superintendent and the assistant superintendent described the district as "a loosely coupled system" (Weick, 1976) because administrators and teachers in the district experienced a great deal of autonomy. Four of the eight individuals interviewed stated that the audit process broadened their perspective regarding the system's need for communication, interaction, and support.

Question 3. Are the Benefits of the Audit Perceived to Improve the Management of the District?

District C implemented three of four recommendations at the macro-management level. The only micro-management level recommendation, to continue an innovative program at the district's high school, was implemented. The two recommendations not implemented were given careful consideration by the management team of the district and

found to be out of line with the district's goals and management priorities. The three micro-management level recommendations were considered by those interviewed as having improved the management effectiveness upon their implementation.

Question 4. Is the Audit Broad Enough in its Scope and Analysis to Enable the District's Board of Education and Administrative Team to Develop or Extend a Process of Systemwide Strategic Management?

Prior to the audit, District C had strong, stable leadership. Due to the philosophy of the superintendent and the district's financial position, the district successfully employed strategic issue management, focusing on specific trends or events as they emerged. The respondents judged the audit as a thorough process that provided "on-target recommendations to improve the system's performance."

ANALYSIS BY CATEGORIES

Voluntary versus Mandated Selection

When comparing the implementation of audit recommendations by whether the district voluntarily commissioned the audit or underwent the audit through state imposition, we found implementation statistics higher for the voluntary districts. Table 11 shows the implementation of recommendations based on audit selection method. It is clear from

Table 11. Implementation of recommendations by level of management.

Recommendation Level	Districts B and C Voluntary Audit	District A Mandated Audit
Mega or Strategic	1 of 2	0 of 1
Macro or Tactical	8 of 10	1 of 6
Micro or Operational	4 of 4	2 of 5
Total	13 of 16	3 of 12
Percent of Implementation:	81%	25%

both the implementation data and the interviews that audit recommendations have a greater likelihood of positively affecting change if the curriculum management audit is not required by external agencies.

No negative, unanticipated, audit-related effects were identified by respondents during the interview process or from survey responses. However, individuals in Districts B and C did identify three positive, but indirect, outcomes of the audit. Although the specific language varied, individuals described the audit report as promoting a "systems" or "district" perspective, as empowering various constituencies to participate in curricular change, and as helping everyone "own" the recommendations.

District Carryover

The last comparison we conducted looked at levels of district financial carryover. The categories were *low* or less than $500,000 available at the end of the fiscal year; *middle* or $500,001 to $5,000,000 available; and *high* or over $5,000,000 available at the end of the fiscal year. Table 12 presents the implementation data displayed by carryover level and management level. It is not surprising that the district with the low financial carryover was also the district with the mandated audit.

Perceptions of District Management

Table 13 indicates the perceptions of district members regarding the improvement of the district's management resulting from the curriculum audit. Unlike previous comparisons, the somewhat mixed perceptions of the audit impact do not break down exactly by financial carryover or voluntary selection status.

*Table 12. Implementation of recommendations by level
of financial carryover.*

Recommendation Level	Less than $500,000	$500,001– $5,000,000	Over $5,000,000
Mega or Strategic	0 of 1	1 of 1	0 of 1
Macro or Tactical	1 of 6	5 of 6	3 of 4
Micro or Operational	2 of 5	3 of 3	1 of 1
Total	3 of 12	9 of 10	4 of 6
Percent of Implementation:	25%	90%	67%

Table 13. Perceptions of district management.

Perception	A	B	C
Competency of Management	ineffective	moderately effective	very effective
Status of District Management Prior to the Audit	not stable	not stable	stable
Improvement in District After Audit	minimal improvement	major improvement	moderate improvement

SUMMARY AND CONCLUSIONS

Based on this study of three districts who completed a curriculum audit commissioned by AASA, we believe we can offer several observations for district administrators contemplating the investment in a curriculum management audit. While this study analyzed only three districts in depth, we reviewed audit reports from dozens of districts not included.

First, there are standard audit recommendations common to the use of the curriculum management audit as a management tool for improvement. If a district undergoes a curriculum management audit, these recommendations will more than likely be part of the final report. Thus, listed below is a generalized audit report including the seven standard recommendations.

Standard I. The school system is able to demonstrate control of its resources, programs, and personnel.

(1) Establish a comprehensive policy framework for curriculum development and management.
(2) Develop and implement a long-range management plan.
(3) Clarify and revise the Table of Organization for the district.

Standard II. The school system has established clear and valid objectives for the students.

(1) Engage in significant revisions of the system's curricular documents.

Standard III. The school has documentation explaining how its programs have been developed, implemented, and conducted.

(1) Develop a comprehensive staff development plan and program.

Standard IV. The school system uses the results from designed or adopted assessments to adjust, improve, or terminate ineffective practices or programs.

(1) Develop guidelines for district testing and utilization of data.

Standard V. The school system has been able to improve its productivity.

(1) Revise district budgeting procedures to be directed more by curricular priorities.

Each of the seven recommendations will be specifically tailored to the individual district. The explanatory section following each recommendation will appropriately link it to the specific management practices of each district. Further recommendations, based on the five audit standards, will address additional issues within the district as found through the auditing process.

Second, we found the majority of audit recommendations fit Kaufman and Herman's (1991) second category of management levels. That is, macro-level, or tactical, recommendations fit the nature of the audit process and its usefulness for district administrators to bring about change in the school district. Of the twenty-eight audit recommendations reviewed, sixteen were classified as macro-level. Indeed, most macro-level recommendations were implemented by the districts included in this study.

One final observation is that the only audit recommendation consistently not implemented by any of the districts pertains to the development of a curriculum-driven budget. Respondents gave three reasons for not implementing this recommendation: (1) a lack of understanding of what the recommendation meant, (2) a lack of skills within the district to implement the recommendation, and (3) a lack of agreement with the recommendation itself, "not realistic in today's educational environment," as one administrator stated. Although the audit report follows each recommendation with an explanatory section, additional information sources and more concrete implementation guidance might enhance the possibility of this recommendation's implementation. However, the lack of concrete examples of districts that have developed and used curriculum-driven budget is perhaps the greatest obstacle to its implementation.

IMPLICATIONS FOR FUNDING AUDITS

The curriculum audit requires a sizable investment of resources. Besides the time commitment and disruption of normal administrative duties, the dollar costs can be prohibitive to many districts. While the majority of districts who have commissioned an audit have paid for it through district funds, other sources are available. We found three kinds of clients who may commission an audit: (1) the school system itself at the superintendent request, (2) an external support group such as a Chamber of Commerce or a corporate partner, and (3) a regulatory agency such as the state department of education.

When the audit is commissioned by the school system or by an external group in consort with the district, the audit's recommendations have a stronger chance of being implemented, resulting in improvement across many levels within the district. In addition, the audit can be expected to contribute to the development or extension of a strategic management posture.

However, when a regulatory agency commissions the audit, the purpose of the audit and the position of the district regarding the audit will directly influence any audit-related outcomes. When the audit is mandated because the district is labeled "deficient," minimal implementation of audit recommendations will probably occur, resulting in minor improvement in the management process of the district. The curriculum audit, while a powerful management tool, is as unlikely as any state-mandated reform package to bring about real change if school administrators are left out of the decision-making process.

REFERENCES

Kaufman, R. and J. Herman. (1991) *Strategic Planning in Education.* Lancaster, Pennsylvania: Technomic Publishing Co., Inc.

Weick, K. (1976) "Educational Organizations as Loosely Coupled Systems," *Administrative Science Quarterly,* 21:1–19.

About the Editors

LARRY E. FRASE, Lead Editor

LARRY E. FRASE—Dr. Frase's experience includes six years as Assistant Superintendent of Schools in the Uniondale School District in New York and the Flowing Wells School District in Arizona and eight years as Superintendent of the Catalina Foothills School District in Tucson, Arizona. Dr. Frase completed his B.A. at the University of Arizona and his M.A. and Ed.D. at Arizona State University. He is currently Professor of Educational Administration at San Diego State University in San Diego, California. He is author or coauthor of eight books and fifty-five professional articles. He is editor of *Total Quality Education: Best Schools in the World*. He serves as keynote speaker at conventions and as consultant to school districts in Canada and the United States. Topics of his writing and speaking include teacher and administrator motivation, school management by wandering around, performance compensation, work environments, teacher and principal evaluation management, and superintendent/school board relations. He is also Book Review Editor of the *International Journal of Educational Reform*. Dr. Frase received his audit training in Tucson, Arizona, in 1989 and serves as auditor, lead auditor, and trainer.

FENWICK W. ENGLISH, Editor

FENWICK W. ENGLISH—Dr. English designed the curriculum audit; conducted the original curriculum audit in Columbus, Ohio, in 1979; and trained the authors in this book in curriculum auditing. His experience includes Superintendent of the Newport Public Schools and the Hastings on the Hudson Public Schools in New York. He also served as a partner in the accounting and consulting firm of Peat, Marwick, Mitchell and Co. for three years where he was National Practice Director for Elementary and Secondary Education for the North American Continent. He earned his B.S. and M.S. degrees in education at the University of Southern California and his Ph.D. in secondary education at Arizona State University. Dr. English is currently a Professor of Educational Administration in the College of Education at the University of Kentucky in Lexington, Kentucky. He is the author or coauthor of fourteen books on a variety of topics such as planning, curriculum management, organizational development, administrative skills, and administrative theory. He frequently serves as consultant to the National Association of Secondary School Principals and the Association of Supervision and Curriculum Development. He is coeditor of *International Journal of Education Reform.* Dr. English currently serves as the trainer and lead director of the American Association of School Administrator's National Curriculum Audit Training Center's five-and-one-half auditor training program.

WILLIAM K. POSTON JR., Editor

WILLIAM K. POSTON JR.—Dr. Poston is Associate Professor at Iowa State University, Ames, Iowa. Dr. Poston's experience includes fifteen years as superintendent of three school districts: Flowing Wells School District, Tucson, Arizona; Billing Public Schools, Billings, Montana; and Kyrene Public Schools, Tempe, Arizona. He earned his B.A. at Northern Iowa University and his Ed.S. and Ed.D. at Arizona State University. He writes widely in professional journals and is author of one book and coauthor of one book. His writing includes such topics as alternative compensation, school management, teacher evaluation, school board and superintendent evaluations, total quality management, and curriculum-driven budgeting. He serves as consultant to numerous school districts. Dr. Poston received his audit training in Montreal, Canada, in 1988. He has served as lead auditor on fifteen audits.

About the Authors

THE contributors to this book represent varied and rich backgrounds. Five of the authors have a combined total of forty-three years of experience as superintendents and are now active writers, researchers, consultants, speakers, and professors. Another three have high-level central office experience in school districts or professional associations.

CAROLYN DOWNEY

CAROLYN DOWNEY—Dr. Downey is currently Associate Professor of Educational Administration at San Diego State University. Prior to that, she served as Superintendent of the Kyrene Elementary School District in Tempe, Arizona, for three years; Assistant Superintendent in the same district; and Assistant Superintendent of Schools in the Apache Junction School District in Apache Junction, Arizona. Dr. Downey has extensive experience in educational research and is a widely sought-after consultant in North America on topics including curriculum development, curriculum alignment, total quality management, and instruction. She is coauthor of one book and author of numerous articles. She received her audit training in Montreal, Canada, in July 1988. She serves as an auditor, lead auditor, and lead auditor trainer.

KAREN GALLAGER

KAREN GALLAGER—Dr. Karen Gallager is Associate Professor of Educational Administration at the University of Cincinnati and the Associate Dean of Academic Affairs in the College of Education. She

299

has participated in seven curriculum audits through AASA, twice serving as lead auditor. She has published two dozen professional articles and book chapters on such topics as the use of technology in schools, education reform, and state education policy. Her book, *Shaping School Policy: Guide to Choice, Politics and Community Relations,* was published by Corwin Press in 1992. Besides her experience in higher education, she has served as teacher and building administrator in Washington, North Carolina, and Indiana. She served as the director of an education oversight committee in Ohio. She received her Ph.D. from Purdue University.

SUE GREENE

SUE GREENE—Ms. Sue Greene is currently the Assistant Superintendent at the University Place School District in Tacoma, Washington. Formerly, she served as Assistant Superintendent for Business and Auxiliary Services in Kyrene Elementary School District in Tempe, Arizona. She has been an assistant principal at the junior high and high school levels in Anchorage, Alaska. She served as Deputy Commissioner of the State Department of Administration, State of Alaska, for three years. She also served as President of the Alaska School Boards Association. She earned her B.A. at Ohio Wesleyan University and M.Ed. at the University of Alaska in Educational Administration. She received her American Association of School Administrator's audit training at Lake of the Ozarks, Missouri, in 1988. She serves as an auditor, lead auditor, and auditor trainer.

JAY KEMEN

JAY KEMEN—Dr. Jay Kemen is a mathematics teacher in the Oakhills School District, Cincinnati, Ohio. He received his Ed.D. in educational administration from the University of Cincinnati in June 1993. Dr. Kemen has served as auditor in two audits commissioned through AASA. Chapter 11 is based on his doctoral dissertation.

BETTY STEFFY

BETTY STEFFY—Dr. Steffy is currently Associate Professor of Educational Administration at the University of Kentucky. She was formerly the Deputy Superintendent of Instruction in the Kentucky Department of Education in Frankfort, Kentucky. Prior to that, she served as the Superintendent of Schools in Moorestown, New Jersey, for three years; the Assistant Superintendent of Schools in Lynbrook, New York; and the Director of Curriculum for the Allegheny Intermediate Unit in Pittsburgh, Pennsylvania. Betty received her B.S., NAT, and Ed.D. from the University of Pittsburgh. She is the coauthor of four books and numerous articles in professional journals. She is coeditor of the *International Journal of Educational Reform.* She completed her audit training in Montreal, Canada, in 1988.

WILLIAM STRESHLY

WILLIAM STRESHLY—Dr. Streshly is Associate Professor of Educational Administration at San Diego State University, San Diego, California. His experience includes principalship of two high schools and Superintendent of three School Districts in California: the Exeter School District, the San Marcos Unified School District, and the San Ramon Unified School District for a period of sixteen years. Dr. Streshly publishes widely in professional journals and is the lead author of two books. His writings include topics such as superintendent/school board relations, assessment programs, management, personnel evaluation, employee relations, and contract negotiations. Dr. Streshly received his audit training in 1990 in San Diego, California. He serves as an auditor for the American Association of School Administrators and consultant to school districts in the area of contract negotiations, superintendent/board relations, and assessment.

VIRGINIA VERTIZ

VIRGINIA VERTIZ—Dr. Vertiz is the Director of the American Association of School Administrators' National Curriculum Audit Center. Her professional experience includes assignments as Assessment Specialist and Assistant to the Superintendent in Arlington Public Schools, Virginia. Prior to that, she worked as a teacher and district administrator at the building and district levels. Dr. Vertiz has written articles appearing in a variety of publications on topics including the curriculum management audit, assessment, and quality management. She recently edited a series of articles on the curriculum audit for *Education.* Dr. Vertiz serves as consultant to school districts and businesses on quality management.

Index

303